Determined Weeds

Samuel Jaye Tanner

Determined Weeds © 2018 by Samuel Jaye Tanner.

All rights reserved.

Illustrations by Michael Swearingen

Happy Valley Improv LLC
PO BOX 354
State College, PA 16804

www.happyvalleyimprov.com

ISBN

978-1-7335531-1-7

Second Edition

DEDICATION

For Dad, Mom, Christie, Jayson, Christa, and the baby that never had a name—you are where I come from.

For Katie, Solomon, and Samson—you are where I am going.

As always, I hope this helps.

DISCLAIMER

This is a true story.

I have disguised the names of some people in this story and left others alone.

I do not want to hurt anybody that is written about here. The people included in this work are my family. I love them as such.

Mostly, I just want this to be as honest as I can make it.

CONTENTS

Wilting

Mom was dying.

Her emphysema had grown worse, and she had congestive heart failure. She had fallen and broken a bone in her neck on Halloween. Now, it was the second week of November. Mom had been in the hospital for two weeks after being transitioned out of nursing care.

I learned of her fall through my Aunt Polly, who had sent me a text message. She wrote to tell me that my mother was very sick.

I was nearly 1,000 miles away in Pennsylvania. Mom was at Region's Hospital in St. Paul, Minnesota.

I had sat with my mother at her deathbed numerous times throughout her life. Each time, her doctors informed me that my mother would not survive. I would sit with her. I would hold her hand and tell her how much I loved her.

In the past, Mom had always miraculously survived.

This time was different, though. I called the hospital after receiving Polly's text. I was transferred to Mom's room. She answered.

"I need to see my grandson, Sam. You need to come home."

My second son, Samson, was born in August. That was one month after my wife Katie and I had moved to Pennsylvania. We left our home in Minnesota because I accepted a job with Penn State. Mom was unable to travel. We were planning to introduce her to her new grandchild when we returned for the holidays in December.

"Can you hold on for another month?" I asked her stupidly.

"I don't think so, Sam."

Mom put me on the phone with her doctor. He could not tell me how much time she had left.

"I'm flying home next week for a conference," I told him. "Will she make it that long?"

"We can't tell," he said.

He put me back on the phone with Mom.

2

"I love you so much, Sammy," she told me. "I'm so proud of you."

I began to cry. I had wept for my mother so much during her life. I was surprised to find that there were any tears left.

"I love you too, Mom."

Polly arranged for us to FaceTime with Mom the next night from the hospital. She called while we were finishing dinner.

Tubes were attached to Mom's nose. She had white hair and distant eyes. I had seen her in this state before. Still, this time felt different.

"Can you see us, Mom?"

"Yes, Sammy."

I showed her my oldest son, Solomon. He had food in his mouth. Solomon smiled when he saw my mother.

"Hi!" he said. This was one of the few words he knew.

"Hi, Solomon," Mom said. "Grandma loves you."

"I want to show you Samson, Mom."

I brought the phone to Samson's bassinet. I held it to his face. Samson smiled and giggled. Mom smiled too.

"He's so beautiful, Sammy," Mom said. "I am so proud of you."

"He sure is," Polly agreed.

Again, Mom told me that she loved me. Again, I told her that I loved her.

I was driving to campus the next morning. My phone rang. It was a nurse from Region's Hospital in St. Paul.

"Your mother needs you to come right now," she said.

I told the nurse that I was in Pennsylvania. I told her I would be returning next week for a conference. I told her that I could not afford to buy a ticket to come out immediately. I told her that my wife and two sons needed me in Pennsylvania.

"Okay. Your mother still wants you here."

I was angry. How many times had I stopped everything in my life and raced to help my mother? What else could I

3

do for her? I had given her everything I could. I had
showed her Samson. She had spoken with Solomon.

I could not explain myself to the nurse. So I told her I
was trying to figure out how to come back to Minneapolis.

"She keeps telling us that she wants to die," the nurse
told me. "We wanted to let you know."

I laughed.

"She's been saying that for years," I told the nurse.

The nurse did not respond.

We hung up. I sat alone in my car. Campus was quiet.
A storm was coming over the mountains, and the sky was
gray. It was starting to rain.

I felt compelled to go to my mother, but what could I
do? Katie had pink eye, Solomon was getting over an
infection, and trying to get all of us to St. Paul would be an
ordeal. I could not just leave on a whim. My family in
Pennsylvania needed me.

I told Polly as much in a text later that morning. She
responded to let me know that she understood.

Polly sent me another text message that afternoon.
Mom was in pain. Polly wanted to know if it was okay to
put my mother in comfort care. Mom would be given
minimal oxygen and have only hours left.

I told Polly that it was okay with me.

I spent the rest of the day in my office on campus,
waiting to hear the news that my mother was finally gone.

Mom had always been a gardener. She eliminated
weeds with relentless determination. Weeds wreak havoc
on the careful symmetry of human design. They fight for
life, intent on imposing their will despite our obstinate
objections.

I was the product of my mother's willfulness. I was also
its victim.

Should I race home to be with my mother? Should I
stay in Pennsylvania to take care of my family? Should I
return to Minnesota the next week as planned?

There was no right answer to those questions. There

was no way for me to explain that there was no right answer, either.

Things were so complicated.

My soul was chaos as I waited for news about my mother.

Heavy clouds rolled in over the mountains as the afternoon turned into evening. A storm was coming, and wind howled against the building that housed my office on campus.

I braced for what was coming next, determined to make my way in an enormous, complicated universe.

Chapter 1

I was sitting in the front seat in Mom's red 1980 Mazda Hatchback. It was a warm summer morning, and I was a little boy.

Mom was standing over me. She had a child's face with big, bright eyes that sometimes changed from brown to green but, more often than not, were hazel. Her short brown hair curled around her smiling face. Mom was about 5'2". She was short and slight in stature. In her thirties, when I was born, Mom had a frenetic, captivating energy. Between that and her sparkling eyes, people gravitated toward my mother.

For some reason, Mom started talking to me about death that afternoon as she was getting ready to take me somewhere in her car.

"You know I would give my life to keep you safe, Sammy," she told me as she buckled my seatbelt and kissed me on my forehead. "I would die before I let anything happen to you."

"I wouldn't want you to, Mom," I told her. The idea of Mom dying frightened me.

"You are that important to me," she told me. "I would do anything to protect you."

I thought for a moment and asked her a question to test her.

"Like if I was trapped under a car, would you lift it off of me?"

"Yes," she laughed. Her huge, hazel eyes sparkled. "I would find superhuman strength."

"What if I was attacked by big green cats from outer space?" I giggled.

"I would fight them off."

"What if a kidnapper tried to shoot me with a gun?"

"Sammy." Mom's voice became serious. "I would stand in front of you and take the bullet."

"Really?" I asked.

"Really," she said.

Even though I was only a child, I *felt* that Mom was

telling me something that was true.

She finished buckling my seatbelt, kissed me again, and slammed the door.

This was one of my earliest memories.

I loved my mother very much.

***

Mom lost the first three children that she carried. The first miscarried before Mom and Dad learned its gender. The second was a little boy who was going to be named Jayson. He was stillborn. The third was a little girl named Christa. She was born premature. Christa was one pound and lived for only one week. Doctors performed surgery on her tiny body to remove as many intestines as they could. It did not make a difference, and she passed away.

"Wendy," the doctors told my mother, "we just don't think you should try to have another baby."

Mom was adamant about having a child. The doctors tried to convince my father to talk her out of it.

"Clayton, her body just isn't healthy enough to have a baby."

Mom was extremely small like both of her parents. She was both short and skinny. Dad was of medium height and slightly overweight.

My dad's name was Clayton Hermann Tanner. He was named in honor of his Jewish aunt. Her name was Clara. As a child, she had immigrated to St. Paul from Ukraine during the Russian Revolution. Dad's grandfather was a Russian merchant. He had saved enough money for his wife and two daughters, Dad's mother Edith and her sister Clara, to escape from the pogroms that Ukrainian Cossacks were conducting against the Jews during the early 20th century throughout Russia. Dad's grandmother did not survive the journey. The family ended up in a Russian, Jewish immigrant community on the lower east side of St. Paul. David changed his last name from Tankenov to

Tanner.

"*You* try to convince Wendy not to have children," Dad told the doctor.

Try as they might, nobody could persuade my mother to give up trying to have babies. She was determined. Mom became pregnant again, this time with a little girl. Christie was born four months premature in 1976. She weighed two-and-a-half pounds. She was immediately taken to intensive care and put into an incubator.

My parents named her Christie because, despite his Orthodox Jewish upbringing, Dad had accepted Jesus Christ as his personal lord and savior in his late twenties. He became a zealous, Jew-for-Jesus freak. This meant that he grew a grizzly beard, started quoting Bible verses, and trusted God to take care of *everything*.

"There's no way that she'll live," the doctors told my parents.

"I wouldn't be so sure," my father told them fanatically. "With God and through Jesus, all things are possible."

The doctors rolled their eyes at my father as he told them that they could move mountains if they accepted that their sins had been forgiven because Jesus was the son of God.

Mom and Dad spent the next four months in the hospital praying over my sister's incubator. Despite assurances by the doctors that Christie would never leave the hospital alive, they brought her home. She was dressed in doll's clothing because she was so tiny. Though she had mild cerebral palsy, she survived, and my parents decided to try to have another child.

"That's not a good idea," the doctors told my mother.

She refused to listen to their advice, and so I was conceived. For the next nine months, Mom gave up cigarettes, did not touch alcohol, and stopped smoking marijuana. She was on bed rest the final six weeks of the pregnancy and shocked her doctors by carrying me full-term.

Mom gave birth to me in a scheduled caesarean section on June 9th, 1980. Her amniotic sac remained intact as the doctors lifted me out of her stomach.

They broke the water after I was out of her womb.

"It's a miracle," the doctors told my parents after they checked me over. "He's fine."

"It *is* a miracle," Dad said.

"He's perfect," Mom said.

My mom convinced my dad to name me Jamie. She did this for two reasons. For one, Mom's first serious boyfriend was named James. Secondly, Mom's mom had a fixation on including incidental "E's" in people's names. My mother's eccentric mother's name was spelled Pattye. Mom's dad's name was Jaye. He legally changed his name and added an E after marrying my grandmother so that they would match. They named their two daughters Wendy and Polly to emphasize the "E" sound. Polly spent 60 years spelling her name "Polly" only to discover that the actual name on her birth certificate was spelled "Polley."

Dad pressured Mom to change my name after one night in the hospital. She acquiesced and agreed to call me Samuel.

In Hebrew, Samuel is Sh'muel and means God listens. My father was convinced that God had listened, and that I was the answer to his prayers.

Mom was adamant that my middle name should contain an "E," so they decided on Samuel Jaye Tanner.

Despite terrible odds, the concerns of her doctors, and all logical expectations or explanations—Mom gave birth to a healthy baby boy.

***

Before I was born, Dad and Mom purchased a large Tudor home in St. Paul for a fraction of what it was worth.

It was built in 1900 and sat in a wealthy, white neighborhood named Highland Park near the Mississippi River. After moving in, Mom single-handedly renovated the kitchen, created ornate stained-glass windows for the living room, finished the basement, and helped design a deck that wrapped around the back of the house. The house had already doubled in value by the time I was born.

My arrival meant that there were four of us. Five, if you included our family dog, Muffy. My parents had everything they needed to begin our family.

Dad was off on the road living in motels, smoking pot, and making a small fortune selling Medicare supplements and long-term care insurance to anybody who would let him sit down at their kitchen table. His clients were elderly, small-town farmers scattered across rural Minnesota. They were enamored with his Jewish humor and charisma. After selling them a policy, he would tell them the story of the gospel.

"I'm an apostle disguised as an insurance agent," he would brag to others.

I saw little of my father. Most of my time was spent with Mom.

Her days consisted of feeding me, changing me, and watching my every move. She also chased Christie around the house. Early in Christie's life, she was described by doctors and specialists as hyperactive, ADHD, special-needs, or whatever other word they could come up with to explain her constant impulsivity. Eventually, Mom and Dad enrolled Christie into pre-school. Mom was able to focus attention on me. This was probably the happiest period of her life.

In the mornings, Mom would sit with me on the hardwood floor in the large sunroom at the front of the house. I would breastfeed, play with my toys, and listen to her make up silly songs as the sun streamed in through the windows that lined the walls. Sometimes, I would watch *Sesame Street* on our television. Oscar the Grouch was my favorite character. Later in the morning, I'd nap. If I was fussy, Mom would sing to me.

"Grouch, grouch, grouch, who is a grouchy man?" Her song calmed me down. After I would fall asleep, she'd go to work on various projects.

Mom made stained glass lamps for local businesses. She also sewed me blankets with satin lining so that I could run my fingers along the edges. This obsessive habit was infinitely calming to me. I would build the satin into peaks and then push it down with my fingertips. Mom cooked, cleaned, and came up with a variety of creative projects to keep us busy.

After lunch we would go outside to our huge backyard, and she would work in her garden as I explored. One of Mom's gardens was always spilling over with vegetables; the other, with flowers. She could describe each flower with meticulous detail. If she was not tending her garden, she was hanging clothes on the clothesline. I enjoyed dashing and darting around the clothes as she hung them up to dry.

Mom was pinning clothes up on the line one summer afternoon. I darted off to hide between two rows of tall corn that were growing in her vegetable garden. When she realized I was gone, Mom started calling out my name.

"Sam! Sammy, where are you? Sam!"

She searched for an hour. Mom combed the neighborhood as I stood still between those stalks of corn. I was smirking.

After a while, I started to call back.

"Mom," I called. "Mom!"

She heard me and came running. When she found me, she wrapped me up in her arms and started to cry.

"I thought I'd lost you," she said.

I told her I was sorry and hugged her back.

We were running errands when we were not playing in the backyard. This included going to the department store. I used to climb into the center of circular clothes racks and hide from Mom behind shirts or pants. I would run my fingers along the fabric and giggle as I played hide and seek.

Once, while I was doing this, Mom could not find me. She frantically ran around the store. Mom looked everywhere. She had the manager make an announcement over the store's loudspeaker. Eventually, Mom found me in the parking lot. I was holding a strange woman's hand.

Mom grabbed me away from the woman and held me close.

"What are you doing?" Mom screamed at the woman.

"Oh, I was keeping him safe for you," she said.

When we were in the car, Mom turned to me.

"That woman was trying to steal you, Sammy. You can't trust strangers."

"I'm sorry, Mom," I told her.

"It's okay," she told me.

In the evenings, Mom would tuck me in and read me books. She wrapped me up in my green blanket with satin lining that she made for me, snuggled with me on the edge of the bed, and read aloud.

One of my favorite stories was about a cat that could drive cars.

Mom made sure that each of the cats had different voices.

Our family cat often jumped up onto the bed for this story. Cato was a stray kitten that Dad had found in a box while he was taking a walk along the paths in the bluffs near the Mississippi River. She was black. Mom and Dad named her Cato because it was the Spanish word for cat. When Cato was not outside terrorizing small woodland creatures, she was curled up in bed with me.

"Read it to us again, Mom!"

She would.

I would giggle hysterically about the cat that could drive until Cato got annoyed and jumped off the bed. Mom laughed with me as she showed me the pictures.

Another of my favorites was *Green Eggs and Ham*. Sam I am? Am I Sam? I empathized with the character Sam because we shared a name, and I would recite the story with Mom as she read.

"I do not like green eggs and ham!" I would squeal in delight. Mom would laugh with me.

Another book was about the Stupid family. The Stupid family was incompetent and would become confused doing even the simplest things. We would howl with laughter as we read.

The story I remember best was *Are You My Mother?* In the story, a baby bird hatches from an egg. Its mother is nowhere in sight, so it goes on a journey to find her. It meets an assortment of animals.

"Are you my mother?" It asks them.

"No!" they say.

Finally, the bird climbs into an enormous bulldozer.

"Are you my mother?" It asks.

The bulldozer makes a loud, terrifying noise and begins to move. The little bird is frightened.

The bulldozer drops the bird back in its nest, where it is reunited with its mother. I always sighed with relief as we reached that page in the story.

After reading me one of these books, Mom would turn on the light in my closet so it would not be too dark in my room, bring my blanket up to my chin, and kiss me on my forehead.

"I love you, Sammy," she would tell me.

"I love you too, Mom."

***

Our house in St. Paul was one block east from a road that ran along the Mississippi River. A path ran along a bluff that overlooked the water. Between the bluff and the water were trees, trails, and overgrowth. Affluent homes cluttered the neighborhoods near this road. Affluent people cluttered those trails and paths. Dad often took my sister and me for walks along the river.

In the first dream that I can remember, I was walking along the Mississippi River Road behind Dad, Mom, and Christie. They were walking too quickly for me to keep up.

I looked over my shoulder and saw a row of bulldozers behind me. They stretched from the street to the river and were moving toward me quickly.

I wanted to call out to my family, but I could not make a sound.

"Mom!" I tried to scream but nothing came out.

"Dad!" My voice wasn't working.

"Christie!" Nothing.

"Help!"

My family did not notice me as they reached a bus stop. I watched as a huge city bus pulled up to them in the distance. They climbed on. It drove them away to safety without me.

I turned around and saw that the bulldozers were bearing down on me. I tried so hard to scream that I woke myself up.

I was lying in my bed, wrapped up in my green blanket, and unable to make a sound. Finally, I was able to screech out a word.

"Mom!" I called.

She came running into my room.

"What's wrong, Sammy?"

"You left me," I said.

"What?"

"The bulldozers were coming and you left me."

"It was just a nightmare," she said.

"It was *real*."

"I'm here now." She held me in her arms and tried to calm me.

I fell asleep in her arms. Though I was safe for the moment, I had the distinct impression that *something* was *wrong*.

Chapter 2

Mom and Dad took Christie and me camping in the summer of 1987. I was seven years old and we went to Luck, Wisconsin. This was where Mom's family used to have a cabin when she was a little girl.

Grandma Pattye and Grandpa Jaye would take Mom and her sister Polly there for vacations when they were children. This was because Jaye had grown up in Wisconsin. He was one of eight brothers and sisters who were farmed out to family members after both of his parents died extremely young due to heart issues. Jaye was two when he lost his mom and dad.

Luck was an hour drive from St. Paul. Mom and Dad decided this would be the perfect place to try out our new mobile camper. It was attached to Dad's white Ford Thunderbird.

Dad was always obsessed with cars. Anytime he brought home a huge commission check, he usually blew most of it on a new car. For a brief period in the eighties, he was fixated on Ford Thunderbirds. Prior to that it was Buicks. After that it was Corvettes. By the time he was forty years old, he had created a list of sixty cars he had owned during his lifetime. His list continued to grow as he aged.

Dad would buy me package after package of Matchbox cars. I would take them to my room and line them up by color or model. Dad would come up and make fun of me for being so organized. Then we would take the cars and race them into each other. I enjoyed the collision. This was the extent of my interest in cars. They did not fascinate me in the same way they did my father.

Anyway, the camper we used to go to Luck was something like a mobile tent. It had a cloth ceiling that could be cranked up using an oversized Allen wrench. It had a small table, two mattresses that served as beds, and a bench instead of a couch.

Dad won the camper because of his prowess as an insurance agent. He was always bringing home new Sony televisions or vacations to Hawaii. The agency awarded its top agents with prizes. The camper was a bonus for my dad because of another year of huge commissions. Despite the fact that he spent most of his time either smoking pot in the basement or watching television on the couch, Dad still outsold the other employees in his agency.

"God is with me," Dad would tell his associates. "You should give yourself to Jesus."

They would roll their eyes with animosity.

We listened to the radio during the entire trip out to Luck, Wisconsin. There was a major thunderstorm moving through the area. The sky grew darker as we left Minnesota and drove east through Wisconsin. Ominous clouds gathered as we got closer to the campground.

"Shouldn't we maybe stop and get a motel room?" I asked my parents.

"It'll be fun to sleep out in a storm," Dad said.

My mom and sister agreed.

I was skeptical.

"Don't you think it might be dangerous sleeping in the camper during a thunderstorm?"

"Shut up, Sam," Christie snapped. Dad was becoming annoyed.

The announcer on the radio mentioned that the area of Luck, Wisconsin was now under a tornado watch.

"I don't know if the camper would be safe if a tornado came through," I said. "Don't you think it would be better for us to get a motel room?"

Dad became angry.

"We're not staying in a motel, Sam. It'll be fine."

That was that. My father had a quick temper. By the time I was seven, I knew it was better to keep quiet instead of provoking him.

We arrived at the campground in the early evening. Dad cranked up the roof of the camper with the Allen wrench, took out his pipe, and packed it with marijuana. He sat in a folding chair outside of the camper. He was shirtless, and his tangled chest hair seemed to blend into his wild black beard and his long black hair. Mom was dressed in a halter top and jean shorts. She sat next to him and opened a wine cooler. Christie and I fought over who got to sleep on the elevated bunk in the back of the camper.

Christie was four years older than I was and threw temper tantrums when she did not get what she wanted. I usually gave in to make peace and found a quiet place to read a book or newspaper.

The sky was dark and ominous, but nobody seemed worried. What followed was a short period of relative calm and hazy domesticity. I wandered off and began exploring the campground. The only permanent building was an old camp bathroom that included one dirty shower stall. Outside, a stream ran through the grounds. I started skipping stones out into the water. It began to rain. I headed back to our camper.

At first the rain was just a drizzle, and my parents ignored it. When it started coming down more heavily, we moved inside the camper. The sky grew black. Outside the plastic windows, we watched as other people at the campsite began packing up their gear to leave the campground. One by one, they started to disappear.

"How come everybody is leaving?" I asked Dad. I was hoping he might get the hint that maybe we should leave too.

"Because they're chickens," he laughed.

I was becoming nervous as the rain pounded the cloth ceiling of the camper.

We listened to the weather report on a tiny, portable radio on the table inside. The tornado watch had been changed to a tornado warning.

"I don't feel safe," I told my parents.

"You're fine, Sammy," Mom said.

Mom opened up another wine cooler, and Dad put more marijuana in his wooden pipe. Gusts of wind started to howl around the camper. Christie fell asleep on the elevated bunk. The roof began to leak, and I watched as Mom tried to patch the damp spots in the camper's ceiling with duct tape.

On the radio, the announcer said that a tornado had been spotted near Luck, Wisconsin. We were told that people in the area should take immediate shelter. Mom and Dad ignored the announcer's warning.

"We're fine here," they told me.

Finally, the campground was nearly empty. As I watched the last family pack their tent into their car, I decided to do something.

I got up from the bench and opened the door to the camper. I stood in the doorway and screamed through the wind and rain at the people who were getting into their car to leave.

"Help us!" I yelled.

My father became furious.

"Sam, stop!"

Dad grabbed onto me, but I would not let go of the doorframe.

"Help us!"

I screamed louder and louder. Finally, because I was making a scene and the people across the campground were concerned, my parents begrudgingly agreed to take us somewhere. They were embarrassed of me. We quickly packed up the camper and got back into the car.

"You're being a baby, Sam. Be quiet!" Dad's face was red as he yelled at me. I sat in the backseat quietly.

The weather proceeded to get worse as we drove. Eventually, Dad could not keep the car on the road. We turned into the parking lot of a school. We ran inside and took shelter in the gym with other people who had been caught out in the storm. Other families from our campground had been there for hours. We stayed in the school's gym until the storm had passed.

In the morning, most of Dad's anger toward me had

subsided.

We learned that a tornado had gone through the campground that night, destroying the only structure on the property, the camp bathroom. That building was much sturdier than our flimsy camper.

***

Later that summer, another thunderstorm came through St. Paul.

Even before the incident in Luck, Wisconsin, I was terrified of storms. I would creep out of my bedroom on the second story of our house whenever it thundered at night. There was a linen closet in the hallway with extra sheets, towels, and washcloths. I would remove a stack of towels and bring them back to my room. I would wrap myself in my green blanket and cower as lightning flashed and thunder boomed. I placed towels over my ears to muffle the sound.

Mom and Dad were downstairs smoking pot the evening of this particular thunderstorm. They were getting high with one of Mom's friends and watching the new Sony television Dad had won from his agency. Dad was probably hitting on her while Mom grabbed more wine coolers from the kitchen. Dad was lecherous.

Before we went to bed, Mom and Dad had let Christie and me watch the movie *Poltergeist* with them. This 1980's classic tells the story of a family tormented by a demonic spirit.

After watching the movie and going to bed, the storm grew worse. I spent the night staring at my closet door with towels wrapped around my ears. Every bolt of lightning made me more certain that the malicious clown in *Poltergeist* was going to sneak out of my closet and swallow me whole. I fell asleep in a sweaty cocoon of linen. My sister was asleep in her room across the hallway.

Christie's screams woke me up in the middle of the

21

night.

My sister's voice filled the house with a piercing squeal.
I was certain that she was being sucked into our new
television set like the little girl from the movie.

I noticed the distinct odor of pine as I crept out of bed.
Mom and Dad came running upstairs.

"Christie?" Dad was irritated.

"Christie!" So was Mom.

I hesitantly walked down the hallway toward Christie's
room.

"Sammy, stay back." Mom's voice had changed. She
sounded less annoyed and more worried.

Dad walked into Christie's room and picked her up out
of bed. He brought her back into the hallway.

I sneaked a glance over their shoulders and saw that
there was a tree in my sister's bedroom.

In *Poltergeist*, a possessed tree comes to life and smashes
through the house to attack the family. I was pretty sure
that was what had happened in my sister's room.

"Is there a poltergeist in there?" I asked Mom.

She ignored me and took me back to my bedroom.
Christie slept with my parents that night. The
thunderstorm continued to grow worse. Instead of
sleeping, I huddled under the covers and watched the
lightning flash outside my bedroom window.

One of the two 100-year-old pine trees that towered in
our front yard had been struck by lightning that night. It
had split at the trunk and collapsed directly into the house,
through the roof, and into my sister's bedroom. My
parents must have been thoroughly stoned, because they
did not notice until Christie started screaming and Dad
remarked that he could smell pine.

The next day, we were barricaded into the house. Parts
of the tree were dangling over both the front door and the
back door. My parents called the police in the morning
when they realized the extent of the damage. A fire truck
arrived, and we were told through a bullhorn not to exit

the house due to the precarious limbs suspended above the entrances.

I sat inside and played with my toys, excited that the house smelled like Christmas. Later in the day, a truck came and removed what remained of the tree.

My sister was frightened to sleep in her room after that. I could not blame her.

"I'm not going back in there," she would say.

"You'll be fine," Dad told her. "God will take care of you."

***

A third thunderstorm roared through St. Paul that same summer. The meteorologists on television called this one the storm of the century. Clouds were charged with electricity, gusts of wind thrashed trees back and forth, and torrents of rain flooded the streets. It started raining in the afternoon. By evening, it seemed like the world was ending. Tornadoes were touching down all over the Twin Cities. I watched from the window above the radiator in the living room. Lightning flashed, and sheets of water poured out of the sky.

Christie was up in her room, and Mom was drinking wine coolers in the kitchen. Dad had gone out to buy pot and was nowhere to be found. As the storm grew worse, Mom came into the living room.

"I have to go out and find your father, Sammy," Mom told me.

"You can't go out and drive in this storm," I told her.

"I need to, Sam," she told me. She reached for her keys in the entryway. "He might be cheating on me."

I could tell that Mom and been drinking too much. I was sure she would be killed that night if she went out into the storm alone. I knew I would not be able to convince her to stay home. Instead, I offered to go with her. She agreed to take me.

"What about me?" Christie asked when we told her we were leaving.

"You stay here in case Dad comes home," Mom said.

I was scared to go out into the storm, but I was even more afraid to let Mom go out by herself.

So we ran out the front door and into the chaotic thunderstorm, leaving Christie at home alone. Mom and I were soaked by the time we were inside of her car.

Mom got behind the wheel of her little red Mazda hatchback. I sat in the passenger seat and put my seatbelt on. Mom did not. The windshield was a wall of water.

Mom started the engine, put the car into gear, and drove off into the rain. I kept my eyes peeled. I knew that we should not be driving in this storm. It was terrifying.

"Be careful, Mom," I told her.

"I will, Sam."

We made it two blocks before conditions grew worse. We could not see anything in front of us because of the rain.

"We should turn back, Mom," I told her. "It isn't safe out here."

"I'm not going back until I find your father." Mom clutched the steering wheel and impulsively plunged forward into the worsening storm.

I whispered prayers to myself because I did not know what else to do. Dad had always said that God would take care of me. I certainly needed *somebody* to watch out for us.

Meanwhile, Mom attempted to navigate the storm by watching the brake lights ahead. She was following other cars because we could not see streetlights, sidewalks, or much of anything.

The car in front of us came to an abrupt stop. Our car did not. Mom sped into the stationary vehicle in front of the gates of The University of St. Thomas on Cretin Avenue in St. Paul. Her head crashed through the windshield. The front-end of the Mazda was destroyed. So was the rear-end of the car in front of us.

After the collision, my chest ached from where the seatbelt had bitten into it. Other than the shock of the crash and a searing red mark, I was fine. I quickly looked over to Mom.

Shards of glass speckled my mother's red, bleeding forehead. The windshield was shattered. She had been propelled out of her seat and into the glass because she was not wearing a seatbelt.

"Mom!" I was terrified. "Are you okay?"

She seemed dazed.

"Mom!"

Her eyes were cloudy.

"Sam?"

"Mom? Are you okay?"

Mom did not say anything. Eventually, she started sobbing. I did too.

"Stay here, Sammy."

Mom got out to check on the car in front of us. She returned.

"It's bad." She sounded like a child. I pitied her.

"Are you okay?"

"Yes," she mumbled.

"I love you, Mom."

"I love you too, Sam."

The police arrived shortly after the accident. I sat in the car to stay dry. An officer gave me a blanket. Eventually, an ambulance arrived and I rode in the back with Mom. She was unconscious. I held her hand, and the EMT told me that she would be fine. I was unconvinced. We ended up in Region's Hospital in downtown St. Paul.

Mom woke up after we arrived. I showed her the welt across my chest.

"Thank God you put on your seatbelt," she told me.

"Why weren't you wearing yours?" I asked.

Mom did not have a response.

The next memory I had was of waking up in a hospital bed.

"Is my mom okay?" I kept asking the doctors and nurses. The evening was a blur.

"She'll be fine," they said. "How do you feel?"

"I'm fine," I said. I was.

Eventually, they let me go into my mother's room. She had bandages wrapped around her head. She was crying.

"They had to pick pieces of glass out of my forehead," she told me.

My dad and sister arrived later in the evening, after the storm had died down. Dad was furious.

"What the hell were you thinking?" he barked at my mom. Dad's face was bright red. He kept screaming at my mother. "You could have killed him!"

"I'm fine, Dad," I told him. "We're going to be fine."

"What's wrong with you, Wendy?" he yelled at my mom. "How could you take Sam out in that storm?"

"We were looking for you," she yelled back.

"It's okay," I told them. "We're fine. Stop yelling."

Dad listened to me and tried to calm himself down. He drove Christie and me home. Mom spent the night in the hospital.

***

Those three storms marked the end of whatever remained of a peaceful, innocent childhood for me.

Mom and Dad started fighting more and more. Mom began going out to bars with her friends, Dad's sales trips became longer in duration, and it was tense when the two of them were in the same room.

Things came to a head when one of them was supposed to get me one day after school. I sat outside as other children were picked up by their parents. Eventually, I was alone. The school secretary noticed me as she came out of the building. She was the last one to leave.

"Are you okay?" she asked.

"I'm just waiting for my mom and dad."

She took me inside and we tried calling home. Nobody answered. The secretary drove me home, and I entered through the unlocked back door.

Mom came home later. She told me that she had just forgotten to pick me up.

I was upset with her, but she told me that she was sorry.

My family was proving to be unreliable, so I started looking for distractions. Surprisingly, baseball provided me with something of an escape.

The same summer those three storms came through the Twin Cities, I became a serious fan of the game. I began to watch baseball regularly in the spring of 1987, and I must have been a good luck charm. After years of failure, the Minnesota Twins became shockingly relevant that year. They won their first World Series. I was seven years old.

It was so exciting when I could convince Dad to bring the 12-inch black and white television set up to my bedroom; that way, I could watch the games away from my annoying sister and dysfunctional family.

"Dad, will you bring the TV up to my room?"

"Are the Twins playing tonight?"

"Yes," I begged. "Please?"

"Why not?" Dad plugged in the television and went back downstairs.

He probably just wanted some privacy as he smoked pot. I did not care. I had a TV in my room and could study the game.

I would watch each inning closely. Each pitch fascinated me. The shortstop, Greg Gagne, did backflips as he turned triple plays. The first baseman, Kent Hrbek, hit 600-foot home runs. Juan Berenguer threw at speeds of 200 miles per hour. Al Newmann could not hit the ball out of the infield, but he had a wacky handshake that he shared with Kirby Puckett. And if Kirby liked him, he was okay by me. It was a magical baseball team.

I learned a great deal about baseball that year. I learned that "E" stood for error in April. In May, I learned there was a machine on the corner of our street that sold newspapers. I could spend hours studying box scores at the kitchen table if I walked up to buy one. Nothing was better than the Sunday edition. I would sit and memorize who was leading the league in batting averages. I would even highlight Twins players so that I could see where they lined up. By June, I was collecting baseball cards. By July, I was organizing them by team. By August, I could rattle off the career statistics of nearly every player on the Twins.

I have three distinct memories about the 1987 World Series. First, Dad brought me home my first baseball glove and a Homer Hanky after a sales trip. I hung the hanky in my room. The Homer Hanky was a gimmick the organization used to promote the success of the Twins. It was a white handkerchief that fans waved in the stands. My second memory is of staying up late and watching all the playoff games. Bedtime was erased by the unique success of the team. Finally, I remember that game seven was the last time my mom, dad, sister, and I watched television together as a family in the sunroom.

Mom kicked Dad out soon after the Twins won the World Series. He was forced to rent a townhouse with a friend in the suburbs of St. Paul.

Christie and I stayed at home with Mom. At first, I was happy to be with my mother. She had always taken good care of me.

That happiness was quickly replaced by discomfort. Mom's drinking became more and more reckless. She would stay out late. When she did come home, she was either drunk or accompanied by some strange man. The three or four months that Christie and I lived with my mother were a confusing blur. I spent as much time as I could outside with a tennis ball and my baseball glove. I would imagine that I was Kirby Puckett or Dan Gladden as I threw the ball up in the air, caught it, and ignored what was happening around me.

It was an unstable time, so I was happy when Dad came up with a plan to return home. After talking to his lawyer, he realized that Mom had no legal right to force him out of the house.

Dad showed up one Sunday afternoon with all of his belongings packed into his new Ford Thunderbird. He started carrying things upstairs to the third-story attic.

"What are you doing here, Clayton?" Mom asked him.

"Moving back in."

"You can't do that."

"Yes, Wendy, I can."

"Dad is back!" Christie screamed.

I was excited too. Living alone with Mom had not felt right.

"I'm home now. For good." He hugged both Christie and me.

We happily helped him arrange his stuff upstairs in the attic. Mom watched nervously as we set up his bedroom.

Dad's return meant that Mom started to keep her distance. She could not bring men back to the house or come home drunk without risking my father's outrage anymore. Some nights, she stopped coming home altogether. She began moving some of her things to Grandma Pattye's house in St. Paul. Mom split her time between Grandma's guest bedroom and her room at home.

It was during this tumultuous time that Dad came home one night with a present for Christie and me. He had purchased the original Nintendo.

It was the spring of 1988. I had been bugging Dad because both of my good friends John and Dookie had a Sega. I had been playing video games at their houses and was extremely jealous.

Incidentally, my friend Dookie's real name was William, but his parents called him Dookie for short. One assumes there was a story involving feces connected to such a nickname.

Anyway, I was extremely disappointed when Dad walked through the door with a Nintendo Entertainment System.

"I talked to the guy at Best Buy," Dad said. "He told me that Nintendo was the future. The salesmen said it was much better than Sega."

I sulked all night. My dad could not do anything right, so I would once again be the odd one out amongst my friends. They would all master *California Games* or *Kidd Alex* on Sega while I was stuck playing *Super Mario Brothers* on Nintendo.

Dad's propensity for Jewish haggling had beat out my attempt at fitting in once again.

That night, Dad and Christie stayed up and played Nintendo in front of the old black and white TV in Dad's new attic bedroom.

"I got all the way to level two," Dad bragged that morning as he came downstairs for breakfast.

Even though he had bought the wrong system, I was so glad that my dad was home. Living with Mom for the past couple of months had been frightening, unpredictable, and profoundly *unsafe*.

I got over my initial frustration about Dad's Nintendo purchase and wandered up to his bedroom that afternoon.

I played *Super Mario Brothers* well into the evening. Dad came upstairs after he had gotten home from work.

"How far did you get?" he asked.

"I got to the fourth world, level three," I told him.

He was astonished.

From that point on, there was little use in my father and me playing video games together. Dad was no competition. Still, Dad kept the Nintendo up in his attic bedroom. That was where I spent most of my time.

After the trauma that had come from living with my mother during her period of self-destruction, it was nice to be relegated to Dad's room. I played *Super Mario Brothers*,

Nintendo Baseball, and *Nintendo Golf* for hours. Time passed, and it was the middle of summer. That big house in St. Paul was over one hundred years old. There was no air conditioning, and the attic was the hottest room in the house. It was also the *safest.* I even started sleeping on the couch in Dad's room.

"Can I sleep up here?" I'd ask two or three times a week.

He would shrug. "Sure."

Mom's room was on the second story, next to my own bedroom. I did not feel good sleeping near her. I couldn't articulate it, but I knew that it was better for me to be closer to Dad than Mom.

One night, Mom came home after a night of serious drinking. She woke Christie and me up because she was yelling at Dad. I came out of my bedroom and stood in the doorway. Christie was standing in her room. Dad was on the landing of the split stairway that led up to the attic. Mom was on the steps leading up to where Dad was standing. She was swearing at him, crying, and visibly upset.

"Wendy," Dad said, "calm down."

Mom started to climb the stairs toward my father. She lost her balance and fell backward onto the floor. She lost consciousness for a moment as Dad came down the steps. She returned to her senses and looked at Christie and me.

"Did you see your father push me down the steps?" she screamed. "He hit me!"

I watched her fall by herself, so I knew that she was lying to us.

"Come on, Wendy." Dad carried Mom into her bedroom, and she quickly passed out.

"Is Mom okay?" Christie asked.

"She'll be fine," Dad said. "Go to bed."

I stood in the hallway silently.

Later that spring, Mom and Dad were having another fight. Dad was accusing Mom of cheating on him.

"Just leave!" he shouted. "Move out!"

I watched them silently as they fought.

"If I leave, I'm taking Sammy with me," she screamed back at him.

"No, you're not," Dad said.

"Do you want to come with your mommy, Sam, or stay here with your bastard father?" she howled at me.

I did not know what to say—I wanted to please them both.

"We are going to live at Grandma Pattye's house," she told me.

Mom scooped me into her arms and ran with me out the back door. She sprinted through the backyard, past the overgrown garden, and back to where her red Mazda hatchback was parked next to the garage. It still had a dent in the bumper, despite the repairs after the accident. Dad chased after us.

Mom put her stuff into the car and opened the passenger door. She was about to strap me in when Dad caught up to us.

"I'm taking him to my mother's house, Clayton."

"No, you're not," Dad bellowed. "He's staying here."

Mom held onto one of my arms and Dad held onto the other. They were both pulling on me as hard as they could. It felt like I was going to be ripped apart as they played tug-of-war with me.

I started crying.

Eventually, Mom gave up and drove away. Dad held onto me as I sobbed into his chest.

A few days later, Mom and Dad gathered Christie and me in my bedroom.

"We've decided to get a divorce," they told us.

Christie was crying. I was not.

"Aren't you upset?" my parents asked me.

"Yes, but this needed to happen," I told them.

Later that week at school, I was called into the counselor's office at Horace Mann Elementary.

"Why are you going to the office?" John asked. Dookie and the rest of my friends were watching.

"My parents are getting divorced," I told them.

"Oh."

Once again, I was singled out because of my strange parents. I shrugged and walked down to the office.

"Sam," my counselor told me, "I understand your parents are getting a divorce."

"Yes, they are," I said.

"Do you have anything you want to talk about?"

"Not really."

"It's going to be okay."

"I know."

The counselor looked at me quizzically. She sent me back to class.

During this period of my childhood, I started spending more and more time with friends to get away from my family.

John and I became extremely close when I was eight. I met him in the second grade when Mom and Dad put me in Cub Scouts.

I was never any good at Cub Scouts. Neither was my father. Our pinewood derby car was the laughing stock of the troupe.

As I wrote, Dad loved cars, so he was excited when he learned that our Cub Scout troupe was participating in the pinewood derby tournament. After forming and sanding the car down, he paid for it to have a professional paint job. The car had a racing stripe and looked fierce, but its wheels were unable to turn because of the dried globs of paint. When it came time for us to compete in the crowded gym of Horace Mann Elementary, the car scraped its way down the ramp only to get stuck in the track before crossing the finish line. My friends watched with a smile and laughed with me when it was announced that Dad and I had placed last in the competition.

To Dad's credit, when it came time for him to lead the

monthly Cub Scout field trip, he took us to a military air base. We spent the afternoon climbing around inside old bomber planes. Dad told us all about how his father, a poor junk dealer, had worked on bombers during World War Two. My friends and their fathers loved it.

"Your dad is the coolest," my friends told me.

"He *is* something else," I said.

"Why does his license plate say 'Yeshua'?" John asked me.

"It's the Hebrew word for 'Jesus,'" I told them.

"Oh."

John was a great hockey player, had a Sega Genesis, and laughed at all of my jokes. We lived a few blocks away from each other. During the third grade, he and I were inseparable.

My group of friends from Cub Scouts and Horace Mann were closely knit. We did things like build forts out of abandoned wood, organize football games during recess, and stay up all night playing *Contra* on Nintendo.

We also started gangs.

Horace Mann Elementary was only a couple blocks away from my house in Highland Park. It was a pleasant little neighborhood school.

In the third grade, my group of friends decided to make a more perfect union. We came up with the idea of the Silly Octopus Club.

I had developed this habit of drawing a cartoon octopus in school when I was bored. I was often bored.

Anyway, the octopus had six muscular arms, two muscular legs, sunglasses, and a mohawk. It wore a gold chain and rode skateboards.

"That thing is awesome," my friends told me.

It was awesome.

We decided to make the drawing our gang's emblem.

We met on a Saturday at Matt's house to formally enact the Silly Octopus Club. There were nearly fifteen of us. It was decided that everybody in the group would have a role.

Matt drew the best, so he was the artist.

Dookie was the strongest, so he was the enforcer.

It was decided that I would be the president.

"I promise not to take this responsibility lightly," I told my friends.

John was the vice-president because I wanted him to be.

And so it was. We announced our presence to the third grade. Ms. Schroeder was very respectful. She even made an announcement to the class. We were invited to the front of the room to announce the creation of our group. I was elected spokesperson.

"We are the Silly Octopus Club," I told the class. "Let it be known."

"What do you guys do?" the class asked.

"Stuff," I said.

"Awesome," they said.

At the end of the third grade, we had a class picnic at a park near the school. Ms. Schroeder asked the Silly Octopus Club to prepare something to share at the event. My father played the guitar and taught me rudimentary blues riffs. John played the saxophone. So John and I got together and wrote a song before the picnic; it was called The Silly *Octopus Blues*. We played it live that afternoon in the park.

This was when I first learned of the great power that came from playing guitar. The chicks dug it. They followed me around for the rest of the afternoon.

"Play something else, Sam," they would coo at me.

I would unleash a wicked G-note. I would follow it up with the melody to La Bamba, a song made popular by a movie of the same name in the eighties. My coup de grace was playing a D chord.

"Holy shit!" the other third graders swooned. My D chord drifted up into the sky.

Playing live music with John that afternoon was a

pleasant reprieve from my bickering parents, the constant tension at home, and the instability of my family. It was a beautiful afternoon.

The Silly Octopus Club continued into the fourth grade. In fact, I had one of my first encounters with the authorities due to the club. By then, the chicks were starting to dig our gang. A couple of them wanted to become members. We took stock of what we knew about girls after they asked to join.

The summer before fourth grade, we had found an old stack of Playboy magazines in the alley behind Dookie's house. We carted them back to camp. We tore through dank and smelly pages, trying to catch glimpses of naked women.

"That's awesome," one of us said.

It was awesome. In 1988, one had to be resourceful to gain access to pornography as a third grader.

Most of what we knew about girls came from trying to thumb through moldy Playboy magazines. This informed our decision to include the girls in our club.

"Sure, you can join," we told the girls. "You guys will be our Playboy bunnies."

"Awesome," they said. With that, the first two girls were admitted to our gang.

This had problematic results. Ms. Aimes came to me one morning before school.

"I know you're the leader of this club, Sam. The other kids look up to you. So we need to talk about the Playboy bunnies."

My face got bright red. Ms. Aimes pulled John aside as well.

"Have you ever heard of the phrase 'sexual harassment,' boys?"

We had not. So Ms. Aimes explained the objectification of women to us. We took her lesson to heart. We changed the titles of the two girls who had joined. The next day, their parents told them that they could not be members anyway. This was probably for the best. The life of a Silly Octopus Club member was tumultuous, to say the least.

One of our gang's biggest projects during the fourth grade was digging a hole during recess. We decided that it would be cool to dig through the playground in order to reach the center of the earth. I organized our efforts.

The first day, we started by digging into the sand. By the end of recess, we had a nice little pit. By the end of the week, four of us could stand in the hole. It was deep enough that we had to climb in and out. People gathered as we worked.

"What are you doing?" the other kids asked.

"Digging a hole."

"That's awesome."

It was awesome.

After two weeks, we were about ten feet down. We were sure that the center of the Earth was only a couple of buckets of sand away. We had built enormous sand castles around the hole to protect it. Finally, the authorities got involved.

Ms. Aimes approached me again.

"Sam, what's your club doing?"

"Digging a hole."

"Well, you need to stop."

"Why?"

"Because it's dangerous."

"How so?"

"Because it is."

By the end of those two weeks, we had created a spectacle. Nearly the entire elementary school had gathered around to watch us during recess. I learned that a group of people doing something together made others pay attention.

The Silly Octopus Club was a powerful collective, and it felt good to be part of a functional family as mine fell apart.

***

My father took me for a walk along the Mississippi River Road in the midst of the disintegration of my family.

He often took me for walks when I was a child. Those walks are my favorite memories of being with him, though he was usually stoned during our excursions. We would spend all morning or afternoon exploring the woods near the river together.

On one particular walk, we stopped at a bench on the bluffs. The bench looked out on the river. It was morning, and the view of the water was spectacular. Sunlight sparkled on the gentle waves as the current pushed the water lazily along its path.

"If you pray in the name of Jesus, Sam, God has to answer your prayer," Dad told me as we sat together on that bench.

Dad's best friend Dave had told my father this same thing when Dave returned from Vietnam. My dad then decided to pray for his mother, and she made a miraculous recovery from her anxiety and depression. Dad was hooked, became what he would describe as a believer, and lived the rest of his life as a Jew-for-Jesus freak.

He told that story about Dave ad nausea to whoever would listen. He considered it his apostolistic charge.

I considered what my father was telling me that morning as we sat on that peaceful bench and looked over the rushing Mississippi River. White clouds hung in a perfect, blue sky.

After the divorce, Mom had moved into Grandma Pattye's house. She had reconnected with her first boyfriend, Jim, who had moved back to St. Paul from San Francisco where he had spent two decades growing out his hair, doing drugs, and being a carpenter. Jim's given name was James. This was the same man Mom had tried to name me after when I was born. Unlike Dad, Jim was not trying to imitate Jesus. He was trying to imitate Jerry Garcia. Mom had dated Jim as a teenager until he moved out West.

Mom began dating Jim again. She was drinking too much and seemed to be heading down a dangerous path. I was worried about her.

Dad had won custody of both Christie and me, despite the fact that it was almost unheard of for the father to win a custody hearing in 1988. The judge took one look at my mother as she pleaded for her children to stay with her and deemed her unfit to take care of us.

I thought for a moment. I told Dad that I knew what I wanted to pray for.

"Okay Sam," he told me. "Let's try."

So we prayed together. Instead of praying for wealth, fame, power, or whatever else my eight-year-old mind might have lusted after, I prayed for Mom. Like my father had done for his mother, I prayed that God would take care of her. I included my sister Christie in the prayer. Both of them were such fragile people.

"Please protect Mom and Christie, God," I prayed. "In Jesus' name, amen."

My prayer hung over the Mississippi River for a moment that morning. Then it drifted up to the sky. I did not know what my request would accomplish.

My childhood was over.

Chapter 3

Mom kept her distance from Christie and me after the divorce. It was nice to have distance from my mother, but I still missed her. Now it was left to Dad to raise us in that big house in St. Paul. He continued to smoke too much pot. He also started going through girlfriends like toilet paper.

"Do you like Sharon, guys?" he would ask Christie or me. This was after we spent an afternoon at the beach on Lake Nokomis in Minneapolis with one of his new girlfriends.

"She seems nice," one of us would say.

"She's twenty years younger than you," the other would tell him.

The next week, he'd bring another one home to watch a movie.

"How about Rachel?"

"She seems okay."

Then we would go out with *another* girl for dinner at Bridgeman's Ice Cream Parlor a couple of blocks from our house. Unlike Mom, Dad never cooked for us. Instead, he took us out for dinner nearly every night. My diet consisted mostly of greasy cheeseburgers and salty fries after Mom left to live with Grandma. I started getting chubby. During dinner, Dad would ask us about the woman he had brought with when she was in the bathroom.

"How about Grace?"

"I guess she's fine…"

At one point, Dad even started dating the mother of one of my close friends from school. Noah's mom was ten years younger than my father, but this did not stop him.

"What if our parents got married and we became brothers?" Noah asked as we raced Micro-Machines through his living room.

"That would be awesome!" I told him.

At one point, Dad took all of us to Noah's grandmother's farm in Northern Minnesota. At some point during that weekend in the woods outside of Duluth, Dad slept with Noah's grandmother. Dad admitted this to me years later. His relationship with Noah's mom ended shortly thereafter.

My sister's undiagnosed impulsivity grew worse without Mom around. My father was constantly yelling at her, and she was constantly provoking either him or me.

One evening, Noah was over at my house. He and I were playing video games in the sunroom. My father was on a date, so Noah, Christie, and I were home alone. Christie was irritated because nobody was paying attention to her. She kept dancing in the doorway so that Noah or I would stop concentrating on the Nintendo and notice her.

I had become adept at ignoring my sister, but two hours of obnoxious dancing was too much for me.

"Sam, look at me!"

Frustrated, I picked up a rubber bike handle that lay on the floor. I threw it at her.

"Leave us alone," I screamed.

The handle struck her face. It knocked one of the teeth out of her mouth. It was dangling from the wire that connected her braces. Christie started to scream. Her face was covered in blood.

"Holy shit!" Noah exclaimed.

We waited for Dad to come home and told him what happened.

Dad found the dentist's home phone number and called. Christie went in the next day to have the tooth put back in place. The dentist told her it was dead. It would always be darker than the rest of her teeth.

I felt terrible. I faced the brunt of Christie's naïve and incessant need for attention because Mom and Dad were not there to watch us. I could humor her, but my patience had begun to run thin.

"I don't blame you, Sammy," my mother told me when I shared what had happened with her over the phone.

During this illusory time, I started figuring out ways to occupy myself that had nothing to do with the antics of my family.

Like I said, Dad had bought me my first baseball glove during the Twins' run in 1987. I spent hours tossing myself pop-ups in our backyard because I did not have anybody to play catch with. Later, I created a chalk outline on the sidewalk steps in the backyard to represent home plate. I drew a strike zone on the steps and fired fastball after fastball into a little green box on the second of three steps leading up to our backdoor. I even learned how to put a wicked curve on the tennis ball. I figured that this rigorous training regiment had prepared me for the next step, so I asked my dad to sign me up for little league.

Dad agreed and put me in a summer league that was close to our home. Games were played at a park near the Mississippi River. He dropped me off at the field for tryouts and left to spend the afternoon with one of his harem of girlfriends. I walked right up to the coach and asked if I could be a pitcher. I had visions of becoming the next Frank Viola.

"Why not?" Coach asked.

Coach was a gruff, frightening man in his forties. His mustache was grizzly, his teeth were stained yellow, and his son had the strongest arm on the team.

It is safe to say that a tennis ball is different from a baseball. That being said, I put my fingers on the seams and started throwing from the stretch. The other kids watched as I fired a couple of fastballs toward the plate. I was nothing special, but most of my pitches were in the general vicinity of the strike zone.

"Try throwing from the windup," the coach spat at me.

"The windup?"

"The windup."

I had never thrown from the windup, but I figured I could give it a try. I situated myself on the mound and tried to imitate the pitchers I had been watching on TV. So, like Juan Berenguer, I itched my crotch, kicked my leg out, and rocketed the ball toward the catcher. Instead of hitting the glove, the ball soared about twenty feet over the backstop and into the busy street where cars swerved to avoid it. Coach rolled his eyes, the rest of the kids sniggered, and I gave up my dream of pitching.

After tryouts were over, the coach gathered all of the players into a huddle.

"I want you to tell me what position you want to play on the team," he told us.

All of the kids told him which positions they wanted. I was quiet. After the debacle of my pitching tryout, I was trying to go for a low profile.

"You," the coach snarled at me. "Where do you want to play?"

I thought for a moment. After my failure to pitch, I figured that I would have to prove myself in the eyes of my peers. I wanted to give an honest assessment of my performance that day. I responded as follows:

"I'll play right field."

This enraged the coach. His eyes got red, he clenched his face, and he began yelling at me in front of the whole team.

"Nobody will hide from me out here! Do you hear that? You won't hide from me!"

Coach stalked off and left me feeling embarrassed. I sheepishly went over to where Dad's car was parked.

"How'd it go?" he asked.

"Um, good."

"That's good."

"Yup."

Dad took me to McDonalds, and then we went home. He spent the evening smoking pot and watching television with one of his girlfriends while I munched on a cheeseburger and ate some fries. Then, I wandered outside and played catch with myself. But something was different now. Coach had instilled a sense of insecurity in me, and it was harder to dream of pitching a complete game shutout in the World Series for the Twins.

Coach stuck me in the outfield, and I spent most of the season swatting at gnats, standing in an empty field, and watching eight-year-olds slap weak grounders back to the pitcher. I made friends with some of the other kids who hit in the bottom of the lineup. We went through package after package of big-league chew together and learned nothing about the game of baseball from our coach. Instead of teaching us anything, Coach started his son as pitcher, put him third in the lineup, and snarled at me every time I slinked by him in the dugout.

My friends John and Dookie played on different teams in the league. When our games were happening at the same time, we would sneak off and hang out together on top of the dugouts where our coaches could not see us.

At the end of the year, our team was playing in a game to advance to the championship. Coach had me in right-center field. Eight-year-olds require four outfielders instead of three.

I spent most of the night plucking grass out of the ground, swatting away mosquitoes, and watching the sun set over the Mississippi River.

Eventually, it was the final inning of the game. Our team was up by a slight margin, and I was looking forward to getting McDonalds afterward. Dad was not actually watching the game because he had a date, but he would be there to pick me up when it was over.

During one play, an eight-year-old on the other team managed to knock a double into left field. A big, meaty looking kid came to the plate. This child had gotten a hit in every one of his at-bats that day. I did not figure to be involved in the play, but I perked up anyway to watch the dramatic situation. To my shock, the kid ripped the first pitch out in my direction. More surprising than anything, I charged to make a play on the sinking line drive. I dove,

45

came up with the ball, and fired it to second base where my teammate was jumping up and down. The other team's runner had not tagged up. We turned a double play, and my team advanced to the championship. Everybody was shocked that I had come up with the play to win the game. Coach growled an acknowledgement of my catch and proceeded to remind the team about how well his son had pitched that day in order to keep us in the game.

That was my first and last highlight as a little league baseball player.

Dad lost the schedule. I learned that I had missed the championship game after calling the coach to find out when it was scheduled.

After that season, I would force my dad to play catch with me to prepare for my next year on the team. During one of these sessions, Dad fired the ball at me and I failed to grab it. The ball bounced off my head. It hurt like hell, and I developed a severe fear of baseballs.

"Want to go play catch?" Dad would ask after that.

"That's okay," I would say, remembering the sound of the ball bouncing off of my skull.

"Are you sure?"

"I'm sure."

And that was that. I continued to follow baseball, but I no longer had much of a desire to play.

"Maybe you could be an announcer?" Dad suggested.

"Maybe," I said.

Still searching for ways to spend my time that did not cause me harm, I started playing more and more video games. Nintendo created a safer, fictional environment for me to inhabit. Little league baseball and my family had proved frustrating.

After convincing my father to buy me *Baseball Stars, Tecmo Bowl,* or *The Legend of Zelda,* I would spend hours building up my first baseman, leading the Vikings to the Tecmo Bowl Championship game, and gathering pieces of the Triforce.

"Sam and Christie, I'm going out on a date!" Dad would call up to us in our bedrooms.

"Sounds good," I would say. Then, I would spend the evening exploring the land of Hyrule, ignoring my sister's impulsive attempts to get my attention, and hoping that Dad would be home before it got dark. Being home alone at night without my father caused me anxiety; it made me feel afraid.

It was better when I could spend the night playing video games with my friends. I would often sleepover at one of their houses. This gave Dad the freedom to go out on dates without worrying about a curfew. It also provided me with a stable place to sleep. I think most of my friends' families felt bad for me because my home was broken. John or Dookie or Noah and I would play video games until early in the morning in the safety of their more traditional homes.

One of my clearest memories of this time was playing *Altered Beast* on John's Sega with him in his bedroom.

John's mom came into the room and grabbed a basket of laundry while we were playing.

"Do you have any more dirty clothes?" she asked John. "Sam, do you need me to wash anything?"

"No, Mom," John said. "Can you please leave us alone?"

After she left, I turned to him.

"You're so lucky to have a good mom," I told him.

I remember how my statement hung awkwardly in the room.

"Sure," he said, "I guess."

In the morning, after John and I had beat *Altered Beast* about seven times, we woke up and went downstairs. John's mom was making breakfast.

She cooked eggs and sausage, and it reminded me of the breakfasts Mom used to make before she and Dad were divorced. After the divorce, I had to fend for myself for breakfast. I usually made a bowl of cereal or ate a piece of toast with grape jelly while Dad slept in.

"You're a really good Mom," I told John's mother that morning.

She laughed.

"You think so, Sam?" she asked me.

"Yes, these are good eggs," I told her.

After spending one of these long weekends at John's house, Dad drove me home and I returned to my room. I put *The Legend of Zelda* into my Nintendo. My character was named "Sam." Sam had gathered most of the Triforce, had almost maxed out his hearts, and was close to beating the game. I was excited to continue my journey. When I went to load my game, I discovered that my character had been erased and replaced with "Poop."

"Poop" had three hearts and had yet to obtain the first sword in the first cave on the first screen of the game.

"Christie!" I screamed at the top of my lungs.

"What?" she asked.

"What happened to my game?"

"My friends and I played it."

Apparently, Christie's friends from across the street had spent the night while I was gone. They got bored and played Nintendo.

"You erased my character!"

"So what?"

"I had almost beat the game!"

"Shut up, Sam." Christie shoved me.

I went to get Dad.

"Christie erased my game!"

"Oh, well, that's too bad." Dad shrugged. He smelled like marijuana.

"Stop being such a baby, Sam," Christie sneered.

I went into my bedroom and sulked all afternoon. I was so angry with my sister and father. In the evening, I started a new quest. It took me another year, but I eventually defeated Gannon, restored the Triforce, and finished the game.

***

My interactions with Mom during this time were rare at best. She would call me once or twice a week, and we would talk on the phone.

"What's new, Sammy?"

"You know. How about with you?"

"Jim and I are doing great."

"Okay."

"I love you, Sammy."

"I love you too, Mom."

Phone calls made up the bulk of my relationship with her. They always ended with the same call-and-response routine that signified my mother's love for me and my reciprocation of that love.

Mom spent her nights going to the bars with Jim and her days working at Midway Bank in St. Paul.

Grandma Pattye had worked at that bank for years after her husband Jaye died in 1974. Grandpa's death occurred two weeks after his 49th birthday. Grandma was 46 at the time. He was gone by the time I was born. According to my Aunt Polly, he had premonitions of his death. At Christmas in 1973, he told the family that this would be his last Christmas. During his birthday party, he turned to Grandma.

"I won't make it to fifty," he told her.

"Don't be silly, Nubby." Grandma's nickname for Jaye was Nubby.

Jaye had a heart attack and died two weeks later. This happened despite a routine checkup that included a normal EKG reading one week earlier. Grandma Pattye started drinking bottles of vodka by herself soon after Jaye was gone.

Grandma Pattye was the only child of my great-grandmother, Dorothy. We always called Dorothy "Gom-ey"—that was how my mother pronounced the word

"Grandma" when she was a little girl. I learned to spell this version of my great-grandmother's name like "Gammy." Anyway, Gammy was the youngest daughter of Norwegian immigrants. Her mother died giving birth to her, and her father re-married a stern, taciturn woman who treated Gammy poorly. They lived in a small town in rural Minnesota. Gammy ran away when she was sixteen. She came to St. Paul and played piano in nightclubs in the 1920's. Her first husband was alcoholic and abusive. This was Grandma Pattye's father. Gammy left him soon after Pattye was born and raised her daughter as a single-mother in a two-room apartment in St. Paul.

By the time I was born, Gammy was an old woman with white hair. She served lutefisk at holiday gatherings, recited old Norwegian prayers, and always had coffee cake or candy corn for me to eat. In her living room, there was an ancient pipe organ she would play for us during family gatherings such as birthdays, Christmas, or Thanksgiving.

Grandma Pattye was also an old woman by the time I was born. I remember her as an eccentric lady who smoked cigarettes at her kitchen table, had thousands of knick-knacks or art supplies hoarded in her attic, and was always quick with a witticism or a joke.

I used to spend nights at Grandma Pattye's house as a child. I would sit in the spare bedroom and play with her ancient typewriter. After filling pages with gibberish, I would bring them out to her in her dining room.

"Read these aloud for me, Grandma!" I would squeal.

She would read aloud the nonsense words with dramatic intonation, and I would giggle with delight. At night, she would turn off the lights, burn candles, and play old Alfred Hitchcock records for me in the front room.

"You know my house is haunted, right Sammy?" she asked me after the record was over.

"Is it?"

"It sure is."

I spent the night with my eyes wide open, tangled in sweaty sheets, and cowering against ghosts on the futon in her spare bedroom. In the morning, Grandma poured me purple soda from Kowalski's, and we listened to 1950's pop songs as we waited for Mom and Dad to come pick me up.

Anyway, Grandma Pattye got a job working at Midway Bank after her husband died, so she was able to get Mom a job there after my parent's divorce.

Sometimes, during a particularly boring day of school, I would lie and tell my teachers that I had a headache. They would send me to the nurse. After convincing the nurse that I needed to go home, I would call Mom.

"I'm sick, Mom," I told her. "Can you come get me?"

"Where's your father?" she asked.

"I don't know."

"Okay, I'll come get you."

Mom came to Horace Mann Elementary over her lunch break and picked me up to bring me back to the bank with her. After hugging Grandma, I hung out in a conference room on the second floor. Mom stopped in to check on me every fifteen minutes or so until the end of her shift. Then she took me home to Dad's house. It was exciting for me to spend the afternoon with Grandma and Mom in a place as stable as the bank, because both of them had to be sober at work. I so rarely got to see them, and I missed them both.

Mom began carefully introducing Christie and me to her boyfriend, Jim, after the shock of the divorce wore off.

Jim had a thick beard, long hair, and looked like the pictures of hippies I saw in the copies of *Mad Magazine* my father bought for me. Jim had a serious nature, and I was both frightened and resentful of his relationship with Mom from the beginning.

"Jim is a really nice guy," Mom told Christie and me one day after they picked us up in the ancient 1982 Pontiac Jim drove.

"Sure," I said.

"He lived in California for the past twenty years. He was in San Francisco," Mom told us.

"Cool!" Christie squealed.

"Okay," I shrugged.

"What was it like?" Christie asked.

"Warm," Jim said gruffly.

"Sammy," Mom told me. "Jim really likes baseball."

"He does?"

Then we talked about the Twins for a moment until I became self-conscious.

It was during this time that I started bringing reading materials around with me wherever I went. Instead of participating in unpleasant conversations or getting bored with the people around me, I would thumb through baseball box scores, the funny section in the newspaper, or a magazine. Eventually, this reading material was replaced with novels by Stephen King or Dean Koontz. I read whatever I could get my hands on. Dad had a strange collection of books around the house for me to choose from, ranging from evangelical tracts to gory science fiction.

Anyway, after engaging Christie and me in contrived conversation, Mom and Jim lit each other's Marlboro cigarettes and brought us back to Grandma Pattye's house. Christie and I figured out ways to stay amused with all of the toys in Grandma's attic while Mom sipped wine coolers, Jim drank Budweiser, and Grandma snuck off to the back room to pour herself shots of vodka in private. I would read whatever I brought with me, and Christie would go outside into Grandma's backyard. Then, Mom took us back home to where Dad was sitting in a cloud of marijuana smoke.

"How was spending time with Jim?" Dad asked me after Mom left.

"Fine," I shrugged.

And then I went upstairs and turned on the Nintendo in my room.

Eventually, Mom and Jim moved in together. They rented a lakefront bungalow about twenty minutes north of the Twin Cities on the shores of Forest Lake. Soon afterward, they were engaged.

It was during this time that Dad began having difficulties making the house payments in St. Paul.

Dad had been selling Medicare supplements as a way to generate a list of clients who might have eventual interest in buying the more lucrative life insurance or long-term care insurance policies he sold. He ended up selling a replacement supplement to an elderly customer that doubled up her existing coverage. The insurance commissioner's office discovered Dad's illegal activity and revoked his life and health insurance license for the year. Dad's income dried up, and he was unable to pay our bills. I distinctly remember coming home from the fourth grade one day to find Dad sitting on the front stoop of our house in St. Paul. Christie was next to him. She was crying, and Dad was holding his head in his hands.

"What's wrong?" I asked.

"We have to move," Christie told me.

"They're taking the house away from me," Dad said.

"Oh."

I went upstairs and turned on my Nintendo. Cato slinked into my room and curled up on my lap as I tweaked my lineup in *Baseball Stars*. Meanwhile, our house was foreclosed, and Dad made plans for us to move into a rental property outside of the cities on Lake Minnetonka.

"You're moving?" my friend John asked me.

"I guess so," I told him.

"Why?"

"Because."

"Oh."

I told all of my friends from the Silly Octopus Club. They were as upset as me.

"Will we still stay in touch?" Dookie asked me.

"Of course," I said.

So the summer after fourth grade, Dad moved us to Minnetonka. Like Mom, we also rented a house on the waterfront. We had a beautiful view of the lake from the deck off the back of the house.

I attended fifth grade at a middle school in Mound, Minnesota. My friends from St. Paul would come and visit on the weekends. We would play video games and go swimming in the lake, but things were not the same.

Christie started smoking pot with the kids that lived in the trailer park a mile down the road from our house. Christie lost her virginity to a kid in the trailer park, while Dad tried to score with his mom.

I stayed inside and kept playing Nintendo.

After finally making new friends at school in Mound, I was upset when Dad moved us again the summer before sixth grade. He bought a house an hour away in Arden Hills.

Arden Hills was a suburb outside of St. Paul. It was adjacent to the richest gated community in Minnesota, North Oaks. Dad purchased the place from a high school friend of his named Mike.

Dad knew Mike because they had gone to school together in St. Paul. Mike had dated my mother when they were teenagers. According to Mom, when Mike left for Vietnam after high school, he had asked my dad to keep an eye on her. My dad's eye was lecherous, so Mom and Dad started dating soon afterward. After years of an on-and-off relationship, Dad proposed to Mom.

"I guess we should get married," he told her.

"Sure," she said.

Years later, Dad's friend Mike returned from Vietnam and made an enormous amount of money as a baseball card dealer. I used to love going to his shop in St. Paul and thumbing through Barry Bonds' rookie cards or full sets of different Twins teams from the 80's. I could usually talk

Dad into buying me something: a Kirby Puckett rookie card, an Ozzie Guillen, a Dennis Eckersly, etc.

Mike took the enormous amount of money he made from the baseball card boom of the eighties and moved out to the suburbs. Just as my father was looking for a place to live after our lease in Minnetonka ran out, Mike purchased an even bigger house in Arden Hills. Dad's friend was selling his old house just as my father was trying to find a place.

Because Dad's credit was terrible, he convinced Mike to sell the house to him on a payment plan. Dad convinced Mike to draw up a contract for the deed. This meant that Mike was selling the house to Dad directly, without involving realtors or a mortgage company. Eventually, Dad made enough money selling long-term care insurance in the early 90's to restore his credit and buy the house outright with a legitimate mortgage.

I remember visiting that house in the suburbs for the first time. Mike and his three-year-old son met us there to walk us through the place.

It was my first experience with the suburbs. I could not get over how clean and new everything was.

"This house is so *nice*," I told Mike.

"It's a great place," he said.

The house Dad had been renting on Lake Minnetonka and the house that had been foreclosed in St. Paul were not nearly as updated and modern as the place in Arden Hills. In comparison, they were grimy, run down, and aged. In the suburbs, the grass was green, the homes were new, and everything felt *different*.

I walked up to Mike's little boy while we were being shown the house. He followed his dad closely as my father signed off on the contract.

"Do you have any idea how lucky you are?" I playfully asked Mike's son with condescending, sarcastic enthusiasm. "You have a rich family that takes care of you and a great big house out here in the suburbs to live in."

"Sam, will you stop?" Dad was harsh. He must have been embarrassed by what I said in front of his friend.

Dad bought the house, and we moved again.

In Arden Hills, I started to lose touch with my friends from Highland Park. The suburban kids around me now were *different*. They were less welcoming, did not laugh when I made outrageous jokes, and were confused by my hybrid, Jewish background. So instead of spending my time as the gang leader of the Silly Octopus Club, I became shy. I started hiding from Dad and Christie. They yelled at each other about something silly while I played the Super Nintendo Gammy bought me for Christmas in my bedroom. Cato would sleep peacefully on my lap. Otherwise, I was reading *The Hitchhiker's Guide to the Galaxy*. Generally speaking, I was figuring out what to do with the adolescent awkwardness of my chubby stomach, growing buckteeth, and strange family.

Christie started skipping school, hanging out with anybody who would give her marijuana or positive attention, and leaving the house for days or weeks at a time. Dad was unable to discipline her impulsive habits, so he ignored them. She began to spend more and more time with her boyfriend, Tim.

"He has three fingers and a hairlip," Dad told Christie sarcastically after meeting him. "He's perfect for you."

"Fuck you, Dad." This was how Christie often responded to my father.

Jim and Mom lived in their bungalow on Forest Lake while Dad was dragging Christie and me from St. Paul to Minnetonka to Arden Hills. I continued to exist in a general state of displacement as all of us settled into our new lives.

Whereas Dad seemed to relish his newly found bachelorhood, Mom and Jim had settled into a more stable, domestic routine. Christie and I would visit them on the weekends. They started out renting the little house on the lake, but Jim was so diligent and handy around the place that he endeared himself to the owner. Eventually, this owner agreed to sell the house to them. Jim was a systematic carpenter. He was constantly repairing the roof, renovating the kitchen, or replacing the windows. He was also working full-time as a handyman in the Twin Cities. Mom continued to work at the bank. Both of them kept extremely busy.

Mom and Jim got married a couple of years later. Their wedding was held on the lakeshore outside a bar that was only half a mile from their home. This was the same bar where they would bring me when I came to visit. Mom and Jim would drink beer, and I would beg for quarters to play the video games in the corner. Jim would show off my baseball knowledge to the other drunks in the bar.

"Sam, come here," Jim would call to me from the counter. It was crowded and smoky. I would be irritated because I had been playing the video game machines in the back.

"Yes, Jim?"

"Tell this guy what Mookie Wilson's batting average was last year."

I would rattle off stats to the amazement of the local drunks and return with a quarter to play another game of Spyhunter.

Anyway, I was the ring-bearer at Mom and Jim's wedding.

I snuck shots of champagne when nobody was looking and caught my mother's garter when she tossed it into a strange gathering of Mom and Jim's relatives.

My weekends in their tiny rambler on that neatly kept bit of lakeshore came to follow a routine. Mom and Jim always picked Christie and me up after work on Friday. On the way up to Forest Lake, Jim would stop at the local video rental store, Video Update. He would pick out a couple of movies for us to watch and rent me a Nintendo. Video stores used to make the system available for rent. This was exciting to me because I was able to pick out six or seven new games to play over the weekend. The clerks at Video Update always recognized Jim when we showed up. He would flirt with the girl behind the counter as I thumbed through the selection of games on the shelf. After Video Update, our next stop was the liquor store. Jim would buy a 24-pack of Budweiser, and Mom would get a 24-pack of Bud Light. Mom and Jim would keep themselves busy with yard work, gardening, or cooking during the day. I would be engrossed in my video games. At night, they would drink themselves to sleep in front of the television while we watched movies together. Sometimes, I could convince them to play *Monopoly* on the Nintendo with me before they passed out. It was the only game they could keep up with. I would transfer their money into my account when they were not paying attention.

"Are you cheating again, Sam?" Jim would laugh.

"No," I smirked.

"He's cheating," Mom would say with a smile.

"You're going to work on Wall Street someday," Jim would tell me.

"He's *so* smart," Mom would agree.

Eventually, Mom and Jim would pass out. Christie slept in the second bedroom, and I slept on the old green Victorian couch in the living room. Prior to the divorce, this couch sat in our parlor room in the St. Paul house. Now, it rested underneath a large bay window Jim had installed to look out over Forest Lake. I would fall asleep every night looking out on the stars.

One night, after Jim had passed out and she was thoroughly inebriated, Mom asked me to come into the kitchen.

"Is that a UFO, Sammy?" She pointed at a bright light over the lake.

I studied the light.

"I think it is."

"What should we do?"

"I don't know."

We watched as the light hovered over the lake for nearly fifteen minutes.

"I have to do something," Mom slurred. She picked up the phone and called the police department.

"I'd like to report a UFO," she said into the phone.

The conversation ended quickly. The police asked if she had been drinking. Mom lurched into her bedroom and passed out. I fell asleep on the couch, the covers around my face to ward off aliens.

By Sunday morning, I had spent two days playing and mastering different Nintendo games. All of Mom and Jim's beer was gone. They would drive me home in the afternoon.

Mostly, I felt unsettled spending the weekends in Forest Lake. More than Mom and Jim's drinking problem, it had never felt like a safe place to me. There was a heaviness in the home that was accentuated by the silence of the lake at night.

In order to fall asleep, I would listen to the radio and try my best to imagine myself as being anywhere but where I was. I would create and play out stories in my head to block out the menacing silence and darkness that came after Mom and Jim passed out.

One night, I was sleeping on that Victorian couch beneath the bay window. It was late in the evening or early in the morning. I awoke to the sound of something in the kitchen.

I turned and looked up from the couch. A figure that appeared to be my mother was standing in the kitchen. She was near the bathroom door. Her face was in her hands, she was weeping, and she was motioning for me to come toward her. Wet with sweat, I tried to stand and go to her but found myself frozen.

"Help me, Sammy," I heard the figure say.

"Mom?" I tried to speak, but no sound came from my throat.

"Help me."

The more I looked at the apparition, the more I was confused. Was it my mother, or was it a ghost?

The figure stopped calling for me and watched me from across the room. This dragged on for an eternity. It vanished suddenly. Once it was gone, I found myself able to move again. Afraid to investigate the apparition and sure that Mom and Jim were both unconscious in their bedroom, I cowered beneath my green blanket until the sun rose.

In the morning, I did not tell them about what I saw. Mom's house in Forest Lake always terrified me after that experience.

I wanted to be near my mother, but I was also afraid of her.

Chapter 4

When I was in middle school, Mom called me every morning during the week at 6:00 AM. It was the early nineties. She was up early because both she and Jim had to drive into the Twin Cities to go to work. I was up early to catch my bus for school.

We talked about nonsense for a couple of moments.

"You have no idea how much I love you, Sam," she told me at the end of our conversations.

"I love you too, Mom."

Mom was at her most sober around 6:00 in the morning. This may have had something to do with the coffee she brewed. It was strong enough to bring the dead back to life.

Mom only drank coffee if she made it herself. She had a careful process that included grinding beans and filling the filter to the brim which led to extremely strong pots of coffee.

"I can't drink coffee unless I make it myself," she would tell people when they offered her coffee at gatherings.

In fact, some of my most vivid memories of staying with Mom and Jim in Forest Lake included walking down the coffee aisle while we were grocery shopping. Every Saturday morning, we would wake up, eat breakfast, and drive into town to go to the grocery store.

Jim would point out all of the fat people waddling into the store for us to laugh at as Mom organized her coupons. She managed to spend next to nothing during our trips to the store because of her meticulous coupon clipping.

Inside the store, I was eager to reach the coffee aisle. I played with the plastic levers attached to the dispensers of their containers as Mom filled up paper bags with coffee, I would munch on the beans that fell into my hands. I even stored the extras in my pockets so I could have a snack by the time we reached the frozen foods section. Mom laughed as I became hyper from chomping away. My addiction to caffeine can probably be traced to those grocery store visits.

We would return home from the store, and Mom would spend a Saturday afternoon preparing Cornish game hens, manicotti, or flank steak while I played Nintendo in the living room. Sunlight streamed in over the lake through the large bay window. Mom's talent for cooking was one reason I was happy to visit her in Forest Lake. The steady diet of fast food Dad fed me was monotonous and unhealthy. Mom's tasty, home-cooked meals were a reprieve.

Anyway, during one of our early morning conversations, Mom told me that she and Jim had decided to give up drinking alcohol.

"We woke up one morning, Sammy," she told me, "and I noticed how yellow the whites of Jim's eyes were. I told him we needed to stop drinking."

Mom's news made me excited. The thought of my mother returning to the sober woman I remembered from my childhood made me ecstatic.

The first couple of weekend visits out to Forest Lake after Mom and Jim gave up drinking were luxurious for me. Instead of passing out on the couch, Jim stayed up and watched the movies we rented with me. Instead of becoming maudlin and awkward, Mom was simply warm and loving at night. She would make me cups of hot chocolate and sip cocoa with me in the kitchen.

Jim gave up drinking cold turkey after he and my mother made the decision to do so. Mom did not. A couple of weeks went by, and then Mom called me one evening.

"Your mother is on the phone," Sarah yelled up to me. I was playing *Super Mario World* on my Super Nintendo in the upstairs loft of our house in Arden Hills.

Sarah was my stepmother. My father married her in 1991, when I was eleven. She was originally from New Jersey, drove a school bus, and had three kids from her second marriage. Dad was Sarah's third husband. Like Christie and me, Sarah's children lived with their father. Sarah was a stern, blonde woman with icy blue eyes. She was in her forties. She was also a devout Evangelical Christian. Dad claimed divine intervention whenever anybody questioned his choice for a second wife.

"God brought us together," he told his friends when they raised an eyebrow at Sarah's brash style of communication. Indeed, they had met through a Christian dating service.

"Damn straight, Jew boy," Sarah would sneer.

Over the first couple years of their marriage, Sarah made Dad give up smoking pot, balance his checkbook, and pay his taxes on time. This was the most fiscally sound period in Dad's career as an insurance salesman. His commissions reached six-figures consecutive times during the 90's.

A good portion of that money went to paying Sarah's college tuition. She received a degree in English education from Bethel College. Bethel was a private Christian school. It was expensive. Sarah was unable to get hired as a teacher when she was finished. So she stayed at home and managed Dad's finances.

Sarah was amicable toward me, but it was tough for me to see past her bitter exterior.

It took me a little while to make new friends after moving from Minnetonka to Arden Hills. By the time Sarah moved in with us, I had made a few close friends. I spent most of my time with two boys I met in class. All of us were in the sixth grade at Sioux Middle School. Their names were Josh and Nick. Both of them followed the Twins and the Vikings, liked to play Nintendo, and laughed when I made inappropriate jokes. Sarah used to berate them when they would call me on the phone.

"Is Sam there?" they would ask.

"Where?" Sarah would retort.

"There?"

"What am I, his answering service?"

"Ummm…" Josh wouldn't have a response.

"Are you?" Nick would bark back sarcastically.

"She's from New Jersey," I would shrug and tell Josh or Nick later.

"So she gets to be a bitch?" Nick asked me.

Josh and Nick often came over to my house to drink Mountain Dew, eat pizza, and spend the night playing video games. Dad usually rented us four or five games from Mr. Movies, and we would stay up all night in the upstairs loft that served as a living room. One night, Sarah met Josh and Nick at the door.

"Make sure you don't put your hands on the walls," she told them as they walked into the house. "I just cleaned them."

Sarah's statement confounded Josh.

"I really want to put my hands on the walls," he told me after she went downstairs. Instead, we played *The Legend of Zelda: A Link to the Past*, *Starfox* and *Tecmo Super Bowl 3*.

My family bewildered Josh. He had three brothers, stable parents, and no idea how I coped with the chaos of my household. One weekend, after spending two nights at Josh's house, his parents drove me home. When we arrived, the doors were locked and nobody was there. A note addressed to me was taped to the front door. Sarah had written it.

"Dear Sam," it read, "We are out of town. Can you spend the night with a friend?"

Josh's parents did not have a choice after I showed them Sarah's note. So I spent a third consecutive night at Josh's house.

"I like your Dad," Josh told me later that night. "He's a nice guy. But your family is really fucked up."

Anyway, one night after Mom and Jim had quit drinking, Sarah's voice called me to the phone.

"It's your mother," she barked at me as she handed me

the receiver.

Mom was slurring her words, mumbling, and crying about how sorry she was. She was reminding me that Sarah was not my mother, and that Jim was more of a father to me than my real dad had ever been. Finally, Jim took the phone from her.

"I'm sorry, Sambo," Jim told me, "your mother isn't feeling well. She'll call you in the morning."

Incidentally, Jim often called me Sambo. This was a reference to little black Sambo—a stock character Jim knew of from his childhood. He meant it as a term of endearment, but after I learned what he was referring to, it had always struck me as a little racist.

"Okay, Jim," I told him. "Talk to you later."

"Bye." He hung up. I knew that Mom had been drinking again.

Mom apologized in the morning and told me that she had made a mistake. She told me that it would not happen again. Another week passed, and she called me slurring again. This went on for weeks, then months, then years.

I learned not to trust Mom when she started talking about sobriety.

Eventually, those morning conversations with Mom stopped. Talking to Mom every day became a chore after I started high school. The inanity of our conversations bored me. Also, it was painful to think about Mom sneaking pulls off of a hidden bottle of vodka while Jim was at work. By then, Mom had lost her job at Midway Bank; she was fired after missing shifts because of her drinking.

One of those last morning phone calls occurred because of her worsening alcoholism. But it was not with her. It was with Jim. I was a freshman in high school. The phone rang at the same time that Mom had always called me during middle school.

I recognized my stepfather's voice. "Jim?"

I was sitting in the living room of Dad's big suburban

house in Arden Hills. It was 6:00 in the morning. Sarah was making coffee in the kitchen, and Dad was sleeping upstairs. I was getting ready for school.

Christie ran away from home when she was sixteen. This was shortly after Sarah moved in. Christie left after becoming more and more contentious with my father, developing a habitual use of drugs and alcohol, and dropping out of high school. Christie first moved in with her boyfriend, Tim. Then she met a man who was ten years older than her named Todd. When I was thirteen, Christie and Todd moved to his hometown in Texas. I had spent years hiding in my bedroom in order to avoid Christie and her constant fighting with Dad. I was happy to see her and the constant chaos she represented leave the house.

So it was a quiet morning in Arden Hills on the day that Jim called.

"Sam, your Mom had a heart attack this morning," Jim told me over the phone.

Despite the distance I had been creating between my mother and me, Jim's statement was devastating. After spending the whole day at school worrying about Mom, I called Jim at the hospital when I got home. Jim told me that the doctors had discovered she had not had a heart attack. Mom had simply overdosed on pain medication. Jim found her collapsed on the kitchen floor when he woke up. He had thought it was a heart attack, only to discover that she had simply taken too many prescription pain pills.

"So she's fine?"

"Yes, she's fine. She'll call you later."

"Okay. Thanks Jim."

"Talk to you later, Sambo."

I was disappointed with my mother. I was also happy she was alive.

***

Grandma Pattye died when I was seventeen years old.

She was experiencing liver failure. This led to complications, and she developed an untreatable form of cancer toward the end of her life. By the fall of 1998, her health was failing. Grandma traveled back to Minnesota to visit her family over Christmas, because she knew she was dying.

At the time, Grandma was living in Florida after having met and married her high school sweetheart during the last few years of her life. His name was Hale.

In 1990, Grandma Pattye sold the house where my mother grew up. I was ten. She bought a condo in St. Paul, eventually met Hale, and left for Florida.

On the day of the closing of Grandma's house, Jim and Mom brought Christie and me over one last time. My Aunt Polly and her second husband, Scott, brought my cousins Leisa and Heidi with as well.

Incidentally, Leisa and Heidi's real father was my Uncle Dan. He worked with my father selling insurance for a couple of years. This meant that he used to come over to smoke pot with my father and play Nintendo with me. In fact, after Polly kicked him out, Dan moved in with us in Arden Hills. He slept on our couch upstairs before my father met Sarah and she chased Dan off. Dan and I would play *Top Gear* on my Super Nintendo for hours. I liked Dan because he was crude and sarcastic, but I was not surprised when he and Polly got a divorce.

Scott was a former minor league baseball player. He was far more stable than Dan had ever been. He became a fixture at family gatherings, and Dan disappeared.

Gammy was also there for the closing. As she aged and could no longer drive, Polly and Scott became responsible for transporting Gammy.

After spending so much time with Grandma in her house, I was sad to know I would never see it again.

My cousin Heidi was my age, and both her and I got

along well. We found an old Ouija board in the basement that was not packed up yet. We started playing with it.

"The ghost in this house is not happy that I'm moving," Grandma slurred at Heidi and me as we toyed with the board on the living room floor.

"Have you been drinking, Mom?" Mom asked.

"This house won't let me leave," she told Heidi and me.

"You're drunk at 10:00 in the morning?" Mom glared at Grandma Pattye.

Polly rolled her eyes.

"I'm so disappointed in you, Pattye," Gammy said as she tried to make her daughter feel guilty.

Heidi and I were too excited about talking to ghosts to care about Grandma's sobriety. We used the Ouija board to ask the spirit in her house to reveal itself.

"Who are you?" we asked the board.

Before the spirit could respond, Mom helped Grandma sign the papers that the realtor had brought over, the closing was finished, and we were helping our parents bring Grandma's stuff over to her new condo in St. Paul.

There was a swimming pool on the main level of Grandma's new building. Heidi and I would go over to her condo, have lunch with her, visit, and swim in her pool. Afterward, we would go up to her apartment and watch television with her.

Grandma gave fantastic backrubs.

"Will you rub my back?" I begged her when I visited.

"Will you pay me?" she snapped back sarcastically.

Then she would massage my shoulders, and I would melt.

"Sam," Grandma told me as she was rubbing my back, "you really should be a writer."

"You think so?" I asked her.

"Yes. You have such wit in your writing."

When I was in ninth grade, I had written Grandma a birthday card because my mother told me to. I used sarcasm in the card because I knew Grandma would *get it*. I rambled on about how young and attractive she was. Grandma framed the card and hung it on her wall next to a picture of me. She laughed out loud and read it to people when they came over. Grandma had a powerful sense of humor.

On Christmas night of 1995, three years before Grandma died, she called her daughter Polly. She was incoherent, but she kept muttering that there was blood everywhere. My Aunt Polly hung up and called an ambulance. Polly and Scott picked up Gammy and met Jim, Mom, and my sister at a hospital in St. Paul. We were told that Grandma was the sickest person in the hospital and probably would not last the night. She had no blood pressure. They put her in an inflatable suit. All of us went into the intensive care unit to visit Grandma Pattye. We said our goodbyes that evening. She was shriveled, her eyes were yellow, and her skin was translucent. Mom wept openly, and so did I.

"Her liver is shutting down," the doctors told us. "There isn't much we can do."

Somehow, Grandma survived the night. She woke up a couple of days later. After she was awake, she joked with us when we visited.

"This isn't going to make me shrink any more, is it?" she laughed.

Grandma Pattye was 4'11" in her fifties. By the time she was in her sixties, she was just under 4'8".

"I just keep shrinking as I get older," she would laugh. "I'm already eligible to attend the midget's ball. Can I get any smaller?"

This was a joke that Grandma used routinely. She was, in fact, considered a legal midget by the time she was sixty.

Miraculously, Grandma survived that stint in the hospital. She quit drinking after she was released.

Hale was the reason that Grandma Pattye started drinking again. Unlike my mother, Grandma Pattye had managed to stop drinking after her brush with death forced her to quit. She had been sober for over a year before meeting Hale at a high school reunion.

Hale convinced her to have a couple of drinks while they were out on a date one night. Embarrassed, Grandma Pattye did not want to admit to him that she had trouble with alcohol. She ordered a drink and quickly fell back into her old routine of hiding vodka bottles around the house. She developed cirrhosis of the liver that eventually led to cancer by 1998.

My last memory of Grandma Pattye was of us sitting together on a bench outside of an Outback Steakhouse. We were at a mall in the suburbs of St. Paul. Gammy had taken all of us out to eat after Grandma came home from Florida.

Grandma sat with me outside of a Best Buy store after dinner. It was a week before Christmas. People were racing by with shopping bags as Grandma and I waited for Mom and Jim to finish shopping for a CD inside the store. We watched as snow accumulated on cars in the parking lot.

"Will you wait out here with Grandma?" Mom had asked me before going into the store.

"Of course," I said.

So I sat on the bench with Grandma and held her hand. Grandma was tiny, shriveled, and weak. She could not walk without help. Both she and I knew that this was the last time we would see each other.

"I just want you to know that I love you very much, Grandma," I told her as I held her hand. Mom had told me not to mention that Grandma was dying. Mom said it would make everybody sad. But Polly and Scott had left with Gammy, and Grandma and I were alone now. I had to say something to her.

Grandma Pattye started crying.

"I know, Sam. I love you too. I am very proud of who you are becoming. Even if you're short."

I laughed, squeezed her hand, and started to cry.

I wiped tears out of my eyes as Mom and Jim came out of Best Buy.

"You ready to go?"

I had recently passed my driver's test. So I got into the 1984 Oldsmobile Cutlass Cierra my father had given me and drove off into the snow. Mom and Jim took Grandma back to Gammy's house.

Two months later, Grandma's doctors told her she only had six to twelve months left to live. Mom, Polly, and Gammy flew down to be with her after learning Grandma had so little time left.

Grandma was put on hospice. Her nurses gave her a supply of morphine drops that she could place under her tongue to dull her pain.

On the second night of Mom, Polly, and Gammy's visit, Grandma's pain grew worse. She was moving in and out of consciousness and calling out for her dead husband, my Grandpa Jaye.

"Nubby," she moaned.

Gammy and Polly were staying at a hotel. Mom was sleeping at Grandma's house. Hale was asleep in the other room, so Mom was alone with her mother.

Mom spent the night squeezing morphine into Grandma's mouth. One drop after another, my mother tried to kill my grandmother's pain.

Grandma died in her sleep that night. She drowned due to the buildup of fluid in her lungs.

My mother called Polly at her hotel room the next day. "I think I killed our mom."

Polly was silent on the other line.

"Don't you have anything to say?"

"What do you want me to say to that, Wendy?"

Grandma Pattye was dead two days after Mom, Gammy, and Polly had flown down to Florida. When I spoke to Mom afterward, she admitted to me she had given Grandma too much morphine to help ease her pain.

"She was hurting so badly," Mom told me. "She kept

waking up and calling out for my dad. She didn't want to live anymore."

Like Polly, I did not know what to say to my mother.

Shortly after Grandma died, my sister Christie gave birth to her only son. Skylar was born in Minnesota. Mom flew down to Texas to bring Christie back home months before she was due. Christie had decided to leave Skylar's father, Todd. He had become increasingly abusive toward my sister.

Todd was hit by a car after Christie left him. He had been riding his bike home from a friend's house where he had been drinking. He was killed instantly.

Christie got in touch with an old boyfriend named Tim after she returned to Minnesota. They had dated in high school before Tim ended up in prison. Both she and Tim qualified for disability; Christie had cerebral palsy, and Tim was born with birth defects. His hand was deformed, and he had developmental issues. So they rented a cheap apartment where they lived with Skylar, Christie's baby. Skylar began spending most of his time with my mother and Jim or my father and Sarah--there was less of a chance that marijuana would be blown in his face as a joke at their houses.

Mom started drinking more heavily after Grandma died. Jim began to complain about finding bottles of vodka stashed all around their house in Forest Lake. This led to multiple inpatient and outpatient treatments for my mother's alcoholism. After a stay at Hazelden, Mom spent a month sober before falling back into her old habits.

"I promise I'll never drink again, Sammy," she would tell me.

"Okay, Mom."

Time passed, and she would often call me slurring her words. I would grit my teeth and listen to her drunkenly sob into the telephone about whatever she could think to mumble about.

"You'll always be my little Sammy," she would say.

"Okay, Mom."

During this time, Jim started to become more of a caretaker than a husband for my mother. I did my best to avoid interactions with her.

My sister was gone, and my father was preoccupied with his wife Sarah and selling insurance. The two of them were always attending Evangelical churches or holding Bible studies in our living room. I slinked around the house when I was home, keeping to my bedroom where I played video games or read books. I also called my friends as a way to get out of the house whenever possible.

"Can I spend the night?" I would ask Josh or Nick.

"Let me ask my parents," they would say.

Both Josh and Nick's parents got used to me spending the weekends with them.

"We should charge you rent," Nick's father would growl sarcastically.

"Don't you have a home?" Josh's mom would laugh.

I would shrug sheepishly and make a joke to change the subject.

Despite my attempts to remove myself from interactions with my family members, Mom's phone calls were persistent. Listening to her go on and on about how difficult her life was, how sad she was, or how I did not call her enough was grueling. This was particularly true if she had been drinking because I knew that, regardless of what I told her, she'd forget it by the next day.

I worked to avoid her as much as I could without cutting ties completely.

***

The lack of support from Mom and Dad made me angry. Josh and Nick's parents were so much more involved than mine were. I tried to figure out how to take care of myself.

I was hired for my first job when I was fourteen years

74

old. The position was that of a dishwasher in a convent for retired nuns. Josh came from a devout Catholic family. He had worked at the convent for a couple of months and gave me a stellar recommendation. Next thing I knew, I was walking down eerie, sacred corridors and scrubbing grease off of dirty pots and pans.

Every so often an elderly nun would hobble by the dishwashing room. She would see my long hair or my Nirvana t-shirt, make the sign of the cross, and hobble away.

The shifts lasted from 4:15 until 7:15 PM. My supervisor was the cook on duty for the evening. This was usually Dean. Dean was nearly 350 pounds, a huge fan of the band AC-DC, and bragged about how much alcohol he could consume after his shifts were over. He was also extremely nice to me.

After serving dinner, Dean would take me out to his car during our break while we waited for the nuns to gum their way through their meals. We would eat Fritos we stole from the pantry, listen to 1980's hair metal, and talk. Dean would tell stories about his mishaps of going through life as a 350-pound cook at a convent, and I would tell him about my drug-addicted sister or my wicked stepmother.

Dad and Sarah could rarely be bothered to drop me off or pick me up from work. So I would ride my bike nearly five miles each way to make it to and from the convent in time for my shift. If it were snowing really hard, Dean would put my bike in his trunk and give me a ride home.

Eventually, I decided I needed to make more than the $4.25 an hour. So after I turned 15, I went back on the job market. My first interview was at a local pizza and hoagie restaurant chain called Davanni's. On the day of the interview, I showed up wearing a black Pearl Jam t-shirt. The manager looked me up and down when I arrived for the interview.

"That isn't how you dress for an interview," she told me. "We can set another time for when you're more prepared."

Embarrassed, I went home. The next interview was set for the following week. I found an old button-down shirt that belonged to my father. Dad drove me to my second meeting with this woman. He was running late, so we ended up arriving about fifteen minutes after the scheduled time.

"You should never be late to an interview," the same manager told me. "I'm afraid this won't work."

This experience thoroughly humiliated me. I blamed my father for my failure to get a job. Dad was never very punctual, and he was the reason I arrived late. He felt awful. He took me out for Chinese food at a restaurant in the same strip mall after I walked out of the Davanni's. From this point on, I was fifteen minutes early for everything. This included my next interview at McDonald's.

I arrived early. The shirt I was wearing was both formal and ironed. I was cautious and polite as I spoke to the store's general manager. She offered me a position on the spot. The job began in June, before my junior year of high school. I clocked forty hours each week that summer as a closer. This meant that I worked late into the evening cleaning the store at the end of the day.

I convinced the store manager to hire Nick two months after me. He and I were a food-service force to be reckoned with. We had an efficient system. Between the two of us, we could have the store spotless by one minute after closing, give out about $50 worth of free food to our friends when they came to visit, and still have time to melt the faces off the Dutch Barbie Happy Meal toys in the deep fryer. Then, we would stuff about forty chicken nuggets in a bag, go back to his house, and play the Nintendo 64 I had purchased with my earnings from McDonald's until three or four in the morning.

Due in equal part to my work ethic and the general manager's shoddy store management, I was promoted to shift manager within three months. This meant I wore grease-stained ties, made a dollar more per hour than everybody else, and had the ultimate authority to delegate who would be cleaning the grill, doing the dishes, or expediting food. Nick would sneer at me when I told him to do something.

"Yes-sir, *shift manager*, right away," Nick would tell me as he lowered Dutch Barbie into the deep fryer.

My promotion also meant customers brought their complaints to me.

During one dinner rush, an old man came up to the register that Nick was working.

"Excuse me, did you know there are ants in the store?"

"Ants?" Nick asked sarcastically. "That's too bad."

Nick's response exacerbated the situation. Nick came back into the kitchen.

"Sam," he told me, "you should probably get out here."

By the time I was out front, the customer was standing on a table in the lobby screaming at the customers.

"Ants! There are ants everywhere! Don't eat the food, it's probably crawling with ants."

"Sir, can I help you?" I asked.

"ANTS!"

"I'm the manager. Can I help you?"

"ANTS!!!"

Eventually, the man tired himself out and left. After sweeping up a pile of ants congregating near the soda fountain, I did my best to convince the rest of the customers in the lobby that there were no ants in the store, even though there were.

One day, an old woman came up to the counter after eating her McChicken sandwich in the lobby.

"Excuse me, can I talk to the manager?"

I smiled.

"That would be me," I told her. I looked about twelve

at the time. The outfit brought that age up to about thirteen. People always had a hard time believing I was in charge.

"Really? *You're* the manager?"

"What can I do for you?"

The woman handed me her half-eaten McChicken sandwich. A worm was hanging out of the processed meat.

"I don't want to alarm you, but I think there's a worm in this McChicken."

Alarmed? I was mortified. It took everything I had not to gag. I figured a lawsuit would follow.

"I'm so sorry, ma'am," I told this woman. "What can I do? Do you want me to refund the sandwich? Do you want me to file a complaint with corporate?"

"That's okay," she told me. "Could I just have a new McChicken sandwich?"

I watched as the woman sat down and ate another McChicken sandwich in the lobby. Meanwhile, I put the sandwich with the worm hanging out of it in the freezer, left a note for the general manager, and never ate anything from McDonald's again. In fact, working at McDonald's made me skinny. Between the revulsion I developed for fast food and the long hours, I started wasting away.

Soon after losing the weight that had accumulated during my unhealthy childhood, I started dating my co-worker, Missy. She was seventeen when we started going out—one year older than me.

I arrived for work one evening complaining about a runny nose. Missy was just getting off from the morning shift. She showed up later that night with homemade chicken noodle soup.

"I made this for you."

It was an extremely sweet thing for her to do. I agreed to go out on a date with her the following week, and we were pretty serious from then on.

Missy's family was far more functional than mine. Her mother and father got along, she had three siblings who were close, and her house was a pleasant place for me to be. I started spending as much of my time there as I could. I would show up for dinner and stay until midnight, watching television with Missy in her basement family room.

During my junior year of high school, I worked nearly forty hours a week. Between school, work, and Missy, I kept so busy that I rarely interacted with my family.

When I learned Missy had been accepted to the University of Minnesota in Duluth (UMD), I decided that I needed to follow her. I started paying attention to my grades for the first time since I started high school. After getting good marks in middle school, I found that my high school classes did not much interest me. My grades didn't bother my father because Dad did not pay that much attention to me. So I did not care either. My grade point average after 10th grade was abysmal. The consequences of this became clear to me when I began to worry about following Missy to college. So I got serious about school. After getting straight A's during my junior year, I was able to bump my GPA up to a 2.1.

Intent on getting accepted into college, I signed myself up for the ACT during my junior year. My friend Mike's parents had scheduled his test for the same day as mine. Mike had started hanging out with Josh, Nick, and me as our group of friends expanded in high school. There was a group of about ten of us who played fantasy basketball and spent time together.

Mike and I woke up early on a Saturday morning, drove to Bethel College, and took the exam. Somehow, the contact lens in my right eye tore during the first section. I took the test with one hand covering a weeping, red eye. At one point, the proctor came up to me.

"Are you okay?" she asked.

"I'm fine," I told her gruffly.

By the end of the ACT, I could not see out of one eye. Mike drove my 1984 Cutlass Ciera home from Bethel for me. His car was parked in my father's driveway. He had driven to my house that morning so we could ride over together.

The seat adjustment switch in the Cutlass was broken. Mike was a basketball player. He was well over six feet tall, and I was just a touch over five. So his knees were jammed in his face as we navigated home. When we arrived in my driveway, Sarah came running out the door.

"Why is Mike driving *your* car, Sam?" she howled at me.

"Because I can't see," I told her.

"Oh. Well, he can't drive it."

Sarah stormed back inside.

"What a bitch," Mike remarked.

"Yup."

Despite the twenty-eight I got on the ACT, my college application was rejected from UMD during my senior year. I called Missy and told her the bad news.

She and I had continued our relationship after she left for college. An angsty teenager, I became seriously lonely without her and moped around school after she left in the fall. Josh's girlfriend at the time was also a year older. Like Missy, she went to college in Duluth. Josh and I had most of our classes together during our senior year, so he and I would commiserate with each other. In first hour physics, we would check box scores in the paper to keep track of our fantasy sports teams, whine about how lonely we were, and pay little to no attention in class.

Missy and I talked four or five times a week, visited each other on the weekends, and managed to remain entangled regardless of geographic distance. Missy transferred to the University's main campus in the Twin Cities after our relationship somehow survived her freshman year.

By a stroke of luck, the University of Minnesota had a program in 1998 called General College. This was its final year before its funding was cut. It was designed for students with good ACT scores, poor grades, and extenuating circumstances. More bluntly, it was designed to help poor students of color get into college. I met some of the qualifications, so I was admitted into college by the skin of my teeth. I signed up to room with my friends Josh and Mike and started looking at FAFSA forms so that I could figure out how to pay for school.

All of my friends' parents were helping them pay for college, so I went to my father.

"You're paying for Sarah's college," I told my Dad. "Are you going to help me out?"

"I can't afford it," he told me. "Call your Gammy. She's filthy rich."

Dad went outside to wash his new Corvette, and I called Gammy.

"Can you help me pay for college?" I asked her.

"I don't have enough money, Sammy," she told me. "Can't you go to people at the University of Minnesota and tell them about your situation so that they can help? They'll see you're such a nice boy."

"Sure, Gammy." How could I explain to my great-grandmother that college tuition didn't work that way?

"I love you, Sammy."

"Love you too, Gammy."

I did not bother calling Mom.

I was angry with my family for not helping me. Still, I knew that sharing this anger would not accomplish anything.

I filled out my FAFSA application for student loans. My father made far too much money for me to get any sort of grants or federal aid, so I was forced to take out the maximum amount of loans to pay for college.

Later that year, when I was eighteen, Mike got me a job working with him as a manager at Subway. Mike had worked there for a year, had been promoted to manager, and convinced the owner of Subway to offer me a position. By the time I quit Subway four years later—during my junior year at the University of Minnesota—I was making $14.25 an hour. That was a significant sum of money to be working in fast food in the late '90's. To augment my job at Subway, I got licensed to sell insurance with my father after I graduated from high school.

In the summer of 1998, after training me so that I could sell long-term care insurance, Dad discovered that he needed triple bypass surgery. The operation was serious, but it was also a success.

After Dad came home, it seemed like there was something different about him. Some of his lively, charismatic spark was gone.

"I was dead for seven seconds," he told Sarah and me. "I wonder if I went to heaven?"

I rented Dad ten or twelve movies from a local Blockbuster, and Sarah waited on him as he recuperated on the couch in the upstairs loft. Meanwhile, he had one of the lucrative seminars he had been conducting for state employees scheduled up North in Duluth, Minnesota.

"Looks like it's time for you to take over the family business," he told me.

Dad booked me a room at the Radisson. He let me borrow his Nissan Maxima so that I would project the classy confidence of an insurance agent. I traveled to Duluth and presented a seminar on long-term care insurance to about sixty elderly people in his place. I wore a suit and tie, gave presentations like my father did, and spent a successful week as a salesman. I sold roughly ten long-term care insurance policies in Duluth and made close to $30,000 in commissions for a week's worth of work.

While the money was lucrative, I learned that I could not count on my father as a boss. I constantly had to look over my commission reports to make sure he was paying me on the sales I had made.

Dad convinced me to let him sign off as the supervising agent so that all of my sales would count toward his annual bonus with the company we sold for,

Blue Cross and Blue Shield. That meant that most of my commissions were technically listed under his name. His intentions were good. He wanted to make the annual bonus and share it with me.

But the devil was in the details. Dad quickly started to forget which commissions were mine and which were his. After learning that I could not count on him to be accurate or consistent in paying me, I gradually stopped putting energy into being an insurance agent. Instead, I focused on my English major at the University of Minnesota.

I transferred out of General College after two trimesters. By the spring, I was taking regular classes in the College of Liberal Arts.

It was during my sophomore year of college at the University of Minnesota that Mom's house in Forest Lake burned down. Mom and Jim had a propane tank in their garage that connected to a heater they used to stay warm when they smoked cigarettes. They forgot to turn it off one morning when they left to go into town to run errands. When they returned, the entire house had burned to the ground.

Mom and Jim used the enormous sum of money they made from their insurance claim to buy an expensive house on a large plot of land in Hudson, Wisconsin. The house had an updated workshop for Jim, was ten times larger than their place in Forest Lake, and was immaculately modern. They were able to purchase brand new furniture, updated appliances, and a small fortune's worth of tools for Jim's workshop.

Anyway, when Mom called to tell me about the fire, I did not ask for the details. She was slurring, and I wanted to get off the phone. After rambling for about twenty minutes about how upset she was, my response was simple.

"That's too bad, Mom."

"Is that all you can say, Sammy?"

I had two papers due in classes I was taking, had to

work a shift at Subway, and was heading over to Missy's house to spend the evening with my girlfriend. In other words, I had too much to worry about to take on the impossible task of trying to make my mother feel better. Besides, I could tell that she had been drinking, and I knew that she would not remember anything I said to her.

"Yes, that's about it, Mom."

"I love you, Sammy," she told me.

"I love you too."

And I hung up the phone.

***

The first poem I ever wrote was about fire. It came to my mind when I was ten years old.

It was a Sunday morning, and Mom and Jim were driving me back to my father's house in Arden Hills. Jim was driving. Mom was in the passenger seat. I was in the backseat reading *The Stand* by Stephen King. We were pulling out of their garage in Forest Lake. As usual, I was relieved to be heading home.

I remember the vivid image of a fire coming into my mind as I watched the garage door shut and the truck pull away. In my head, I remember imagining a detailed description of flames. I tried to describe fire in my imagination with the same detail that Stephen King used to illustrate an atomic explosion in his book.

I found a piece of paper once I got home and wrote down my poetic description of fire. Gazing at my mother's garage inspired it. When I was finished, I realized that I had just created my first poem. I kept it buried in a drawer in my bedroom at Dad's house. It would not be my last piece of poetry.

I wrote one poem a day from age sixteen on. They all were saved in folders on my computer. The poetry was terrible, but it became a sacred vessel for me to let my thoughts out without fear of commentary or assessment.

Determined Weeds

Years later, long after I had graduated from high school and squeaked my way into college, that propane tank exploded in Mom's garage. Her house in Forest Lake burned to the ground.

The first thing that came to my mind after I heard about the explosion was that poem I had written as a child.

Chapter 5

I was nineteen when the year 2000 arrived. People were giddy with the dawn of a new millennium.

"I wonder if the aliens will finally arrive," a friend mused to me at a party as he handed me a joint. The image of my father flashed into my mind, and I passed the joint along without taking a hit.

I was at one of the many house parties Josh and Mike held at the house they were renting in Dinkytown, just off the University of Minnesota's campus. I was holding a red plastic cup of cheap beer I had paid five dollars for.

"Are you ready to go yet?" I asked Nick through a cloud of smoke.

He and I drove to campus parties together because we both lived with our parents in Arden Hills. We also commuted to school together. Like me, Nick had been admitted to the University through the General College program. Unlike me, he never made it out. After Nick dropped out of college, I either drove with my girlfriend Missy, who also lived with her parents, or by myself.

Anyway, Nick had driven with me to Josh and Mike's New Year's party.

"C'mon, Grandma," Nick growled at me as he blew smoke in my face. "It's early."

My friends often called me "Grandma" because I did not like staying out late or drinking. I would rather have been home. We called Nick "Grandpa" because he was a stubborn asshole.

My persistent nagging eventually convinced him to leave.

The aliens did not come with the dawn of the new millennium, so I rolled over in a tiny, single bed in the unfinished basement of my father's house in Arden Hills to answer a ringing telephone. This unheated space had served as my bedroom throughout my adolescence and into my early twenties. Dad and Sarah mostly left me alone down there, and I did my best to stay out of their way.

Missy called me early on that Sunday morning in the

winter of 2000. Missy's early phone call disturbed my new black kitten. She was sleeping underneath the covers with me. Her full name was Fluffalufagus, but I called her Kitty. This change in names can be attributed to our first visit to the vet.

An extremely attractive girl had been sitting at the receptionist's desk. When she asked for the kitten's name, I became embarrassed. I did not want to let on that I was a weirdo who named his cat Fluffalufagus. So I told her that the cat's name was Kitty. The name stuck. I only used Kitty's full name when she did something irritating, like jump on my lap while I was battling a boss in *Final Fantasy Nine*.

"FLUFF-A-LUFAGUS!" I bellowed.

I was nineteen when I first brought Kitty home. The day before, I had picked out a different kitten at the Humane Society. Missy had come with me.

"It's like we're picking out our first child," she told me as she stroked an orange kitten with white spots. "We should get this one."

That kitten died the next morning.

"It died?" the person from the Humane Society asked on the phone after I called to inform them that their product was defective.

"Yes," I said.

Indeed, the morning after I brought that first kitten home, it was huddled in the corner of my basement, shivering, looking at me with innocent, helpless eyes.

"Help," it mewled at me as I held it.

I took that kitten to the vet to try and save it. They euthanized it instead. The same attractive receptionist gave the dead kitten back to me in a shoebox. So I called the Humane Society to figure out my next move.

"Well, you could return it," the receptionist told me over the phone.

"Return it?"

"Yes, you could exchange it."

"Okay?"

"Make sure you bring the body."

So I brought that tiny kitten in its shoebox coffin back to the Humane Society and came home with Kitty.

Later, I learned that my stepbrother's enormous dog had picked up that first kitten in its mouth while I was out and flung it across my basement bedroom.

"They were playing," Sarah's oldest son told me years later.

That is how I ended up with Kitty. I picked her out because she looked like a tiny version of my childhood companion, Cato. Like her, she was black and lanky with yellow eyes.

Cato had wandered off one day after we moved to Arden Hills. She never returned.

"She was old," Dad told me at the time. "She wanted to leave on her own terms."

So I named my new cat Fluffalufagus after that big-ass elephant thing on Sesame Street, placed her in my car, and drove her back to Dad's house. I was too stupid to keep her in the box that the Humane Society gave me. My new kitten wandered around the '94 Honda Civic I bought with the money I made selling insurance. She was a spry young kitten, and she mewed and brushed against my feet as I drove through heavy traffic, West along 694.

Kitty could not stop pooping after we got home. My stepmother Sarah made fun of her.

"Shitty kitty," she laughed as Kitty left her mark everywhere she went, especially on my bed.

One of the most generous things my stepmother ever did for me was to take Kitty to the vet. She returned with medication, and I used a syringe to feed it to Kitty twice a day. Kitty stopped pooping everywhere and started staking out her claim in that basement with me. At night, when it was freezing, she limped under the covers and curled into the space between my chest and arm. We kept each other warm after my huge, heated waterbed sprung a leak and I was left with a tiny single bed, pressed up against a freezing brick wall.

Anyway, I pushed Kitty aside and picked up the phone.

"Hello?" I mumbled into the receiver.

Missy's voice sounded anxious. She started to mutter something about needing to talk to me. This led to her suggesting that we should break up.

It was a rare Sunday morning that I did not work an opening shift at Subway. I had been looking forward to sleeping in. Missy's comment ruined my lazy mood.

In my early twenties, I had traces of my father's sarcastic temper and it affected the way I started treating Missy. As we grew older, she became a psychology major who was following in her father's footsteps. He was in a middle management position at a local food company called Sysco. I was turning into a frenetic and emotional English major with the uneven disposition of both my parents. Things became confusing when I tried to talk with her about what I was passionate about. She was not interested in Blake's poetry, *The Brothers Karamazov*, or *Wretched of the Earth*. She never understood what I was trying to discuss with her, and this frustrated me. I probably knew our relationship was finished after watching *American Beauty* with her. On the way out of the movie theater, I spoke first.

"That was one of the most beautiful things that I have ever seen."

"It was gross," Missy said.

We got into a heated argument. Her reaction to the movie was one of the final straws. At twenty, I could not imagine being in love with a girl who did not appreciate *American Beauty*. Despite this, I was afraid to lose somebody who had actually cared about me for such a long time.

During our four years together, Missy and I had gone through any number of fights that ended with one of us threatening to break up with the other. But her voice sounded different when she called me on that Sunday morning.

"After four years," I told her, "the least you can do is tell me this in person. Will you come over?"

Missy agreed and arrived at my front door thirty minutes later.

I pleaded with her. We had just spent Christmas together. We were close with each other's families. She had been leaving ads for wedding rings in my car, hinting that she was ready for us to get married; now she wanted to end things?

"I don't love you anymore, Sam," she told me. "I don't know if I ever did."

"We've been together for four years."

"I have to go."

"If you walk out, this is over. Don't leave," I begged her.

She was not convinced. I stood in the doorway of Dad's house. She drove away in the 1994 Chevy Lumina I had helped her pick out from a used car lot.

Dad and Sarah were at church that morning. I was alone. I made a pot of strong coffee and went up to Dad's office where the computer was. I put Bob Dylan's *Time Out of Mind* on Dad's stereo and wrote a paper for a class on linguistics and rhetoric that analyzed *Super Mario Brothers* as a representation of working-class archetypes. I turned the stereo up as loud as it would go.

"Well, I been pacing 'round the room, hoping maybe she'd come back."

Dylan's unearthly voice filled the room. His words seemed to perfectly capture whatever numbness was spreading inside my chest.

Dad came upstairs after he got home.

"What the hell happened to you?" he asked. "You look terrible."

"Missy broke up with me," I mumbled.

"Oh."

The next morning, I woke up early and drove to school. I had a class on American literature at 8:00 in the morning, another on post-colonial literature at noon, and a German class until 8:00 at night. After dragging myself through that long day, I walked back to the commuter lot where my car was parked. I put the keys in the ignition, turned them, and nothing happened.

A little known feature of the 1994 Honda Civic was its lack of any sort of warning system to make the driver aware that he or she had left their lights on. My battery was dead.

I walked through the snow back to where a friend of mine lived with four other roommates on campus. On my way, a semi-truck drove through a puddle and covered me in icy, muddy water.

"Really?" I looked up at the frozen moon hanging in a wintry sky.

My friend finally jumped my car, and I got back home around midnight. I collapsed in my freezing bedroom after what had felt like an eternally miserable day. Kitty jumped up and fell fast asleep on my face.

The end of my relationship with Missy was devastating. I became gloomy, stopped eating, and went through my days like a dead man. I buried myself in my readings for class and focused on academics. Still, everything in that freezing basement reminded me of Missy. Four years of her gifts to me and pictures of us cluttered the space. So I snuggled with Kitty and suffered through the dull agony my mind produced whenever I thought about Missy.

I found myself on various insurance appointments during this time. Though I was focused on college, I still went in my father's place whenever he was unable to attend a sales call.

On one such appointment, I put on a tie and drove up to a large house in North Oaks. Visions of huge commissions danced through my head as I scoped out the mansion.

An older woman met me at the door. She took me into an ornate living room. After thirty minutes of pitching the woman the most expensive long-term care insurance policy we sold, she looked at me with concern.

"Are you doing *okay*, Sam?"

Her question took me by surprise.

"Actually, not really."

I stopped my presentation about insurance and shared that my girlfriend had broken up with me. After my story, the potential client smirked at me.

She told me that she was an extremely spiritual person. Thanks to my father, I was well versed in Evangelical Christianity. So she and I started talking about God.

"Do you mind if we pray together, Sam?"

Was I going to say no? A sizeable commission was at stake.

I closed my eyes and prayed with this strange woman. After a moment of silence, she asked me if there were any words or phrases in my mind. To my surprise, there were.

"Sing a new song?" I offered hesitantly.

"Yes," the woman smiled. "Can we try something else now?"

Again, was I going to say no?

The woman told me to close my eyes and visualize a spiritual cord that connected me with Missy. I did. The woman asked me to visualize scissors in my hand. I did. The woman asked me to imagine myself cutting the cord. I did.

The moment that I visualized this act, I heard an almost seismic "Bang!" in the air above me. Startled, I opened my eyes. The woman was smiling.

"See?" she asked. "You are free now."

Shaken, I left the house with a check. It was the largest sale I had made as an agent. I shared this story with my father. He shrugged and reminded me that the God of Abraham was powerful and listened to my prayers.

"Your name means 'God listens,' Sam. Don't forget that."

Three months passed, spring arrived, and I started hanging out with a girl named Julie.

Julie was a friend of another girl named Tina. Both of them had been in my section of British literature and were in the same section of American literature I took later. Unlike Missy, both of them had enjoyed *American Beauty*. They were also the same height as me. Meeting anybody who was into what I was into *and* was also the same height as me seemed unlikely. I made it a point to talk with both of them during class.

One afternoon, I ran into Tina on campus when I was walking back to my car after American Literature. We talked about how both of us wanted to be high school English teachers. She invited me to hang out with her and Julie later in the week. Julie and I were dating soon after that.

Julie had a black cat tattooed on her right shoulder, was a strong writer, and had sparkling eyes. I was hooked. After six months, she convinced me to move out of my father's house and live with her.

"There's something off about her, Sam," my father told me after meeting her.

"Damn straight," Sarah chimed in.

I ignored them both, even though I knew that they were right. Julie and I rented a basement flat on Grand Avenue in St. Paul, near where I grew up in Highland Park.

I got a job working at the original Dunn Brothers coffee shop near Macalester College. Dunn Brothers was a local coffee chain, and I enjoyed flirting with the Macalester girls, listening to bad live music, and drinking too many cappuccinos. I would come home from a closing shift at 1:00 in the morning and twitch in bed for hours as Julie was fast asleep.

Both Julie and I were admitted into the secondary

English education master's program at the University of Minnesota. I wanted to be a high school English teacher, and Julie did not know what she wanted. She just followed me.

Whereas Missy and I had gone out to my mother's house in Forest Lake a number of times for dinner, I only brought Julie out to meet Mom once. Julie's little cousin rode along. We drove out to Mom's house in the early afternoon. My mother had been drinking that morning. Mom told Julie how much they looked alike as she stumbled around her front yard. I was embarrassed and quickly made an excuse to leave.

"Sorry about that," I told Julie and her little cousin on the drive home.

Though I enjoyed talking about books and music with Julie, her constant mood swings became hard to live with. One moment we would be watching *The Cosby Show* on the couch, and the next she would be in the bathroom with a knife threatening suicide. This was especially true if she was not taking Paxil regularly.

The moment that ended any pretense of a relationship was when Julie threatened to kill herself on the morning of my friend Nick's funeral. Nick killed himself when he was twenty-three. The disturbing irony of Julie's threat that morning was not lost on me. After our year in St. Paul together, I convinced Dad to let me move back into his basement.

Dad purchased a much larger house down the street in Arden Hills while I was living with Julie. It had five bedrooms, three bathrooms, and a huge, finished basement. Sarah convinced him to buy this more expensive house. They had plenty of room for me.

"We should charge him rent," Sarah told my father.

"I can't afford that and my student loan payment," I told them.

For once, Dad disagreed with my stepmother and let me move back home for free.

The Christmas before I moved back home, Julie's mom had made a blanket for me as a gift while Julie and I were still dating. It was a warm quilt and served to replace my green blanket that had long since disintegrated.

My breakup with Julie left me lonely in my father's basement. I played *Madden 2002* on my Playstation and downloaded Wilco songs with Kazaa on the computer that Tina's boyfriend Todd helped me pick out. Kitty chased mice in the storage room underneath the stairs. Looking at the blanket that Julie's mother gave me made me sad.

So I decided to do what I had not done in years—I asked my mom for something. I called her on the phone in the morning with the hope that she had not started drinking yet.

"Mom, would you be willing to make me a blanket for Christmas?"

"A blanket?"

"You know," I said, "like the one that burned up in the fire?"

Mom had made a biscuit quilt a couple of years back. It won an award at the Minnesota State Fair. When family or friends would visit her at her house in Forest Lake, she would always take them to her bedroom to show off the quilt. She was proud of the meticulous work that went into sewing each individual biscuit by hand.

"It took the blue ribbon," she boasted.

The quilt was destroyed when her house in Forest Lake burned down.

I imagined that it would be somewhat cathartic for Mom to make me a quilt. I also figured that it would give her something productive to do. She was unemployed, had given up most of her hobbies, and had spent most of her time trying to hide vodka or prescription pills from Jim in their new house in Wisconsin. Something felt cosmically right about the idea of Mom creating a blanket for me in my twenties, just as she had done with my green blanket when I was a toddler.

It was summer when I called to make my request. I wanted to give Mom time to complete the project.

"It would be great to have a blanket like that, Mom," I told her. "Something that would last forever."

"I'd love to make that for you, Sammy." Mom sounded excited. "Thank you for asking. It'll give me something to do!"

Mom went to work. The project was enormous. She purchased fabric and supplies. When I visited her in Hudson for holidays or family gatherings, her sewing room in the basement was filled with biscuits that she was building for the quilt.

"Your mother is working very hard," Jim told me.

"It looks like it," I responded.

If it had not been for her drinking, she probably would have been able to complete the blanket in a matter of months. Her work was interrupted by an inpatient treatment for alcoholism, a car accident on the way home from the liquor store that hospitalized her with a broken neck, and constant fights between her and Jim about her use of pain medication. As Christmas of 2002 approached, our phone conversations usually ended the same way.

"Don't worry, Sam, the blanket will be finished by Christmas."

"I'm not worried, Mom. Whenever you finish is fine."

By my early twenties, I had learned that it was useless to rely on Mom to keep her promises. So I figured that there was little chance she would actually complete the blanket. As a young man, I was finally learning to cope with the inability of both my parents to provide me with the things they wanted to provide me with. I put on a brave face and told both of them that everything was fine. I continued to learn how to get the things I needed without their help.

That Christmas came and went, and Mom had not finished the blanket. She brought up the project when we talked at Christmas. Members of our family were gathered at her house for the holiday.

"I'm so sorry, Sammy. I'm still going to finish the blanket."

"It's fine." I held the phone away from my ear so that I would not have to listen to her emotional slur of words. "Don't worry about it."

Over time, I began to forget that I had even asked for the blanket. I was busy completing my student teaching at a suburban high school North of St. Paul. I was finishing my coursework and looking for teaching positions in the Twin Cities.

"Are you going to move out soon?" Sarah would come down to the basement and ask me while I was leading the Minnesota Vikings to another Super Bowl victory in *Madden 2002*.

"When I get a job," I would tell her.

Dad stayed upstairs in his office, cold-calling potential insurance clients or recording a Messianic Jewish radio program that was aired on a local Christian radio station.

"Jesus came for the Jews, too," Dad laughed sarcastically. He sat behind a microphone at a mahogany desk in his large office.

His sidekick and friend, Paul, was always with him during this time. Paul was an Evangelical zealot who gravitated toward my father's sarcasm and endless love for Jesus. Like me, Paul was convinced by my father to get his insurance license after he lost his job. Unlike me, Paul had five children and a wife to support.

"That's right, Clayton; Jesus came for all of us," Paul would chime in on the radio program.

I enjoyed interpreting the Bible and appreciated both of their senses of humor. Sometimes I joined Dad and Paul on their show. As I grew older, it was one of the few ways I tried to connect with my father.

"It's almost as though the New Testament is arguing for a communal society," I said after preparing analysis of a passage he chose to focus on one week. I had been reading Marx in school. "It's ironic because most right-wing, American Christians are violently anti-communist, but the early believers in the Gospels were almost Socialists."

Dad tried to listen. He even began to agree with me. His friend Paul's eyes glazed over as I spoke, and when I finished talking they changed the subject to politics.

"George Bush is a Godly man," Paul said.

Then *my* eyes glazed over. I only participated in a few shows before I realized that sharing radical ideas did not help Dad and me to connect in the ways I had hoped.

During this time, my mother continued to call me once or twice a week. I would hold the phone away from my ear. I would say "sure" or "okay" to feign interest as she rambled on about her various medical conditions. Mom told me stories about the new Main Coon cat—Marty—she had bought to replace the one that burned up in the fire. Finally, Mom would complain that I never called her.

In the summer of 2003, I finished my teacher licensure program. I submitted nearly one hundred applications for teaching jobs. Finally, I was hired as an English and a drama teacher at Sparrowdale Cardinal High School in Minneapolis that July. I went upstairs to Dad's office and shared this exciting news with him after accepting the position.

"You know all teachers are liberals, don't you?" he sneered at me.

Sarah came in when she saw that Dad and I were talking.

"Does that mean you'll move out now?" she asked.

I called my mother after telling Dad and Sarah.

"I got a job as a high school teacher, Mom."

"Did you know that Jim is hiding my pain pills from me?" She slurred her words.

"Oh." I immediately recognized that it was a mistake to call her.

Mom began to tell me a confusing story about how Jim

had bought a safe to keep her pain pills from her. She slurred her words as she accused him of trying keep her in pain.

"Okay, Mom."

"I love you so much, Sammy."

"I love you too, Mom."

"You'll always be my special little guy."

"Okay."

My teaching career started in the fall of 2003. I moved out of my father's basement and into a bachelor's apartment behind Bryant Lake Bowl in Uptown, a trendy neighborhood in Minneapolis. My energy was focused on my students and my classroom. I am sure this was, in part, a way to create as much distance as possible between my family and the person I was becoming.

It was painful to experience my mother.

***

Before Christmas of 2005, Jim called me.

I was on winter break. This meant that I was lazily sitting in my apartment, shaking off the stress of teaching high school, and playing *Civilization* on my computer.

"Your mother is sick. She's in the hospital," he told me over the phone. "You need to come over here right away. We are at Region's."

I got into my Honda Civic and drove to downtown St. Paul. I arrived in the intensive care unit shortly after the call. Jim was talking with a doctor.

"Her liver is essentially pickled," the doctors were telling him. "She's probably not going to live through the night."

Jim and I walked together to the waiting room. He looked ashen. We sat down on a couch underneath a window in the visitor's lounge with a clear view of the St. Paul skyline. Jim told me what had happened. When he woke up that morning, he had found Mom passed out on the kitchen floor.

"That wasn't all that rare," he told me, "but this time she was turning purple."

He drove her to the local hospital in Hudson. They immediately put her in a helicopter to transfer her to St. Paul.

The night before, Mom and Jim had been stringing lights around their Christmas tree in their living room. Mom had always put enormous energy into decorating for the holidays. As a child, I took great pleasure in her ornate and elaborate Christmas, Halloween, and Easter decorations.

"She always gets worse before holidays," Jim told me. He was speaking of her drinking. He did not need to clarify. I knew what he was talking about. "I thought I had found all the bottles of vodka that she had hidden," he continued, "but there must have been more."

The doctors put my mother into an induced coma that night. Mom was unconscious. In the hospital room, I stood next to her bed and held her wrinkled hand. Her eyes were closed and she was pale. She looked far older than fifty-five. Mom looked like a corpse.

Staring at her shriveled body was eerily similar to watching Grandma Pattye dying, as she had been in an identical situation at the same hospital nearly ten years earlier.

Somehow, like my grandmother, Mom survived the night. Her doctors continued to keep an eye on her, and she lived through the next couple of days. Though she was unconscious, I spent that Christmas going to the hospital each and every day to visit her lifeless body.

I would stand beside her bed, tell her goodbye, and tell her that I loved her. I prayed underneath my breath.

Jim never left the hospital room. He slept on the couch.

"What will I do without her?" Jim asked me when I came to visit.

I didn't know what to tell him.

"You can still come over for holidays," he said.

"Sure," I said.

Jim did not have any children of his own that he knew of. He did have two sisters, but my mother was his real family after he had returned from California.

Members of my family such as Gammy, Polly, her husband Scott, my sister, and Christie's boyfriend Tim arrived throughout the week. Despite the doctors' continued assurance that Mom would not survive, she continued to struggle. Like a determined weed, my mother clung to life.

"There really isn't much hope she'll live through this," the doctors kept reminding us as December turned into January.

January turned into February, and Mom remained in a coma. They moved her from intensive care to a unit across the street. Then they transferred her to Minneapolis.

My visits continued. After winter break ended and I resumed teaching, I stopped by to see her lifeless body once or twice a week. Each time I arrived, Mom looked more and more emaciated. I was saying farewell to her corpse.

My final visit was on a Sunday afternoon in February. It was still winter, but the sun was out and the snow was beginning to melt. More out of habit than anything else, I was going to visit my mother and tell her goodbye once more.

When I showed up, I was shocked to see Mom sitting upright in a wheelchair. The nurse was combing her thin, gray hair. She weighed a little over sixty pounds, and her skin was translucent. But her hazel eyes were open and sparkling.

I could tell at once that she was sober.

Due to the length of the coma, the inordinate amount of pain medication and alcohol had completely cycled out of Mom's body. This may have been the first time since I was a child that my mother was completely clear-headed.

Mom did not say a word. She looked at me and started to sob. I started crying, too.

"I'm sorry, Sam." Mom's voice was sharp. "I'm so sorry."

I walked up to her, hugged her fragile body, and started weeping even harder. The enormous emotional energy that I felt surprised me. I gave into it.

As we wept, Mom did not tell me what she was sorry for. She did not need to. I knew what her apology meant.

Mom was being sincere—she was apologizing for *everything*.

She meant it. Mom wanted to be better than she was.

So I meant it when I told her that it was okay, and that I understood.

It was, and I did.

For one hour, we held each other and wept.

"I thought you were dead, Mom."

She squeezed me.

"Wendy will be fine," the nurse told us, "as long as she quits smoking and drinking."

I knew, as I left, that those two things would be impossible for my mother. This would probably be the only moment in my life that I would ever see her completely sober again.

But in that moment, *everything was okay*.

Walking out of the hospital room that morning, I understood something profound that I could not articulate with words.

In a matter of months, I had said goodbye to my mother. Then she woke up from the dead and I made peace with her. It was as though our relationship was resolved.

Now what?

***

While Mom was still at Region's and the doctors were telling us that she was dying, Jim turned to me and told me something strange.

"Even if she dies, Sam," Jim said, "I'll finish the blanket she's making for you." Jim was as meticulous as my mother when it came to making things.

As my mother survived in a comatose sort of limbo for three months that winter, Jim continued to work on the quilt. He seemed intent on finishing my mother's final project.

"It's a beautiful quilt. Your mom is a talented woman," he told me.

"I know," I said. "Thanks Jim."

After my mother's miraculous recovery, Jim and Mom finished the quilt in the summer. Though Jim had done most of the work, the quilt was a present from both of them.

They showed up at my apartment in Uptown on a school night. They brought the quilt and dinner. It was the only time they visited my apartment in Minneapolis.

Jim prepared bratwurst in my small kitchen. Mom had made homemade baked beans like she used to when I came out to Forest Lake on childhood visits. We sat around the little hand-me-down dining room table that had belonged to Gammy. We ate. Mom proudly put the blanket on my bed.

"I even gave it a satin lining, Sam," Mom said, "like your green blanky used to have when you were little."

The quilt was the softest, most comfortable blanket I had ever had. The night they gave it to me, I was excited to climb into bed. It was a luxurious evening of sleep.

I woke up the next morning at 4:00, went for a run, showered, and spent the day teaching high school. When I came home, I went into my bedroom to look at my comfortable new blanket. I noticed it was wet. I realized what had happened the moment I smelled the quilt.

"FLUFF-A-LUFAGUS!"

Kitty bolted from underneath my bed into the living room.

My cat had spent the afternoon urinating all over my new blanket while I was at school.

The quilt was far too large to jam into the washing machine in the apartment's basement, so I placed it in the trunk of my car with the intention of taking it to a dry cleaner.

Mom called me that evening to ask how I was enjoying my blanket. It was disheartening to hear her slurring her words so soon after almost dying due to her alcoholism.

"It's great, Mom," I told her. "It's the most comfortable blanket I've ever had."

"Good," she mumbled, and then started to speak incoherently.

I held the phone away from my ear, let her babble for a couple of minutes, and made an excuse to hang up.

"If she takes another drink, she'll die," the doctors had said when they released her.

Mom had listened intently.

"If she ever smokes again, her lungs will collapse," the doctors had told us.

My mother nodded sincerely.

Still, Mom began smoking cigarettes in the garage and drinking as soon as she returned to Hudson.

So the quilt festered in the trunk of the 2004 Mazda Tribute I had purchased after selling my Honda Civic. I kept meaning to find time to drop it at a dry cleaner, but, as was the case when I was caught up in teaching high school, I could not seem to find a moment for myself.

Eventually, I found myself directing a children's theatre project at Primville Area High School. Two friends from college recruited me to teach at this school. Michael was a drama teacher at Primville. We met in an adolescent literature class. Tina had also gotten a job at Primville after she finished college. I was lured to a new high school with the promise of a more robust theatre program and working with my friends after teaching for four years in Sparrowdale.

Anyway, we needed to transport our actors and our set over to a local elementary school for a performance. I was forced to volunteer my Mazda Tribute as tribute. I took the blanket out of my trunk, stored it in the auditorium at the high school, and filled my car with chairs, props, and costumes.

I thought the quilt would be safe, so I did not worry about putting it back in the trunk after the performance was over. A week later, I went to find the quilt.

It was gone.

I looked everywhere. After striking the set for our fall play, the quilt had somehow gone missing.

Had somebody thrown it away? Had somebody stored it in our prop room? After days of searching, I realized that the quilt was gone.

"How's the blanket, Sam?" Mom would slur when she called.

"Wonderful, Mom," I would tell her.

"I love you so much, Sammy."

"Love you too, Mom."

I hung up the phone.

The distance between my mother and me began to grow more and more pronounced after I lost that quilt. I spent less and less time interacting with my family because I was immersed in my career as a teacher. I rarely answered Mom's phone calls and did my best to avoid calling her back. I ignored my sister completely, spent very little time in contact with my father, and tried to make the best of my circumstances despite the limitations of my upbringing.

I loved these people very much. I was also angry with their inability to support me.

Chapter 6

My great-grandmother Gammy lived until she was 103. She died in May of 2009. By then, I rarely saw or spoke with her. I was busy being a high school teacher and learning how to be an adult.

Gammy was placed in a senior living community near my Aunt Polly in St. Paul after old age forced Gammy to move out of her house.

Polly and Mom were Gammy's only close family. Gammy outlived her daughter and all of her siblings. The responsibility for visiting Gammy or helping her with her finances in the final years of her life fell to Polly and her husband Scott. This was in part because Mom lived in Wisconsin and in part because she was unable to take care of *herself.*

Polly's generosity was enormous when it came to helping her family. Aside from taking care of Gammy, Polly was also raising her grandson Christian because of Leisa's—Polly's daughter—struggle with drug addiction and mental illness. Polly's kindness also extended to me. In 9th grade, I complained to Polly during Christmas that my father did not pay for me to get a yearbook. Polly snuck into my high school over her lunch break one afternoon to order one for me. Years later, when I moved out of Dad's house, Polly and Scott showed up to help.

It was a sweltering summer afternoon. Dad watched television upstairs, and Sarah drank lemonade in the kitchen while Scott and Polly helped me pack my belongings into Scott's pickup truck.

"Couldn't she have at least offered us some of her lemonade?" Polly asked after we arrived at my apartment in Uptown.

"That's Sarah," I laughed, embarrassed by my father and stepmother.

Anyway, Gammy had always seemed ageless to me. When she turned 100, a large group of family and friends celebrated in the community room of her assisted living facility. Polly organized a surprise party for her. Gammy cried when she watched the slideshow of pictures Polly had accumulated from the past century of her life. Shots of Gammy wearing formal gowns and playing the organ in St. Paul nightclubs flashed on the screen. Images of my mother and father in better times scrolled by. Snapshots of Christie, Leisa, Heidi and me as adorable, innocent children filled the screen.

Everybody looked so *normal* in the show Polly had prepared.

Looking around the room, I was amazed at the difference time had made. Christie was overweight, had yellowing teeth, and wore an old hooded sweatshirt that smelled like cigarettes. Her boyfriend Tim had long, stringy hair. Mom was stooped with age and her eyes were vacant because of pain medication. Leisa was in red sweatpants, and Heidi was standing off on her own, eager to leave. Christian and Skylar were playing with their phones in the corner. Despite this odd assortment of family, Gammy moved around the room with her typical grace, socialized, and even played the piano for everybody at the end of the party.

"I can't believe I can still play after all these years," she laughed.

"Your great-grandmother is an amazing woman," one of her friends from the senior community told me.

"Yeah," I shrugged.

Gammy might have been amazing, but she was also notorious for her guilt trips.

"Wendy," she used to say, "you must stop your drinking and smoking. You're disappointing your Gammy."

Mom would roll her eyes and sneak outside to have a cigarette.

"Sammy," she used to scold me, "you never call your Gammy."

"Sorry about that," I would tell her, and then quickly change the subject.

Gammy's guilt trips were not effective. Mom kept drinking and smoking, and I rarely found time to call my great-grandmother. I only saw her on holidays or at family gatherings. Despite my lack of attention, she would always send me a card with a crumpled twenty-dollar bill in it on my birthday. She continued to do this even as she spent through her savings while living in the facility. I felt bad taking her money.

After she turned 103, Gammy fell and scraped her leg while she was putting away Christmas decorations. When the cut did not heal, she went to the doctor. She was immediately taken to a hospital and told she had contracted Methicillin Resistant Staph Aureus.

"What can you do for it?" she asked.

"Nothing."

Gammy was moved to hospice. We came and visited her. All of us were shocked—she had been in such good health.

"I can't believe I'm going to die from this scrape," she laughed sarcastically.

"Oh Gam," Polly laughed and kissed her on the forehead.

I hugged her tightly as we were leaving.

"I love you, Gammy," I told her.

"I love you too, Sammy."

Gammy was sedated at the end of her life. I said goodbye to her like I had said goodbye to both my mother and my grandmother. I prayed silently to myself over their lifeless bodies, kissed them on their wrinkled foreheads, and whispered that I loved them. The difference, of course, was that my mother survived her encounter with death.

At the time, I was not sure what I was praying for. I guess I asked that the Creator of the universe concern Himself with the wreckage of these women as their lives were coming to an end.

Gammy's body was burned, and a funeral was held in a

church near Polly's house. After the funeral, Gammy's immediate family drove to a cemetery in St. Paul where Grandma's ashes were also kept. Gammy wanted her ashes to be placed with Pattye's ashes in the mausoleum. It was a small, ragged group that gathered near that mausoleum on a cool, cloudy day in May. Jim helped Mom to her walker after they pulled up in their car. Polly and Scott stood chatting with the preacher to distract him as Christie, Tim, and Leisa snuck off to get high in Christie's car. Heidi made small talk with me as Christie's son Skylar, now an adolescent, chased Leisa's son Christian around ancient tombstones.

I felt out of place.

A couple of plots away in the cemetery, a huge family was formally gathered for a different funeral service. Somebody was playing the bagpipes, and the wind was carrying the sound to us. It made me sad to compare the dignity of the group that was saying goodbye at the nearby service with the sad amalgam of people standing near Gammy and Grandma's plot.

My great-grandmother deserved better.

Somebody suggested I read the blessing. The preacher handed me a small book. I read a prayer.

"Ashes to ashes," I said awkwardly at the end of the prayer, "and dust to dust."

The cemetery attendant who met us at the mausoleum walked over to the box where Grandma Pattye's ashes were kept. He unlocked it.

I was sitting next to my mother on a stone bench as the preacher placed the container of Gammy's ashes into the slot. We were in front of a granite tomb that contained the ashes of hundreds of dead people. After the box was opened, Mom stood and walked over to touch her own mother's ashes. She picked up the container and looked at her mother's urn for the first time since it had been locked away more than ten years prior.

Mom started to cry, and something miraculous

happened. Her face transformed. The wrinkles seemed to disappear, and the age and obstinacy drained from her face. She was no longer a weathered old woman. She was a child. I watched as my mother caressed the box and mouthed the word "Mom."

Something about watching Mom look at what remained of *her* mother's body triggered something of a primal reflex. I started to weep.

Incidentally, I often cried when I was a child.

"You're so sensitive," my mother used to tell me.

"You're overreacting," my father would snap at me.

Over the years, it became more and more difficult for me to cry. However, books and movies would still cause me to tear up. I read A *Farewell to Arms* when I was sixteen and wept for an hour after the final paragraph. I finished the novel *Everything is Illuminated* in a coffee shop when I was twenty-one. I was in tears throughout the final 100 pages. In my thirties, sitting at my computer and writing about my friend Nick's suicide would make me cry. Stories seemed to activate emotional energy that I had long since repressed.

Anyway, watching Mom with her mother's ashes broke through my carefully composed façade. My weeping was ferocious. I folded over on myself. I sat on a stone bench and put my head in my hands. I began to have something of a panic attack. Surrounded by a sad gathering of people on an icy May afternoon, I howled with sorrow. The intensity of my reaction astonished me. It had the same effect on others.

Polly hugged me and walked away. Christie and Tim lit another cigarette. Jim did the same.

Mom hobbled over to the bench and sat down next to me. She put her arm around me and spoke softly in my ear.

"It's okay, Sammy," she soothed me. "Let it out."

Her words caused me to weep even harder. This surprised me even more.

Emotion overcame me. For years, I had repressed my emotions. I did not want to upset my mother or my father. I wanted to please them. I knew it would be useless to share how I really felt. Suddenly, feelings came pouring out of me. I was sad, angry, ashamed, resentful, embarrassed, and overcome with emotion.

For forty-five minutes, I was unable to move as an enormous catharsis poured from my body. I grieved for Gammy, for Grandma, for my own mother, and for the tragic insignificance of these people who had populated my childhood.

Perhaps I was grieving most for my mother. Seeing her as a little girl calling out for her own mother gave me a glimpse of the child buried beneath the accumulated waste of years.

I remember thinking that she could have been something else. It was a shame she became what she was.

***

The fall of 2010 marked the beginning of my eighth year teaching English and drama in a high school. The wild ups and downs of that career in public education had led me to a doctoral program. Once again, I was enrolled at the University of Minnesota. I needed to make better sense of what I had done and what had been done to me in schools. I was committed to the art of education. I was also leery that my creative approach to teaching was too out of place in traditional schools. I was worried that my approach to teaching would eventually cost me my job. I decided that graduate school was a smart, strategic career move.

"Besides," I told my friends, "this will give me an excuse to start writing a book about my strange experiences as a teacher."

My principal agreed to reduce my schedule so that I could both supervise student teachers *and* teach at the

University of Minnesota in order to offset the cost of my tuition. God knows that the last thing I needed was more student loan debt.

So I set myself to the enormous task of teaching both high school and college, directing plays in a high school theatre program, chasing a PhD, and writing a book about my stories of working in schools.

"You need to do what you think you need to do," my fiancé Katie told me at the time. This was after I warned her that going back to graduate school would be time consuming and might not be the most lucrative financial decision.

After my relationships with Missy and Julie, I had taken my twenties to slow down and figure out what I actually needed from a partner. That careful trepidation led me to Katie. We met through a mutual friend. Though she was eight years younger than me, her unconditional acceptance and support were part of what I discovered to be necessary in a partner—she was able to put up with my eccentricities. Katie was slight in stature, had strawberry blonde hair, and was very quiet. She was also perceptive. I felt a connection with her as soon as we met.

Polly called and asked me to meet her for coffee after Gammy's death.

"I have something I want to give you."

When I arrived at the coffee shop, Polly took out a box.

"When you're ready," she said as she smiled, "I think this would make a wonderful engagement ring. It belonged to Gammy and it would look great on Katie. Gammy would have wanted you to have it."

I thanked Polly for thinking of me and took the ring. Any number of times afterward, I put it in my pocket with the intent of asking Katie to marry me. Something always seemed to get in my way. Finally, after taking her out for Ethiopian food one night, she and I went for a walk together near the Mississippi River in Northeast

Minneapolis. The path led to a dead-end. Painted in graffiti on the rocks that blocked the way were the following words: "It is time to move forward."

Shocked by this clear communication from the universe, I waited for Katie to turn her back. I placed one hand on her shoulder and pulled her towards me, holding the ring in the other.

She smiled. She cried. She said yes, we kissed, and we were engaged.

Katie had moved into the house I purchased in Northeast Minneapolis after I took my second teaching position at Primville Area High School. It had taken me a long time to muster up the will to propose. Actually setting a date was also difficult for me.

"When should we actually get married?" Katie asked.

"Soon," I mumbled.

So during the winter of 2010, Katie joined me when I drove out to Hudson to celebrate Christmas morning with my tiny family at Mom and Jim's house.

Skylar spent that Christmas Eve with Mom and Jim, as he often did. In fact, Skylar spent nearly every weekend with Mom and Jim. Despite my mother's instability, her house was far calmer than my sister's. By 2010, Skylar was thirteen years old.

Christie and Tim arrived after Katie and me. They smelled like cigarette smoke and had been fighting about a guitar Tim had pawned. They often ran out of their welfare money before the end of the month and were forced to pawn off the things they owned. This was especially true when they were unable to talk my father or mother into giving them money for cigarettes, pot, or food.

Polly and Scott drove out to Christmas at Mom's with their daughter Leisa and her son Christian. Heidi came separately with her boyfriend.

Mom's Christmas decorations littered the house. There was a ceramic tree she had made sitting on an end table.

An intricate wreath she wove hung on the door. A
Christmas tree that was carefully decorated with over sixty
years of accumulated ornaments stood in front of the large
bay window in the living room.

As a child, I enjoyed my mother's obsessive
commitment to celebrating the holiday. I looked forward
to decorations, presents, and cookies. The Scandinavian
excess that marked my mother's approach frustrated my
father. His major complaint dealt with the absence of Jesus
in the way she celebrated Christmas.

"What the hell does a tree have to do with anything?"
Dad would always complain.

Anyway, Jim had decorated the house this year. Mom
was unable to do so. In fact, she looked terrible when
Katie and I arrived. She was fragile and weak. Mom could
not move without a walker, her eyes were hazy, and she
had lost a great deal of weight.

Mom pulled me in to kiss her when I arrived. The smell
of cigarette smoke, alcohol, and her bony shoulders made
me recoil.

After arriving, I went downstairs to Skylar's room to
hide. He and Christian were playing Xbox 360.

"Did you remember the games?" he asked me.

"Of course."

Skylar had asked if he could borrow some of my Xbox
360 games. I brought him *Oblivion*, *Madden*, and *Fallout 3*.

I played Xbox with him and Christian while Jim
finished preparing brunch upstairs. Katie sat on the floor
with me as I crushed Skylar in a game of *NBA 2K10*.

"You're cheating, Sam!" Skylar complained.

"No, I'm just amazing," I responded as Steve Nash
drained another three-pointer.

Polly came down and looked at the ring on Katie's
finger.

"It's beautiful, isn't it?" Polly asked Katie.

Katie smiled and nodded.

"We're just so glad that he met you," Polly told her.

116

"That last one was a little off," Scott quietly laughed. Ten years younger than my Aunt Polly, Scott was both strong *and* silent. He was hulking.

"Julie?" I asked. Both Missy and Julie used to accompany me to family holidays.

"Katie is an improvement," Polly said.

Katie laughed.

Jim looked exhausted that Christmas, and Mom seemed more confused than usual. Jim talked to me about a book he was thinking of writing. He had always thought of me as intelligent. As a child, he always commented on my ability to memorize baseball statistics. He and my mother were the only members of my family who attended my graduation ceremony from college. They met me outside of Northrop Auditorium after the ceremony. My girlfriend Julie was there with us.

"I'm so proud of you, Sam." Mom hugged me.

"That was pretty cool." Jim shook my hand.

Anyway, Jim told me about his book because he thought I could help. I listened politely.

"It's about the kids from my old neighborhood. I want to write about what happened to them as adults." Jim showed me a black and white picture of a group of kids on the lawn outside of a house in St. Paul.

"Look." Jim pointed at a kid on the edge of the group. "Here's your father."

Dad had grown up in the same neighborhood as Jim and my mother. All of them knew each other as children in the '50's and '60's. In the picture, Dad was a chubby, awkward looking boy surrounded by white faces.

"We used to call him the Jew," Jim laughed.

Mom was having trouble breathing. Her wheezing was more noticeable than ever.

"You need to take me out of this house," she kept mumbling to Polly when Jim would leave the room. "Jim has me trapped in here."

Jim had lost his job as a foreman for a stucco company

in the Twin Cities in 2008. The company was losing money and forced to downsize. Afterward, he spent most of his days either doling out pills for my mother from their safe, or working on carpentry projects in his workshop.

In the fall of 2008, I got Jim a job buildings sets for plays at the high school. Jim told me he had worked in theatres when he lived in California and missed having creative projects. He built the set for the first play I directed after getting hired at Primville. It was for a production of Friedrich Durrenmatt's *The Visit*. In fact, after the show closed, we used the extension he built for the play to serve as a miniature stage in my drama classroom. That stage lasted over the next eight years.

Jim embarrassed me when he tried to bill the school for his work after volunteering to build the set. He was strapped for money. It was the last time he worked on a play, because we could not afford the rate he charged.

Anyway, he and my mother had visited my house during the summer before their Christmas party. They came to check out the work that had been done to my garage. A tree had fallen on it during a storm on the 4th of July, and insurance had paid a carpenter to repair the roof.

"Looks good to me, Sam," Jim told me.

"I should have used the insurance money to pay you to do the work." I felt bad after realizing that Jim could have used the money.

Jim said something cryptic to me as he was leaving.

"Do you think your mind ever gets so full that it becomes impossible to remember new things?" he asked.

"What do you mean?"

"Lately, I'll read the paper and forget what I just read," he told me.

I did not know how to respond to his strange remark. I stared at him as he stood in my backyard. His white hair was thinner than I remembered. His mustache no longer had traces of brown, or even gray. It was pure white.

Anyway, I asked Jim to put air in my tires before I left

that Christmas. My tires were low, and I knew he had a compressor in his workshop.

"You know you can do this at a gas station," he laughed.

"I would mess it up," I shrugged. I have always been embarrassingly terrible at anything that involves servicing a car.

Jim filled the tires, and he and my mother stood at the doorway as the rest of the family left. They waved as Katie and I backed down their long driveway. We made our way down a dirt road, through the countryside surrounding Hudson, and back to the freeway.

"My mother is so sad to me," I told Katie. "I can't imagine what she and Jim do in that big house all day."

Katie held my hand and listened as we drove toward Minneapolis.

***

I was teaching a section of my Drama Workshop course that winter. It was scheduled during first period. So at 8:30 on a Wednesday morning, my students were spread out across the auditorium. They were building scenes. The space looked like my classrooms often did—it was a messy cacophony of creative energy.

I walked up to two ninth grade girls who were working on a scene. I paired them together because one often played a caricature of a ditzy girl while the other usually took up more masculine mannerisms. I wanted to see how their energies would mesh.

"Can I watch what you have?" I asked.

"It's terrible," one of them laughed.

"I'm sure it's fine. I'll give you notes."

They started to perform.

One of the doors to the auditorium crashed open as I was watching them. The associate principal marched into the space. A science teacher followed him. I watched their slow approach with trepidation. The appearance of administrators always worried me. This one was an ex-marine. He walked with purpose.

"Mr. Tanner?" The assistant principal approached me.

"What's up, John?"

"Mr. Tanner, do you have any personal items in your classroom?"

He seemed serious. Whenever principals were serious, it usually meant that I was in trouble.

"Um, I guess my jacket is down there. My backpack. How come?"

"I'll go get your jacket and backpack for you. First, I need you to come directly to the office with me. Mrs. Williams will take your class." John motioned to the science teacher who had entered the auditorium with him.

My heart started racing. They were removing me from my classroom? I figured this was it. I had been suspended twice from my job at Primville for the serious offenses of using *The Office* to teach comedic timing in an acting class and using the word "bullshit" in front of a 9th grader. After eight years of getting in trouble for the most arbitrary things, I worried that I was finally being fired.

"What is it, John? Is something wrong?"

"I'll tell you when we get to the office, Sam. Just follow me."

The two girls watched in confusion as John led me out of the auditorium. The rest of the class stopped working and watched as I was escorted out of the room.

"John," I said, "you gotta tell me what's going on. Am I in trouble?"

"I can't say anything until we get to the office, Sam."

I was silent. My mind was racing. What had I done this time?

Each of my previous run-ins ith school administration had been more surprising and more traumatic than the last. Had I made a joke that made a student uncomfortable? Had I said "shit" without realizing it?

Those were some of the crimes I had been accused of in the past.

So I was thinking about alternative career paths as I walked into the principal's office.

"This way, Sam." John led me through the office and into the conference room.

The principal was sitting at a table with my Aunt Polly and her husband, Scott.

I paused. These were the last two people I expected to see in the principal's office.

The last time I had seen either of them had been at Christmas.

Something dawned on me.

"I know what this is," I said as the three of them looked at me.

Mom had looked terrible at Christmas. She was skinny, confused, and in as rough of shape as ever. Finally, after all of the false alarms, Mom had died.

"No," Polly smiled sadly at me, "I don't think you do."

The principal frowned at me.

"Jim took his life this morning, Sam," Polly told me calmly.

I paused as her sentence settled in. I thought about my mother.

"We need to get to Mom," I said.

I scrawled out haphazard plans for a substitute teacher on a sheet of paper and handed it to John. It would be a week before I returned to school.

I would never return to the moment before Jim killed himself.

***

Jim put a bullet in his brain on a Wednesday morning. He shot himself with a revolver that he had kept hidden from my mother in the dash compartment of his truck.

It was January 26th, 2011. Jim woke up. He shaved off

the mustache that he'd had as long as I'd known him. He put an entire bag of food in the cat's dish until it spilled over the edges. He wrote a short, meticulous note addressed to the first responders. Mom told me later that he had hugged her and told her how much he loved her before going down to the garage. He placed a towel underneath a workbench so as not to make a mess. Jim set his head on the towel, put the revolver in his mouth, and pulled the trigger.

Mom found him thirty minutes later. She had been upstairs working on a puzzle in the dining room. Her two lovebirds were chattering away in their cage near the sliding glass doors that led to the deck. Like her mother, Mom enjoyed having birds as pets.

Mom's mind was so cloudy from pain medication that she did not hear the gunshot. She knew something was wrong because she called for Jim and he failed to respond. So Mom crawled down the stairs. She was unable to walk up and down them due to a recent hip surgery, so she was forced to inch her way down to the front landing in their split-level house.

"Jim!" she kept crying out.

Mom went out to the garage and found his lifeless body. Confused, she fell to her knees and grabbed him. She tried to give him mouth-to-mouth. Then she realized that there was a wet substance surrounding him that she thought was water. Mom felt a hard object underneath his head. At first, she thought it was a phone. Then she realized it was a gun. After figuring out that Jim was covered in blood and not water, she dragged her emaciated body up the stairs. It took her over fifteen minutes to get to the phone. She called the police. Then she called my sister Christie and my Aunt Polly.

I rode out to Hudson that morning with Polly and Scott. I called Katie from Polly's phone because I did not own a cell phone. Katie immediately left her job to meet me out at Mom's house. She was working as an elementary school teacher. When we arrived, Mom was huddled on the front step. She was weeping and covered in Jim's blood.

My first thought was that she looked like she had killed a man.

Mom was screaming over and over again that she wanted to die. She kept trying to go to Jim's body in the garage.

A police officer came up to me immediately after I arrived.

"Can you keep her from going into the garage?" she asked me. "We need to keep Jim's body where it is until the paramedics arrive."

"Sure?" I was overwhelmed.

I sat down next to my mother. Her ratty t-shirt was soaked with blood.

"It's going to be okay, Mom," I told her.

"Oh Sammy," Mom howled as she buried her face in my chest. She wept ferociously and I held her tightly.

"It's okay."

"Why did he do this, Sammy?" she moaned. "Why?"

"I don't know, Mom."

"Why didn't he take me with him?" she howled.

When the paramedic asked me if I wanted to see Jim's body, I said no. My sister jumped at the opportunity. She snuck into the garage between crying and puffing away on a cigarette in the living room.

"I guess there are no rules anymore?" Scott sarcastically asked Christie.

Jim did not allow smoking in the house. Instead, he and Mom always went out into the garage and smoked on two folding chairs near a space heater.

Christie rolled her eyes at Scott. Her face was in shock when she came back from the garage.

"It's weird to see him like that."

Polly called Jim's sisters, Donna and Barb. They arrived.

"This is unbelievable," Donna said. She hugged Mom.

"I'll call a cleaning service," Barb said.

"If you pay me, I'll clean up the body," Tim said.

Mom kept crying and crying. I was not sure what to do. I went upstairs and played with Marty, Mom's Main Coon cat. Events moved rapidly. The morning was a blur.

"You're going to have to take care of your mother now," Barb told me.

I was silent.

Eventually, the paramedics took Jim's body away. The police stayed and asked my mother a few questions. As they were doing so, I looked at the note that Jim had written before killing himself. It contained four carefully etched sentences that read as follows: 1) Get Wendy to a "safe house," 2) Keep doors closed so Marty can't get out, 3) Call my sisters Donna and Barb and my sister-in-law Polly (contact information was listed), and 4) The access code to the garage is: 6363. Underneath these four items, Jim wrote the following sentence to my mother: God love you and God forgive me.

"I want the gun," Mom kept telling the police officer in charge.

"I can't give it to you. It's evidence," the woman told her.

"It's my property. I want the gun."

Polly and I asked the police what we should do with Mom before they left.

"We can't just leave her here," Polly said.

"You could bring her to the hospital?" The officer was unsure of her suggestion.

So we locked up the house after the responders had left and drove Mom to the hospital in Hudson. She was still wearing her bloody t-shirt and wailing.

"I want to die, Sammy," she told me over and over again as I sat next to her in the backseat of Polly's car. We pulled up to the hospital, and Mom held onto my arm as I led her through the snow into the hospital's lobby. She was so fragile.

The staff recognized Mom immediately. She had been in and out of the hospital at least once or twice a month over the last couple of years. They were shocked when we told them about Jim.

Mom pointed at the woman behind the front desk. "He used to flirt with her when we picked up my medication." The receptionist's face became pale when we told her why we were there. The woman made a phone call, and orderlies came out to greet us.

Mom was given a gown and placed in a room.

"I need something for the pain," she kept screaming at the nurses.

As they were sedating her, Mom looked up at me.

"Is this a dream, Sam?" she asked. "If I try real hard, can I wake up?"

She closed her eyes and squinted her forehead.

"This isn't real, this isn't real, this isn't real." Mom kept screeching this mantra, trying to bring Jim back.

"This isn't a dream, Mom," I told her. I held her hand. "You're going to be okay."

"No, Sam. I want to die. I just want to die."

"You're strong, Mom. You can handle this."

"No, I want to be dead. I want to stop feeling." Mom kept weeping.

I thought for a moment.

"Katie and I are getting married, Mom. Don't you want to see your grandchildren?"

Her eyes lit up.

"Is Katie pregnant?"

"No," I laughed. "But after we get married, we'll try. I want you around for my child. Don't you want to see that?"

"Yes, Sam, but this hurts so much."

"I know, Mom." I squeezed her hand. "It will be okay."

"Why did he do this?" she asked me.

"My friend Nick killed himself, remember?" I asked

125

her.

"Yes."

"It's impossible to rationalize suicide," I told her. "You can't try to make sense of it."

"How did Nick do it?" Mom asked.

"Like Jim," I told her. "He shot himself."

Eventually, Mom fell asleep after the medication kicked in. Polly and I met with the social worker in a cramped and tiny office in the hospital. Christie and Tim went outside to smoke. Skylar followed them. Katie came with me.

"What can we do with Wendy?" Polly asked the social worker. "She can't go home alone."

"Do you have any family who can stay with her? Can one of you do it?"

Polly looked at me.

"I live in Minneapolis," I told them.

"Could you go out and stay with her for a while?" the social worker asked.

"It's a big, beautiful house," Polly told me. "It would be a great place for you and Katie to start your family if the move became permanent."

"I don't know. I teach in the Twin Cities, and I'm just starting graduate school at the University of Minnesota," I started to say. "I have so much on my plate."

"You and Katie would have to talk about it," Polly told us.

I went outside and talked with Katie alone.

"Mom has that huge house in Hudson," I told her. "They used their insurance money from the house in Forest Lake to pay down the mortgage. We could take over the payment and move out there. Eventually, that could be our house. We would have to take care of Mom, though."

Katie listened and nodded. She was overwhelmed too.

I went back into the social worker's office.

"We'd have to think about it," I told Polly and the social worker, "but it is a possibility."

126

"What can we do in the short-term?" Polly asked.

"If she's deemed suicidal," the social worker told us, "we can put her on a seventy-two hour hold."

"She's been threatening suicide since we arrived this morning," I told her. "Does that count?"

We waited at the hospital for hours. My mother slept, and it grew dark outside. Katie and I were sitting with Polly in the waiting room. Christie and Tim left with Skylar in the afternoon.

Around six o'clock, a doctor went into Mom's room and spoke with her. He came out and agreed that she should be kept on a hold.

"She wants to kill herself," he told us. "The only place we can transfer her to is a psychiatric hospital in Amery. It's about an hour away."

The hospital called a taxi. I rode in the backseat with my mother.

The sky was growing darker. It had been snowing all day. Temperatures were near freezing.

We sat on a plastic, uncomfortable blue bench in the back of the cab. Katie and Polly followed us in Polly's car. The nurses had given Mom back her bloodstained t-shirt and pajama pants. I sat with her as we drove through the Wisconsin countryside, surrounded by darkness and snow. We did not talk. She held onto my hand. She was like a child.

After arriving in Amery, we were admitted into a secure facility that looked more like a prison than a hospital. A woman led us to a room in the back of the building. She handed us a brochure detailing the services that were provided such as meals, massages, and medication control. Mom signed a stack of papers.

"Don't leave me here," she begged me.

"It's just for the night, Mom. We need to figure out what we're going to do."

"Please," she said. My mother's face looked haggard,

her eyes were blurry, and her clothes were dirty.

"We'll get you out of here soon," I told her.

"You have to be here, Wendy," Polly said. She kissed her. "Maybe they can give you a shower and wash your hair?"

The blood in Mom's hair had dried. It was crusty now.

"We can do that," the woman said.

Polly, Katie, and I left Mom with the woman who had admitted her, and we walked down a white hallway lit by fluorescent lights. Outside, it was freezing and dark.

"This has been a hell of a day," I laughed humorlessly.

"You can say that again." Polly hugged me.

I wiped tears out of my eyes as Polly led us to her car. I sat in the backseat.

We used the hour it took to drive back from Amery to start planning what we could do next. By the time we were back at the hospital, Katie and I were trying to think through the cost and benefit of leaving our house in Minneapolis and moving out to Hudson for Mom.

With all of our student debt, the opportunity to take over Mom's beautiful house in Hudson seemed financially prudent. The mortgage was already paid down, it was on a large plot of land, and it would provide plenty of room for Katie and me to start a family. Katie often talked about running a daycare out of our home, and Mom's house would provide plenty of space to do so. If we lived with Mom, we could also help with her finances and watch over her.

The idea of having a comfortable place to start a family appealed to Katie. The financial security of the real estate move made sense to me.

A question kept nagging me as Katie and I talked with Polly. After all this time, was I really going to let Mom back into my life?

Katie and I did not get back to Minneapolis until midnight.

Fluffalufagus met us at the door. She was extremely

pissed off that I had not been there to feed her dinner. Her sister Yara perched on the chair in the entryway. Katie and I had purchased Yara the previous Christmas. She was a neurotic Norwegian Forest cat. Yara was the Hebrew word for fear. The name made sense after she spent her first night at home wedged into a crack between a wall and a mirror because she was so terrified of her new environment.

After feeding the cats, I called my principal's cell phone.

"I'm not going to be able to come to school tomorrow," I told her.

"Don't worry about it, Sam. Take as much time as you need."

I wrote up sub plans and emailed them to the department chair. Katie and I walked upstairs. We climbed into bed.

"What are we going to do?" I asked her.

"I don't know," she said.

Once again, my family was disturbing my life. I was angry, sad, and exhausted.

Katie and I curled up together and fell asleep.

Chapter 7

Katie and I met my aunt early the next morning at a neighborhood coffee shop near her house in St. Paul. It had snowed the night before. It was a cold, winter's morning.

Jim's suicide had removed us from our routines. I was getting ready to drive to Wisconsin instead of waking up at 4:45 in the morning to teach high school. Katie was taking the day off from teaching elementary at a local charter school to join me.

I was pulled over for driving fifteen miles per hour over the speed limit on the way to meet Polly.

"You need to slow down, Sam," Katie told me as the police officer approached the car.

I fumed silently.

"Do you know how fast you were going?"

"No," I replied.

"I clocked you at fifteen over the speed limit. Why were you going so fast?"

"I'm on my way to help my mother," I barked back.

He wrote me a ticket, and we were ten minutes late to our meeting with Polly.

"Sorry," I told her as we took our hats and mittens off and sat down.

Polly hugged both of us. She laughed sympathetically after I told her why we were late.

"How are you guys after yesterday?" she asked.

"You know," I shrugged.

"I do," she said.

We started discussing what we needed to do after ordering coffee. Polly had been on the phone with the facility in Amery. Mom's seventy-two-hour suicide hold carried over into Saturday. Polly learned that they did not release patients during the weekend. That gave us until Monday to prepare for Mom's discharge.

"She can't be left alone now," I told Polly. "She couldn't take care of herself without Jim. After this, who knows?"

"He had really become a caregiver for her."

"It seems like it."

"I wonder if that's why he did it? Maybe she was too much for him?"

"Who knows?" I asked. "It's impossible to rationalize suicide."

Katie and I continued to consider moving out to Hudson and staying with Mom as we talked.

"She'll qualify for Social Security soon," Polly told us. "Between Jim's carpenter's pension and your mother's Social Security, managing her bills won't be difficult. After the fire, they put $150,000 of their insurance money into that house. So the mortgage payment is probably cheaper than your payment in Minneapolis. It might be good for you guys to move out there and take it over. It's a beautiful home. It has four bedrooms, two bathrooms, and all of that land."

"I bet we could raise enough money by selling Jim's tools to pay off our student debt," I added. "There has to be over $100,000 of equipment in his workshop."

"At least," Polly agreed.

Katie quietly listened to the conversation.

"It's a smart financial decision for us. The house is an upgrade, isn't it? Especially if you want to run a home daycare later on?" I asked Katie.

She nodded. I could tell she was not convinced.

"It could make for a wonderful place to raise a family. Besides, who knows how much longer Mom will live? She's so weak. Her body has been through so much."

"It's morbid to say, but I don't think she'll live much longer after this," Polly agreed.

Katie was quiet.

It took the three of us nearly an hour to drive out to Hudson after having coffee. We rode together in Polly's Jeep Liberty. After arriving, I started going through Jim's desk. I found their banking information. They had roughly $30,000 in savings bonds and their checking account. I organized their mail and came across Jim's meager life insurance policy through his carpenter's union. It was worth $6,000.

"Did you find the combination for the safe in the office?" Polly asked me after I finished going through files. She and Katie had been cleaning out the refrigerator in the kitchen.

"No."

"When I called her, Wendy told me that she really needed to get into the safe."

"Because Jim kept the pain meds in there?" I laughed.

"Probably," Polly said with a smile.

We found Mom's adult diapers in their bedroom closet. The mattress pad on her bed was stained. Polly started a load of laundry as Katie and I fed Mom's chattering lovebirds and changed Marty's litter box.

After leaving the house, we stopped at the funeral home in Hudson where Jim's body was being kept. We met with the mortician and agreed to have Jim's remains cremated. They told us that we could pick up the ashes in a week. Finally, we drove an hour East to visit Mom in Amery, Wisconsin.

The staff greeted us at the entrance.

"We've been medicating her," the nurse told us. "She was extremely uncooperative and kept demanding that we give her something for the pain."

They led us to Mom's room. My mother was a zombie.

"How are you doing, Mom?" I asked.

"We've come to visit, Wendy." Polly put her arms around her sister.

Mom looked at us vacantly.

All of us were taken to the staff psychologist's office to discuss Mom's condition. The psychologist was not in the room, so we waited for her to arrive.

Mom was drifting in and out of consciousness in a chair in the corner.

"Mom," I told her, "Katie and I are thinking of moving

in with you to help you out. What do you think of that?"

Confused, my mother looked up and smiled with glazed eyes. Katie held my hand.

A frumpy woman with frizzy hair and glasses came into the room. The chair groaned as she plopped down behind her desk and opened a folder.

"So we're here to talk about Wendy, right?"

"Yes," Polly said. "I'm her sister."

"And I'm her son," I added.

"It looks like Wendy is suicidal?" The psychologist fumbled through a stack of papers.

"Her husband took his own life yesterday," Polly replied.

"Yes, I see that."

"Right now," Polly continued, "we're trying to figure out what's going to happen with her. She has so many health issues. Her husband was really acting as a caregiver for her by the time of his death."

"That's common for spouses as they age," the psychologist interjected.

"I'm sure," Polly kept explaining politely. "Jim— Wendy's husband—added a note in his letter requesting that we find a place for Wendy. We're concerned that she is no longer able to take care of herself. The two of them have been living in Wisconsin for the past eight years. Both Sam and I live in the Twin Cities. Neither of us can take Wendy in. I'm raising my grandson and working; there's no room for her in my home. Sam just started graduate school. He's also a high school teacher. Wendy's daughter is really not capable of watching her. So we're interested in our options."

"We wouldn't be able to keep her here," the psychologist said quickly.

"Why not?"

"There's nothing wrong with her. We did some tests, and it's clear that she may have early onset dementia. She's been through extreme trauma but, other than that, she's fine."

Mom's eyes closed as she passed out of consciousness in her chair. A pool of drool was forming on her shoulder.

"We're extremely worried about leaving her alone. Is there a better place for her to stay?" Polly continued.

"This is a time to reach out to family members." The psychologist smiled. "Call up some retired aunts. They love this sort of thing. It makes them feel helpful to take care of people. It gives them something to do."

"We're the only members of Wendy's family," Polly said. "There really is nobody else."

"She'll be fine when she gets home," the psychologist continued. "It'll be nice for her to get back to a comfortable environment. Just turn the television on. That will keep her occupied. Set up a schedule with your family so that people can coordinate visits to keep her company."

Mom slumped over in her chair as the psychologist spoke.

After listening quietly, the anger in my voice surprised me when I finally chimed in.

"Her husband killed himself yesterday. She's never lived alone in her life. Her history with alcohol and drug abuse is so extreme that Jim had been locking up her pain medication so that she wouldn't accidentally overdose. We are the only family that she has, and we live in a different state. Yesterday, she was asking the police for the gun Jim used so that she could shoot herself. You've filled her full of drugs"—I motioned to my comatose mother— "and now you're telling us that she's *fine*? We should drop her off at home and turn the television on? Is that *really* your solution?"

Polly was always polite. My blunt speech seemed to take her aback. My anger surprised me, but this advice was ludicrous. Despite all her faults, Mom deserved better care after what had happened.

"I'm sorry. There's really nothing else that we can do."

"Are there facilities we can look at? Assisted living? I

used to work in long-term care insurance, and I know that Mom struggles with her activities of daily living."

"We can't institutionalize somebody simply because their husband killed themselves."

"Jim was her primary caregiver by the end. Look at her." I motioned to Mom again. "You're *really* just going to send her home?"

"Sorry," the psychologist apologized. "She's fine. You'll have to make arrangements."

We brought Mom back to her room. She passed out on a small cot with white sheets near the window. She was still wearing the shirt that was stained with Jim's blood. Her body was emaciated. She looked like a walking corpse. Mom was comatose when we left.

Katie sat in the front seat and Polly drove as we made our way back to Minneapolis. I watched the icy countryside pass as we crossed over the St. Croix River and back into Minnesota. It was snowing again.

A black truck raced by in the opposite direction. There was an American flag sticker on its windshield. A handsome face disguised by black sunglasses and a white mustache raced by. Was that Jim?

"What were you thinking?" I asked Jim inside my head.

After Polly dropped us off back at my car in the parking lot of the coffee shop, we met Katie's mother and father for dinner at a restaurant in downtown Minneapolis.

I told them what had happened. Katie's father was quiet as he listened. He was a gruff man. I was surprised when Katie later told me that her father had started to cry as I talked about seeing my mother on the steps, weeping and drenched in her husband's blood.

Katie's mother kept asking questions about what our plans were.

"I moved in with my mother after my father died," Katie's mom shared.

Katie's grandfather had passed away unexpectedly in his fifties. A powerful patriarch, the loss deeply shook their large family. Her grandmother was devastated, so Katie's mother, father, and two siblings moved into her small basement in a suburb of Minneapolis to care for her.

"We're considering moving in with my mother," I admitted.

After eating dinner, Katie and I drove back to Northeast Minneapolis. I fed my ravenous cats, and we curled up on the couch in the living room.

"My mother would be super jealous if we moved in with *your* mom."

"Do you really want to move with me out to Hudson?" I asked Katie.

"I guess so," she said. She sounded unsure.

"I would have to commute back and forth from the Twin Cities. I have work and school. You would be spending some time alone with Mom in that house."

Katie was quiet.

"What about Jim's ghost?" I laughed humorlessly.

Katie did not say anything.

"The mortgage payment would be half of what we pay here." I motioned around. "We'd have twice the space, and we wouldn't have to worry about a leaky roof or a 100-year-old house. Instead of having neighbors peering in the window, we would have a huge plot of land."

"That would be nice," Katie agreed.

"Considering how little we have financially; it might be smart to move out there." I was trying to convince myself.

Exhausted from another long day, we went to bed early. I curled up with Katie, thankful to have her close to me as I found myself moving back into the chaos of my mother's life instead of trying build my own.

Fluffalufagus hopped up onto the bed and fell asleep between us.

***

Over the weekend, Polly, Katie, and I continued to stay

in touch as we tried to prepare for Mom's release. Mom remained in a medicated stupor in Amery.

Polly researched the types of care options available for my mother. This included in-home nursing to help with Mom's medication, psychologists, and support groups. Polly also visited assisted living facilities in St. Paul.

"She really needs to be supervised," the nurses at Hudson Hospital had told us the day of the suicide. "We all knew that Jim was taking care of her. She'll need somebody else to watch her now. Somebody needs to monitor her medication. And she needs to stop smoking. Her COPD has been getting worse."

Polly and I listened to their advice and took it into account as we considered Mom's situation. Jim's suicide note came to mind. Wendy needed to be in a "safe house."

I looked through Mom's financial records, ordered death certificates for Jim, and submitted the claim for his small insurance policy.

Katie and I continued to talk about what it would be like to live with Mom.

"I feel uncomfortable around her," she admitted to me. Katie paused and continued. "There's a heaviness about your mom."

In the midst of all of this chaos and upheaval, I called my father to talk with him about what had happened.

"Jim killed himself?" Dad remarked. "Jesus Christ."

"I know."

"Mom finally drove him to it?"

"Who knows?"

"How is she?"

"A mess."

Dad was living in Clearwater, Florida by the time Jim put a bullet in his brain. It had been nearly six months since Dad had finalized his divorce with Sarah.

More than a year earlier, Sarah and Dad invited her kids as well as Katie and me over for dinner on a Sunday afternoon. Soon after arriving, we realized the invitation was a veiled attempt to make us participate in one of the weekly Bible studies they held in their living room.

"Fuck this," Sarah's oldest son had said when he walked inside to find fifteen Christians gathered in a circle with their Bibles open. He walked out.

Sarah's other son and daughter stayed. So did Katie and I.

"That was strange," Katie told me after the Bible study finished and we were free to leave. "I thought we were having dinner."

"That's Dad and Sarah." I shrugged.

Dad and Sarah had moved twice since I was a teenager. The first move took them down the block into a bigger, even more luxurious suburban house in Arden Hills. After that house increased in value, they sold it and used the money to buy Sarah a car, pay off her remaining student loans, and purchase a vacation home in Florida near Sarah's brother. They bought a smaller house in Arden Hills. Sarah did not work during this time. Rather, she kept pressuring my father to make decisions about his money that always seemed to benefit her.

Dad invited me over a couple of weeks after the sneak attack Bible study. Sarah was upstairs in the kitchen. We were down in his basement office.

"The Bible study was Sarah's idea," he admitted.

"You could have just told us."

"Sarah thought you'd be more likely to come if we didn't."

"Do you like this new house?" I asked him. His guitars and records were packed away in a tiny room behind his desk.

"Sarah doesn't let me come upstairs," Dad told me. He was confined to the basement. He hardly seemed himself. "She's afraid I'll make a mess up there."

"In *your* house?" I laughed.

Sarah and Dad got into a fight because he had left a dish in the sink while I was visiting. He and I went into the

garage and smoked a cheap cigar together. He had turned
the volume up on his record player.

"I got this record player at a thrift shop," he bragged.
"I Jewed the price down."

Phil Collins was howling through his speakers: "*I don't
care anymore.*"

"That's how I feel about Sarah," he told me.

As I left Dad's house that afternoon, it seemed to me
that he was living in captivity. It made me sad to see him
caged. As much as his wildness had made my childhood
difficult, it was also the thing that I respected and loved
about him. His quick wit, charismatic personality, and
mercurial energy were traits I respected as I aged.

Concerned, I invited Dad to join me for a talk on the
patio of the Aster Café in Northeast Minneapolis. This was
a coffee shop in one of the first buildings constructed by
early white settlers in the 1800's. The structure sat on one
of the last cobblestone streets in Minneapolis. Across the
Mississippi River from downtown, the area had not quite
gentrified yet. This was, in part, due to the stench of
sewage from the river. The coffee shop was a pleasant
meeting place aside from the smell—it was quiet, served
beer, and had a wonderful view of the city.

So I started spending time at the Aster in my late
twenties. I would meet with friends, colleagues, and former
students to make better sense of the difficulties I was
having in my teaching career. It was so pleasant to sit
outside and drink coffee and beer. I would gaze at the
water, write, and meet with people to talk about how
difficult adulthood was.

Dad started joining me regularly after our first talk. I
ordered Summit Extra Pale Ales for myself, and he drank
Bud Light. Dad harassed the waitresses, I apologized for
him, and we talked. Our relationship seemed more like it
had been when I was a boy, after Mom and Dad got a
divorce. Dad and I were like friends back then, before he
and Sarah were married.

"I guess I wasn't such a great father," he laughed. He recounted the story of the time he physically forced me to wash my hair under a faucet in a campground. This was when he took my cousin Heidi and me on a camping trip with my Uncle Dan. My father and my uncle smoked pot, and Heidi and I kept each other entertained while they drifted in and out of coherence. We were eleven. One morning, I refused to use the decrepit campground shower. So Dad grabbed me by my hair and forced me under a faucet. I howled and wept.

"But at least I was there for you," he defended himself. "Unlike your mother."

"I wouldn't be who I am today if it weren't for you and Mom," I told him. "And I'm happy with who I am."

Dad was quiet.

"This is the way things are supposed to be," I told him. "I'm not angry or resentful toward either you or Mom. You did what you could with what you had."

"If you think I'm bad, you should have met *my* father."

I was quiet. I let Dad talk about *his* dad. Tears formed in his eyes as he spoke.

"He was a big fat Russian Jew. An immigrant junkman. He drove an old, rusty pickup truck. I was so embarrassed that he parked it in front of our house. He hardly said a word. He ignored me most of the time. When he didn't, I wish he would have."

I kept listening.

"Your mother's parents seemed normal on the outside, but they weren't. Her dad drank way too much, and Pattye was in her own world. I always thought Gammy was a witch," Dad laughed. "She was nice on the outside, but there was always something *off* about them."

I let my father continue.

"Your mother was great when you were little. Something happened before the divorce. She went off the deep end."

"You did the best you could," I told him. "I've dealt

with any frustration or anger I had toward either of you. I think I understand what you are. And I love both of you."

Afterward, we smoked cheap cigars down by the river on a park bench. It was during this time that Dad admitted he was miserable. It took about three or four months of our talks for him to realize that his marriage with Sarah was coming to an end.

They split up soon after that. Sarah took the house, half of his money, and got a job working as a teacher's aide at an elementary school. The school was in Primville the same district where I taught. Dad rented one side of a duplex in Minneapolis before moving down to the house he owned in Florida.

Dad did not need to worry about selling insurance anymore because of his residual commissions and social security. So he spent his time evading calls from my sister asking for money by walking on the beach and leering at young women in bikinis.

I opened up an email from him early one morning at school. Attached was a picture of two scantily clad women walking along a beach.

"This is what I do now," the message read. "Thank you."

I would call him once or twice a month after he left Minnesota. Dad was usually busy pursuing some woman that he had met on a Christian dating website.

"You'll love this one," he bragged.

I would offer a generic response, because I knew he would be chasing a different woman the next time we talked.

Sometimes, his psychiatrist prescribed him heavier medication that altered his mood. I would wait a couple of weeks to contact him for fear that his bipolar personality would answer the phone. Eventually, Dad always cleaned himself up.

Anyway, I called my father after Jim's suicide to get his advice about moving out to Hudson. He listened to my story and gave me financially prudent advice.

"It would be nice for you to take over that house," Dad told me. "She can't live alone anymore."

"I know."

"Would Katie move out there with you?"

"That's what we're thinking. She's always wanted to run a home daycare. We would have plenty of room out there."

"That's a good idea."

"Yeah."

"How's the weather out in Minnesota?"

"Freezing."

"I don't miss winter," Dad laughed. "Keep me posted."

"I will. Love you, Dad."

"Love you too."

I found myself preparing to move to Wisconsin as the weekend came to a close. I had called my realtor about selling my house. Katie seemed to be okay with the idea, and everybody seemed to think that it would be both financially smart and emotionally generous for me to help my mother.

I could not sleep that Sunday. I was terrified. Katie was breathing in rhythmic bursts beside me in our bed. Fluffalufagus was sleeping in the corner of the room. My mind was anxious.

Monday was coming. Maybe I would live with my mother in Wisconsin and commute to the Twin Cities to teach and attend graduate school. Maybe Mom would have to be institutionalized and all of her assets would be liquidated. Maybe she would not survive the night.

Jim came into the bedroom when I finally fell asleep. I dreamed he was hovering over me, not saying a word. I woke up startled. The room was charged with electricity.

"Go away, Jim," I yelled inside my head. "I love you, and I'll help, but go away!"

I wished my family would just leave me alone.

***

Early the next morning, I went for a run through the frozen neighborhoods of Northeast Minneapolis. It was silent.

"Your will," I called out to my father's God as my feet pounded against the icy sidewalks.

A silent, wintry moon stared down at me. Stars spread out across the sky.

Katie woke up early. I showered and we waited for Polly to pick us up. The three of us were going to bring Mom home.

We arrived in Amery two hours later.

"I can't believe how cold this winter is," Polly said.

It snowed all morning. Temperatures continued to plummet.

"Fitting, isn't it?" I laughed.

All of us agreed that after bringing Mom home, Katie and I would spend the night with my mother in Hudson.

We passed through a security checkpoint at the facility. A nurse took us to Mom's room. Her eyes were still hazy, but she was more lucid than before.

"I *need* to get out of here," she barked at us. "They told me I could leave. They aren't letting me have my medicine."

"Well, someone's spunky today." Polly tried to laugh.

"We're taking you home, Mom. Katie and I are going to spend the night," I told her. "We're thinking of staying with you to help figure things out."

"I'd like that, Sammy. I could even teach Katie how to cook."

Katie was silent.

"We can help with your bills and keep an eye on you." I became emotional as I spoke to Mom.

"You're such a good son, Sammy. I don't know what I'd do without you."

Mom's face changed and she turned frantically to Polly.

"We need to stop by the hospital on the way home so I can get my pills."

"Okay, Wendy," Polly said.

"They didn't give me the right medication here. I need to see my doctor in Hudson immediately."

"That's fine, Wendy."

Mom started crying.

"It'll be okay." Polly hugged her.

"Why did Jim do this?" Mom looked at me.

"I don't know, Mom."

"I haven't smoked in three days," she said.

"You aren't supposed to smoke," I reminded her. "The doctors in Hudson told us that your COPD is getting worse."

"I need a cigarette, Sam."

We had to meet with the psychologist before Mom could be discharged.

"Everything looks fine," the psychologist said after a cursory glance through a folder on her desk. "You ready to go home, Wendy?"

"Yes," Mom said.

"Remember, find a couple of retired aunts to help out." The psychologist smiled at us. "And turn the television on."

I ignored her comment. What else could I say?

They returned Mom's personal items to her at the door. A nurse handed her the bloody shirt, her purse, and a pack of cigarettes.

"Good luck," she told us. They opened the doors, and we walked out into the parking lot. It was snowing harder now. Though it was early in the afternoon, the sky was overcast and gray.

"Give me your arm, Sammy," Mom demanded.

Fragile, Mom supported herself on my arm as she hobbled toward Polly's car.

"I need a cigarette," she reminded us.

"You can't smoke in my car," Polly told her.

"*Really*, Pol?" Mom sneered and called her younger sister by the diminutive nickname she used when she was angry.

"Really."

"Sammy, get me a cigarette out of my purse."

A tension started building in my chest. Was this what the rest of my life would be? Feeding my mother cigarettes as she destroyed her wasted lungs? If teaching high school had taught me anything, it was that I was not going to contribute to stupid, destructive decisions. I set boundaries with my students. I could set them with my mother.

"I'm not giving you a cigarette, Mom. You aren't supposed to smoke."

"Fine, I'll get it myself."

I let go of her arm and Mom reached into her purse to grab a cigarette and a lighter. An icy wind rushed through the parking lot. Polly started the car, and Katie climbed into the front seat to stay warm as Mom struggled with the lighter.

"I can't get it, Sammy," she said. "Help me."

Eager to get back into the car, I shielded the flame and lit her cigarette. She took a puff and exhaled noxious fumes into the freezing air.

Both of her hips had been replaced, so she stood at an angle. Her slanted posture meant that standing was tenuous. Mom had advanced osteoporosis. In fact, before Jim's suicide, she had been approved for experimental treatment because her bones were so brittle. Jim drove her to a hospital in Central Wisconsin where she received special shots meant to strengthen her bones. Mom's skinny body appeared as though it would collapse at any moment. Looking at her, I could not believe that my mother was still alive.

"I'm freezing, Mom."

"This'll only take a second," she barked back. After finishing her cigarette, she climbed into the backseat. I sat next to her.

"We need to stop at the hospital so I can get my pills," she snapped at Polly as we pulled out of the parking lot.

"I know, Wendy."

All of us were silent for a couple of minutes.

"I've been looking into some options for you," Polly finally said to break the silence "I found a couple of assisted living apartment complexes in St. Paul that are close to me."

"I'm not living in a nursing home," Mom shot back.

"There are some really nice places, Wendy. We could go look at them together."

"I don't care. I don't want to move. Jim wouldn't want me to move. Besides, Sam and Katie will stay with me."

We were silent as the car raced through the snow.

Katie turned around to look at me, and I could see that her eyes were red. She was crying.

An anxiety started spreading through me. Talking about moving out to live with Mom was one thing. Actually doing it was another. Like usual, being around my mother made me feel like *something* was terribly *wrong*.

Back at her house in Hudson, Mom hobbled upstairs and went straight for a cabinet in the kitchen. Before Polly or I could say anything, she opened a bottle of unmarked pills and popped three or four of them.

"I'm out of pills, Polly. We need to go see my doctor *now*."

"We'll leave in a second, Wendy."

I fed Marty and checked her mail.

Katie walked with me to the mailbox at the end of the long driveway. She was shaking.

"I don't think I can do this," she told me.

My mind had raced as we drove out of Amery. Seeing Katie crying in the car had made the decision for me. After years of keeping my distance to protect myself, I could not give up the life that I had built and return to my mother's dysfunctional world. Moreover, it seemed sinful to ask Katie to join me.

It was getting dark now. I felt exhausted.

Back inside, I approached Polly as Mom searched for something in a drawer in the kitchen.

"I don't think we can do this," I told Polly.

"I saw Katie's face on the way home," Polly told me. "I don't think you can either."

"What else can we do?"

"I'm not sure."

My sister did not have a job. She and Tim spent most of their time watching television or playing on their computers. Skylar played video games in his room. How hard could it be for them to do those things at Mom's house?

"Christie doesn't really have anything else to do," I told Polly. "Maybe she could come out here?"

"Do you think she could handle taking care of your mother?"

"Honestly, I'm not sure. But I don't know who else would."

"Do you want to call her?"

I called my sister.

"You want *me* to come out there?" Christie was surprised.

"Her house is five times the size of your apartment. It's a beautiful, clean home. You and Tim don't work. You might be comfortable out here. She just needs somebody to watch her. Katie and I can't do it. I'm asking you, Christie—please come out here. Just for tonight."

"Does Mom want me out there?"

"She wouldn't say it, but she needs somebody, Christie. I can't do it."

"The *perfect* child can't handle it?" Christie asked sarcastically.

Mom often reminded my sister that I was special and that she was a burden. I learned to dismiss Mom's comments. Christie did not.

"We need you, Christie."

"Let me talk to Tim." She hung up the phone.

Christie called a couple of minutes later.

"We don't have enough gas in our car to make it to Hudson," she told me. "And we don't have any money until next month."

"But are you willing to do it?"

"If someone meets us somewhere and fills up our tank."

"That's fine."

We decided to meet at a gas station between us.

"Thank you, Christie," I told her as I hung up. "I mean it."

"At least she'll have somebody out here tonight. We can figure out something else tomorrow," I told Polly. She was changing Mom's sheets in the bedroom.

"I'm going to take your mother to the hospital to get her medication," Polly told me. "How about you take Jim's truck and meet your sister?"

"Sure. Thank you, Polly."

"It'll be fine, you guys." Polly hugged both Katie and me.

"Can we leave now?" Mom asked.

I turned to my mother.

"Mom, I think Christie and Tim are going to come out and stay with you tonight."

"I thought you and Katie were staying here, Sammy?"

"I think it'll be better if Christie is here."

"Whatever. Polly, can we leave *now*?"

Katie and I went out to Jim's big, black 2007 Chevy Suburban in the garage. He never let anybody drive the car. I started the engine and tentatively backed it down the snowy driveway. Katie sat next to me as I struggled to keep the big truck in its lane on the freeway. It was dark, and temperatures were below zero by the time we arrived at the gas station. I parked the Suburban with Katie to wait for my sister.

We waited for Christie in my car for thirty minutes. We

149

hardly said a word. Katie held my hand, and I watched as people came and went from the gas station. Finally, I called Christie on Katie's cell phone.

"Traffic is fucking terrible," she yelled. "We'll be there soon."

"Okay."

Christie arrived thirty minutes later.

"Thank you so much." I shook Tim's hand. His three fingers felt awkward in my grip. Still, I was so happy to see him.

"I told your sister that your mom is fucking crazy, but we can help her out," Tim told me.

"Tim didn't want us to come. I had to talk him into it," Christie said.

"I'll do it for Christie," Tim said.

"Hi Sam," Skylar said from the backseat. "Get any new video games lately?"

"Not really."

"You should get some."

"So I can share them with you?" I laughed.

He nodded. I swiped my credit card at the pump and Christie took the nozzle out of its holder.

"Thanks so much," I told them after they finished filling up their gas tank. "I'm grateful."

I was.

Katie and I got into the truck and drove back to Hudson. Christie passed me. She was swerving in and out of traffic. They beat us back to Hudson by five minutes.

"What took you so long?" she complained after we pulled up next to her in Mom's driveway.

"You try driving this thing." I pointed at the truck.

Polly returned with Mom fifteen minutes later. Mom said hello to Christie, took out a handful of pills, and went to bed.

"Thank you so much, Christie," Polly said.

"We don't want to stay out here forever," Tim said.

"Just turn the television on," I told him. "This is a nice

place. Relax out here."

"We'll be in touch tomorrow," Polly told them.

I hugged Christie. I hugged Skylar too.

"Jim was one of the few people Skylar looked up to," Christie said.

"How are you doing, Skylar?" I asked him.

He shrugged.

I shook Tim's hand again and put on my jacket.

It was nine o'clock by the time we were back in Polly's car. Once again, I sat in back and Katie rode in front with Polly.

On the ride home, Polly told us that the hospital would not fill Mom's prescriptions because they were not yet due. But Mom started crying. Mom yelled at them and explained that her husband had killed himself and she needed the medication. They gave her OxyContin and sleeping pills.

"I don't understand how she convinces people to give her medication like that," I said.

"She's always been like that," Polly said. "Even as a little girl, she was always able to manipulate people to get what she wanted."

Polly shared that Mom had been hospitalized in her early twenties for anorexia. My mother had become addicted to diet pills. Her parents put her in a treatment facility after she lost an extreme amount of weight in a short period of time. They were going to keep her for thirty days to treat her for anorexia and addiction. Mom convinced the staff at the facility to let her go home after only two days.

"Mom and Dad were so disappointed in her when she came home," Polly told us. "I was too."

I let out a long sigh.

"This has been a long and terrible day," I said.

"You can say that again. How are you doing, Katie?"

"This was hard," Katie agreed.

"You guys can't live out there."

"No," Katie admitted.

"I realized that when I saw the look on your face after we picked up Wendy back in Amery."

Katie laughed.

After that, we rode home in silence. All of us were tired. Polly dropped us off back at our house in Northeast Minneapolis.

"You guys get some rest, okay?"

"Okay. Love you, Polly."

"Love you too, Sam."

I called the principal of Primville Area High School on Katie's cell phone.

"I don't think I can come to school tomorrow," I told her.

"That's fine, Sam. Don't worry about it."

Katie and I did not say anything to each other as we went upstairs. Once more, we collapsed exhausted.

I was so relieved to be home, away from my mother. I felt ashamed for entangling Katie in my family's mess.

I had no idea what to do next.

Chapter 8

I woke up early the next morning. Visions of my haggard mother crept through my dreams during the night.

In one dream, there was a dead deer in my basement. I went down to clean it up, and my mother was waiting for me. She was soaked in blood and appeared to be both human and demon. This apparition chased me upstairs and out onto the street. I was jolted awake. Katie was sleeping.

I brewed a pot of coffee and called Christie after jogging.

"How was the night?"

"It's creepy out here," she snapped. "How long do Tim and I have to stay?"

"Polly and I will figure something out," I assured her.

"You better."

"How's Mom?"

"She's still sleeping."

"Don't smoke in the house, okay?"

"Fine. I'm serious, Sam. It's creepy out here."

"It'll be okay, Christie. Thank you so much. I couldn't have handled being out there."

"Sure."

"Love you."

"Love you too."

Katie took another day off of work as well. Polly called soon after I hung up with Christie.

"We have an appointment with an elderly care coordinator in Hudson at the hospital," she told me. "They can talk to us about finding your mom a place to live."

"Sounds good," I sighed.

Polly came to my house. I offered to drive. The three of us were in my 2011 Honda CRV and heading toward Hudson by 9:00. Our daily trips to Wisconsin were becoming monotonous. I missed my classroom. The chaos of a public high school was calm in comparison to the aftermath of Jim's suicide.

"The commute to Hudson would be annoying," I

admitted as we merged into traffic on I-94. "We couldn't have lived out there."

We were referred to an elder care lawyer in the area after meeting with a caseworker at the hospital in Hudson. She agreed to see us that same afternoon.

"It's so nice to have Katie here," Polly commented as she handed Katie a folder of forms that the coordinator had prepared for us. "She's so organized."

"And you're all over the place?" I laughed.

"I have seriously undiagnosed ADHD." Polly laughed too. "I get it from my mother."

"Grandma was crazy," I agreed.

"She was a very unique woman," Polly said politely. "You would have loved her, Katie."

We stopped by the funeral home in Hudson to pick up Jim's ashes. They gave us a box that contained what was left of Jim and copies of his death certificate. We wrote a check from Mom's account to pay for an obituary that would be posted on the mortuary's website.

Jim's remains sat in a plastic bag in the backseat as we drove to the lawyer's office. Her name was Jenny. A large, welcoming figure, she greeted us warmly at the door and told us that she specialized in managing legal issues for the elderly.

"Business must be booming," I laughed.

"People *are* living longer these days," she said.

Jenny offered us coffee or tea, and we sat down around a round table in a large, modern conference room. Business clearly *was* booming. Jenny's office was littered with contemporary furniture. It looked like an IKEA showroom. After introductions, I shared Mom's story with as much detail as I could.

"It sounds like it's been a rough week," Jenny laughed empathetically. I liked her immediately.

"You don't know the half of it." Polly smiled.

"Sam, you have a pretty strong understanding of your mother's financial situation," Jenny told me after listening

to my story. I had given a detailed account of Mom's
assets, debt, and my concerns about her ability to qualify
for senior housing options.

"In a past life, I sold long-term care insurance."

"Sam is working on his PhD now," Polly bragged.

"What's your field?"

"Education," I told her. "I'm a high school teacher."

"You're too busy to be dealing with this," Jenny
laughed again.

"We could use some help with Mom," I agreed.

Jenny proved to be more than helpful. By the end of
the conversation, we had a plan.

My sister Christie was designated as disabled by Social
Security. We knew this because her cerebral palsy allowed
her to collect a portion of my father's Social Security
retirement benefits.

This designation meant that we could set up a special
needs trust in Christie's name. This kind of trust allows
parents to transfer their assets to their children without
penalty. Typically, if an elderly person gives all their money
away, the government can still claim it for up to five years
before that person would be allowed to qualify for
Medicaid assistance. Transferring all of Mom's assets to a
trust in Christie's name offered a way to both protect her
money and assure that Mom would be eligible for care
options.

Specifically, we could protect the nearly $300,000 in
assets that would come from selling her house, Jim's tools,
and other incidental properties. Mom could qualify for free
housing in assisted living apartments, and she could use
the trust money in case of emergencies. If she were to pass
away (and judging by her current state of health, this
would inevitably happen soon), the money would be
protected and could be used to help Christie with monthly
bills or expenses as she got older. Typically, Christie had
relied on Mom and Dad to give her money for groceries
each month. The trust would eliminate that need. Also,

there was a slim possibility that some of these assets could eventually help to pay down my substantial student loan debt that Mom had never offered to help me with.

"So this means we can move her money into this protected trust, get Mom moved somewhere with nurses to help take care of her, and she won't have to worry about maintaining her finances?"

Jim had been paying all their bills, and I was sure that Mom was too cloudy to handle the monthly expenses she was incurring. This would also create a way for that problem to be taken care of without my constant attention.

"That's right, Sam. You'll need to get her to sign off so that you can become her power of attorney. She'll also have to sign off on the trust. Once she does, all of her assets will be safe. Then we can find an assisted living home for her. I have a number of connections in this community, so finding a good place won't be a problem."

"This seems too good to be true," I told Polly and Katie.

"Thank you so much, Jenny." Polly hugged the lawyer on our way out.

We drove straight from the lawyer's office to Mom's house. It seemed like we were making progress for the first time since Jim shot himself.

I called Christie to ask if they needed anything.

She asked me to stop and buy them McDonald's. When I arrived, Mom was awake but cloudy from the medication. She was hunched over on a chair in the living room. Her crooked body seemed even skinnier.

"Eat this, will you?" I put a Big Mac in front of her.

After her coma nearly ten years earlier, Jim had brought her a Big Mac from McDonald's each day for lunch to help her gain weight.

Mom started crying when we gave her the box containing Jim's ashes. She placed them on a buffet table in her living room as I checked in with my sister.

Christie and Tim had turned the extra room in the basement into their bedroom. Skylar was sleeping in the room next to Mom's. This was the room he had slept in when he visited his grandparents on the weekends.

"We've been smoking in the garage like Jim used to," Christie told me after taking the bag of fast food out of my hands. "But Mom likes smoking in her bedroom."

"It's weird out there in the garage, man," Tim said. "It's so quiet. All you can hear is the ticking clock. That sound probably drove Jim to kill himself. It's creepy out here, Sam."

Skylar was playing Xbox 360 in the basement when we arrived.

"You want to play a game with me?"

"I don't think I have time, bud."

I asked Mom how she was doing.

She started to cry.

"I just can't believe this is happening, Sammy," she said.

"I know."

"I just want to die."

I hugged her and called everybody into the dining room.

"We have some really good news," Polly said.

We explained the plan with the trust.

"All of my money would be given to Christie?" Mom sneered.

"No, it would be placed in a trust for protection."

"I would have all of her money?" Christie's eyes lit up.

"No, it would just be a trust in your name. It would help us to find Mom a permanent place to live. Eventually, you'd inherit that trust. So Mom, between Christie and the trust, we could end up taking care of you. Also, you would be able to help out Christie after you're gone. It's mutually beneficial to both of you. Isn't that great?"

"You aren't putting me in a nursing home!" Mom snapped.

"No, but you're going to need people to help take care of you."

"I can live on my own just fine," Mom said. "In fact, after I sell the house, maybe I'll buy a place on a lake? Or what if I meet a man?"

"Okay, Mom." My voice was stern. Mom was unable to live on her own, let alone care for a house on a lake. As always, her comments seemed divorced from the reality of the situation. I continued. "For now, we need to figure out how you're going to exist financially. This is a good plan."

Mom's tone softened in the face of my direct, paternal statement.

"I'll take care of things, Mom. Trust me," I told her.

"I do, Sammy."

"You'll need to give me power of attorney."

"That's fine, Sammy."

After our talk, Mom took more pills. She used her walker to amble to the bedroom and pass out.

"We'll be in touch after we set up the next meeting with the lawyer to start this process," Polly told Christie.

"How long are you going to make us stay out here?" Christie asked.

"We'll figure it out, Christie. Just try and make sure nobody smokes in the house. It'll be much harder to sell."

"You try and tell Mom what to do."

"Look, if we figure this out, it could be extremely financially beneficial to you," I told Christie. "All you have to do is stay in this house and keep an eye on her until we get everything in place."

"She's so fragile, though. And her pills make her crazy."

"We'll find a place for her as soon as possible."

"Do you think she's going to die soon?" Christie asked. "She looks terrible."

"Honestly, I don't know how she's still alive." I did not. Her body was decrepit.

"You can't worry about that," Polly broke in. "Just

159

keep an eye on her. We'll call tomorrow after we set up another meeting to sign the papers with Jenny. If you need to borrow some money for pizza or something, feel free to use her credit card. There's a little money in the checking account."

Outside, we got back into my car.

"I always feel so relieved when I leave that house," Katie said.

"I know!" Polly exclaimed.

"She's so *heavy*," Katie said.

We drove back to Minnesota in relatively good spirits. After a week of struggling, we finally had a feasible plan. Jenny's idea to transfer funds into a trust would ensure that Mom would be taken care of. Christie would benefit, too. As long as Christie could handle staying with Mom and keep an eye on her until everything was in place, things would be fine. Well, financial things.

The sun was shining as we drove through the frozen countryside. It was still cold, but temperatures were rising above zero.

Things were looking up.

***

Jenny was unable to meet to sign the trust until Saturday afternoon. So Katie, Polly, and I went back to work.

Not only was I taking three doctoral classes *and* teaching high school full time, I was *also* directing a production of Thornton Wilder's *The Skin of Our Teeth*. Taking a week off from these responsibilities to tend to my mother had left me struggling to catch-up. Going back to work was exhausting. Like the title of Wilder's play, I felt like I was hanging on by the skin of my teeth.

"Where were you, Mr. Tanner?" some students asked me.

"I'll tell you about it later." My response was ominous,

but I did not feel like talking.

After coming home from school, there were at least five phone messages waiting for me on my answering machine. They were from Christie, Tim, and my mother.

"This is why I don't get a cell phone," I told Katie. "I hate having to react to my family."

Listening to the messages, it became clear that the living situation was not working.

"Mom keeps trying to overdose on her pills," Christie complained into my machine. "I kinda want to let her, you know? I mean, I like OxyContin too, but she takes *so many*! It might be easier if she dies."

"You need to get us the fuck out of here, Sam," Tim's voice howled from my answering machine. "This is destroying our life and it's your *fuckin'* fault."

"Christie and Tim are stealing my money," Mom slurred. "They need to leave. This is your fault."

After listening to the messages, I turned to Katie.

"It's only been two days!"

I called Christie back first.

"Polly told us we could use some of her money," Christie told me. "It's so boring out here. We need to drive into the cities to relax, you know? Have a couple of beers. Unwind. We take Jim's truck. It's diesel, so it's expensive to fill the gas tank."

"Why don't you drive your own car?"

"Tim likes driving Jim's truck."

"Wasn't Tim's driver's license revoked?"

"Yes."

"He really shouldn't drive Jim's truck."

"*You* try living out here, Sam," Christie exploded. "This is your fault that we're out here. You lied to us. You told us it would only be for a little while."

"It's only been two days," I told her.

"Whatever."

"Just limit the money you're spending. Mom needs it to pay her bills. And make sure you get Mom to the lawyer's

161

office on Saturday."

I called Mom on her cell phone after my talk with Christie.

My mother was incoherent because of the OxyContin. Her words jumbled together. She cried. She told me that Christie and Tim needed to leave because they were stealing her money. It did not matter what I said to her—she would forget it by the next day.

I hung up and collapsed on the couch.

"This is what I had to do as a little boy when I lived with Mom, Dad, and Christie," I told Katie. "I was always the peacemaker."

This situation repeated itself, and each day grew more and more volatile. I focused on my work at school. Finally, Saturday came. Polly, Katie, and I drove out to Jenny's office in Hudson.

By the time we arrived, Christie, Tim, Skylar, and my mother were already gathered around the table in Jenny's conference room. They had arrived early and were talking with Jenny about spicy chicken nuggets from Burger King.

Christie was enthusiastic. "Those are my favorite fast food!"

Christie was wearing sweatpants and a sweatshirt. Tim's hair was long and uncombed, and he was wearing an old starter jacket. Skylar was in a t-shirt. His hair was shaggy.

"They're mine, too." Jenny was being polite with my sister. "I eat way too many."

We greeted Jenny. It was clear that she was relieved to see us.

"I've been getting to know Wendy." Jenny referred to Mom, who was sitting in an office chair at the end of the table. My mother was lost in a thick leather jacket. She had lost even more weight over the week and, like Christie, also smelled of cigarettes. Her face was caked with makeup.

I was embarrassed of this strange family as we sat in Jenny's clean conference room.

"Your mother is such a strong woman," Jenny told me as I took my jacket off. "It sounds like she's been through a lot."

Mom started crying again. She was more sober than when I had seen her last.

"We didn't let her take her OxyContin or sleeping pills before the meeting," Christie told me later in the parking lot. She also told me that Mom had been passing out, falling, and complaining about Negroes trying to climb into the house through the windows. Even to Christie, it was clear that Mom needed to sober up if she was going to be seen in public.

I was quiet as Jenny facilitated the discussion. Having provided her with context, it was clear that she was letting Christie, Tim, and my mother vent. Jenny was smart enough to see that these people did not really understand the legality of the concepts we were discussing. As the members of my family complained about each other, she guided their conversation toward signing the documents that would establish the trust and give Polly and me joint power-of-attorney.

I spoke gently to push them back to the purpose of our meeting when Mom told a rambling story about Jim, or when Christie complained about how unfair it was that she was living in Hudson.

Jenny left the room to make copies after Mom agreed to sign the papers. Some of the frustrations that my mother and my sister had been penning up came rambling out to me.

Apparently, my sister had confronted my mother's doctor the day before about the number of sleeping pills he was prescribing for Mom. The doctor, explicitly concerned about my mother's weight, health, and mental state-of-being, agreed that a nurse needed to start coming out to the house to administer the medication. This bothered my mother, who wanted exclusive control of her pills.

"Jim used to hide my medication, too," she sneered at us. "I can handle it myself."

Mom also revealed to us her frustration that she had not been able to ask her doctor about something she was thinking seriously about.

Botox surgery.

My sister put her head into her hands and started laughing. My aunt was speechless. I struggled for words. My mother's decrepit body looked so frail. She was losing weight. And now she wanted Botox surgery?

She blushed immediately after expressing her desire.

"Don't laugh, Christie."

"I'm sorry, Mom, but Botox surgery?"

I tried to understand her desire for plastic surgery. Was she trying to beautify herself to find a new partner?

Mom had never been alone. She had always had a man in her life. Whether it was my father, Jim, or the men she was having affairs with, she was used to being desirable. In her mind, this desirability was associated with having Botox surgery and being skinny. A doctor first diagnosed my mom's bulimia when she was sixteen. Her need to be attractive to men was something that had been a part of her ever since.

When Jenny came back into the room, Mom was crying and Christie was laughing. I could not take my mind away from the image of my mom, barely living, speaking earnestly about her desire to get Botox surgery.

We signed the documents, and Katie organized our copies in a manila folder. We thanked Jenny and followed Christie to Mom's house in my CRV.

Back at the house, Christie was complaining that she and Tim had run out of money. They needed cash for food and gas.

"How can you be out of money? You don't have any bills to pay out here."

Christie had only tried to ask me for money twice before that moment.

Once, when I was living with my father, they asked six-year-old Skylar to call me.

"I'm so hungry, Uncle Sam. Can you give my mom some money to buy me food?"

I was in my early twenties. I was a poor college student and the last person they should have been asking for money.

"Put your mom on the phone," I told him.

"What is it?" Christie asked.

"Don't ever do that again," I told her, then hung up. I was offended that they were using Skylar to manipulate me.

Years later, Christie, Tim, and Skylar showed up at my house in Northeast Minneapolis on a Sunday morning.

"What are you guys doing here?" I asked her.

"We need money," Christie said.

It felt like they were going to rob me.

"I'm not Mom or Dad, Christie. I won't give you money to spend on drugs."

"We need gas and *food*, Sam."

"I'm not giving you money."

"I told you he wouldn't give us anything, Tim," Christie yelled at her boyfriend on my front steps. She was angry and embarrassed. I would not let her into my house.

"Don't ever do this again," I told her.

I felt horrible for them, but I was not going to enable their behavior.

Christie left that morning and never tried to ask me for money again—that is, until we were standing in Mom's kitchen after our meeting with Jenny.

"If you need money, why did you buy a new TV?" I asked them.

There was a 42-inch high-definition television in their makeshift basement bedroom.

"We needed something to ease the stress, you know?" Christie asked.

"*I* can't afford a television like that," I told her. "Mom

165

has a big television in the living room. Just watch that."

"We wanted one of our own."

"You aren't paying bills, and you're living here for free. There's no way you should be running out of money."

"That's easy for you to say, *Sam*. You don't have to be out here."

"No. I'm working seventy hours a week to pay my mortgage, paying down my student loan debt, and trying to make my way without any support from anybody," I wanted to scream at her.

Instead, I said nothing. Christie needed to vent, so I let her.

I was struggling to keep up my relatively meager standard of living. I was trying to make sure Mom and my sister were being taken care of. Still, my sister wasted money. It was frustrating to me.

Christie was also upset because I had not immediately driven out to Hudson after her string of messages about Mom all week. She had no conception of how difficult it was for me to make time for this while I was working.

My interaction with Christie and Mom made me retrospective. I had worked hard my entire life to make my way despite my family. Doing so had required me to spend thirty years building boundaries against the destructiveness of my father, mother, and sister.

Polly understood this when I talked with her about it on those frozen drives between St. Paul and Hudson. She had been doing a similar thing for sixty years with her alcoholic mother and narcissistic sister.

Experience had taught me that it was not safe to be open around these people – financially or emotionally.

"Look," I told Mom and Christie, "clearly this living situation isn't working. So we have to sell the house and find a permanent place for Mom to live."

"I told you, I want to buy a house near a lake," Mom said as she took pills out of the cabinet. She swallowed several and stumbled to her bedroom to take a nap before we could say goodbye.

"She needs to be in an assisted living facility," Polly said.

"She takes *so* many pills," Christie said. "Tim and I need a break. Can you guys stay here for a little while so we can go get cigarettes?"

"Fine," Polly said. "But we need to get going when you get back."

"I bet you do," Tim said angrily.

Polly called a realtor that Jenny had suggested to us after Christie and Tim left. I went through Mom's mail and paid bills with her checkbook. Polly scheduled a meeting with the realtor for the following week. Wednesday was the only day I did not have a college class.

Skylar and I played Madden 2010 on my sister's new TV while we waited for Christie and Tim to return. I was the Eagles, and he was the Vikings. Michael Vick ran for 200 yards and passed for 300 more. By the time Skylar's parents returned, I was obliterating him.

"You cheat, Uncle Sam."

"No, I dominate," I told him.

"Look what we bought you," Christie laughed as she came into the room. She was holding a used baseball cap that read "I'm in charge."

"I figured it fit, you know? You're kinda like Dad right now. Taking charge."

"Thanks," I told her. I could not think of anything else to say.

Tim pulled out a stack of ten lottery tickets.

"If I win these, it'll fix everything," he said.

"Sure."

They both smelled like marijuana. Their moods had improved drastically.

I shook Tim's hand and hugged Christie and Skylar. We told them about the meeting with the realtor next week.

"We'll get you out of here soon," I promised them.

"Can you believe she wants Botox surgery?" Christie laughed.

"Try and limit her smoking in the house," Polly said. We had found cigarette butts on the floor near her bed upon our arrival.

"It's hard," Christie said. "But we'll try."

Polly, Katie, and I were back on the road to the Twin Cities by late afternoon.

"What are you going to do with that?" Katie pointed to the hat with a smirk.

"I don't know. I don't wear hats."

Katie laughed.

"That's just my sister. I feel bad for her," I said.

I hugged Polly after we dropped her off back at home.

"We're making progress, Polly," I sighed. "I hope Tim and Christie aren't spending too much of Mom's money."

"Even if they're buying stuff, it couldn't be that much," Polly told us. "I told them they could order a pizza or something if they needed to. Maybe fill up the gas tank. Don't worry, we'll figure everything out. Today was good."

"I'm exhausted," I laughed.

"Me too. You guys relax now. I love you both."

"Love you too."

I tossed the hat in the closet when Katie and I got home.

***

I had deleted over thirty messages from my answering machine by Wednesday. Christie also had my email address and sent me constant messages after she realized I responded to emails immediately.

My mother was demanding that we plan a memorial service for Jim. Both Polly and I suggested having a funeral at Fort Snelling in St. Paul. Jim was a veteran, so his funeral service would be free. Mom would not consider parting from his ashes.

"He would want me to scatter his ashes in Forest Lake, California, and Hudson. When I die, we'll mingle the rest of my ashes with his. We need to have a memorial at my house."

"What do you think his sisters would want?" I asked her.

"He was *my* husband!"

Meanwhile, Mom called the funeral home in Hudson and deposited $4,000 for her own funeral service.

I called her back after she told me about the deposit. "Mom, you know that you can be buried for free with Jim at Fort Snelling because you were his wife, right?"

"Jim liked Wisconsin," she mumbled.

"You can't afford to give away $4,000."

"Don't tell me what to do with my money. They gave me a deal. Besides, Christie's stealing from me."

During this phone call, Mom also told me that she wanted to sell Jim's tools in an auction.

"Let me handle it, Mom."

During the week, I had called a local consignment shop in St. Paul to sell Jim's tools. I wanted to make sure that the trust was established so that proceeds would be protected as Mom negotiated her living situation.

"I need money now, Sam."

"I know your financial situation better than you do, Mom. You actually can't have extra money lying around. You could lose it all, depending on where we find a place for you to live. Let me handle it."

"By letting Christie steal all my money?"

"Can you put her on the phone?"

"Fine."

Christie coughed in the background as Mom handed her the phone.

"What do *you* want?"

"How's Mom?"

"She fell again last night. She takes her sleeping pills before bed in the kitchen and falls before she can get to her room. There's a big purple bruise on her forehead. And now she thinks that Tim and I are stealing from her. She *owes* us for putting up with her shit. I wish she'd just die."

"How much money are you using?"

"It's *my* money, anyway. You said that if we stayed here it would all be mine."

"Not exactly, Christie. Some of it could be left to help you, but you can't spend any more money right now."

"We're just using it for gas and food."

"Christie, that's not your money."

"We need something to deal with the stress, Sam," she screamed. "You don't know what it's like out here."

"How much have you spent?"

"I don't know. Besides, you need to worry about Mom. She keeps trying to take the keys to the Cadillac. She hasn't driven in years. Jim made her stop after her last accident. You need to take the car keys away from her. With all those pills she takes? She'll kill somebody. We have a friend in the Cities who'll buy the Cadillac. He offered us a thousand bucks."

"Do not sell her car." I was stern.

Mom and Jim had two vehicles, his truck and the Cadillac that Mom drove before Jim took the keys from her.

"Whatever," Christie scoffed.

"We'll be out there on Wednesday to meet the realtor."

"Also, the laundry machine is broken. There's a puddle in the laundry room."

"Can you call a repairman?"

"Can *you*?"

"Christie, I'm busy, and you don't have anything to do out there. Just find somebody in the Yellow Pages."

"*Fine!*" Christie hung up and I sighed heavily. I looked around my quiet house in Northeast Minneapolis. Kitty was chasing Yara up the stairs. Katie was sitting on the couch.

"This is insane," I told her.

Katie stood up and began massaging my shoulders.

"I just want to set up Mom's finances and find somewhere safe for her to be. She doesn't deserve this. *I* don't deserve this."

Polly, Katie, and I drove out to Hudson to meet the realtor on Wednesday evening after school.

Christie was smoking outside when we arrived.

"Did you take care of the laundry machine?" I asked her.

Christie told me that a repairman had come over to fix it on Tuesday. When he had quoted the price to my mother, Mom started weeping.

"My husband just took his life!" Mom told him.

After the repairman agreed to lower the price, she stopped crying, turned to Tim, and winked.

"She's so manipulative," Christie complained.

"That's sick," I said. "She used Jim's suicide to save a couple of bucks on her laundry machine?"

Inside, we sat with Mom and the realtor. The realtor was convinced that we could get $250,000 for the house.

"List it at $300,000," Mom said.

"It won't sell, Wendy," the realtor told her.

"Do it anyway," Mom barked.

"$250,000 will be fine," I said. "Mom, we need to sell the house quickly so that we can find a new place for you."

Mom and Jim had paid down the mortgage on the house when they first bought it. She would clear nearly $150,000 if somebody offered the asking price.

"I want a house on a lake," Mom told the realtor.

"Wendy, how could you take care of a lake front property in your condition?" Polly asked.

Mom ignored Polly. I ignored Mom.

"Do you need anything else from us?" I asked the realtor.

"You really shouldn't smoke inside anymore," she said.

"I haven't been," Mom lied.

"Maybe you could buy some candles?" The realtor asked me.

"We'll bring some on our next visit," Polly said.

We set up a time to have pictures of the home taken, agreed on a date for an open house the following Sunday, and finalized the listing price at $249,999.

After the realtor left, I found myself standing in Mom's kitchen.

Mom had been going through her old belongings. A photo album from the sixties that contained images of her childhood sat on the kitchen counter. My aunt started thumbing through it. There were pictures of Grandma Pattye, Grandpa Jaye, Polly, and Mom.

Skylar was eager to show me something he had found in the album. He turned to an image that gave me pause.

It was the portrait of a shadowy figure. It looked like the photograph had failed to develop properly.

The closer I looked, the more demonic the figure appeared. The being had two black orbs for eyes. A ragged nightgown cloaked a stooped figure. Its face was ashen pale, and a chilling smile revealed black teeth.

Skylar looked up at me and smiled.

"Scary, huh?"

I thought about the figure I had seen in Mom's Forest Lake kitchen all those years ago when I was a child.

"What the hell is this?" I held the album up to my mother.

Mom stopped stumbling around the kitchen and glanced at the picture. She did not even blink at the photograph. She looked away from the picture and turned to a different page in the album. I tried again.

"Who was that, Mom?"

"I think I was doing my hair," she mumbled.

I looked at Katie with wide eyes. Mom grabbed a large butcher knife off the counter to cut a slice of Hawaiian bread she had bought from the grocery store on a trip with Christie.

"Can I help you?" I asked.

"I'm fine, Sammy." She swayed as though she were about to fall and continued to work the knife.

I stared as my confused mother weakly clutched a gigantic knife.

Mom took a sleeping pill and went to bed after eating the piece of bread.

"You have to get us out of here," Christie begged me as we started to leave.

"We will, Christie."

"You fuckin' better," Tim said.

"We will."

An irrational fear warmed my chest as we left Mom's home. I was certain that, like in the dreams I had been having, Mom would take the form of a demon and chase me as I fled her house.

Katie and I held hands as we walked to my car beneath a frozen, wintry moon. Polly followed. The dark windows of Mom's house stared at us as we sped away down the lonely dirt road that led to the freeway.

Chapter 9

"She really shouldn't be smoking," the doctors told Christie and me. "Her lungs are like tissue paper."

I sighed.

Once more, I was in Hudson Hospital. It was the end of March, and winter was finally ending.

An ambulance had picked up Mom that morning. Christie called me at school to let me know. I drove out to Wisconsin as soon as I was finished teaching.

"I didn't know what to do," Christie said. "She was passed out next to her bed. Her foot started swelling up. It was big and purple. I dialed 911."

"She would have died if you hadn't," the doctor told us.

"Why?" I asked.

"Her liver is failing. And she has Sepsis. Has anybody been supervising her medication use?"

"I'm doing my best," Christie snapped. After the doctor left, she turned to me. "I kinda wish I didn't call, you know? If she'd die, this would all be over and I could have my money."

"It's not your money, Christie."

I felt bad for my sister. She was doing her best, but she was in over her head.

Polly arrived at the hospital after me.

"How is she?"

"Unconscious."

"You guys better fucking fix this shit quick," Christie yelled at us. "Tim and I can't do this anymore. She treats us like shit. It's awful living out there in that house. Now I know why Jim killed himself. I'd have done it too, if I had to put up with Mom's shit all the time. She's always trying to sneak pills. Put her in a nursing home."

"We're trying, Christie," Polly said.

Nobody had made an offer on Mom's home after the first open house. The same thing happened after the second. Showings were few and far between. Meanwhile, I was responding to daily calls or emails from Mom,

Christie, and Tim complaining that the situation was not working and I needed to fix it.

Later, I discovered that Christie was regularly using Mom's debit card. She and Tim would drop Skylar off at school in Hudson—he switched schools after the first week of their stay—and drive Jim's truck to Minneapolis. The stress of being around my mother was taking its toll, so they relied on the coping mechanisms they had developed over time. Their routine included going to strip clubs, buying pot from their dealer in the Twin Cities, and returning in time to pick Skylar up from school. Between the diesel fuel for Jim's truck and the money they were spending on fun, Christie and Tim were quickly using up Mom's meager savings. Meanwhile, Mom's health was deteriorating. She was mean, confused, and continued overdosing on OxyContin and sleeping pills.

Between teaching high school, directing plays, and attending graduate school, I was working sixty to seventy hours each week. I tried to keep the situation in Hudson peaceful with daily phone calls and sporadic visits. I hoped for an offer on Mom's home. If it sold, Christie and Tim could go back to their apartment in the Twin Cities and Mom would qualify for medical assistance, at which point she could be admitted into a senior apartment.

The realtor suggested that we hold another open house on the first warm day of spring. So we scheduled the event for the first day of April after two uneasy months.

Mom had decided that Jim needed a memorial service. This was the week before being taken to the hospital for liver failure. She invited all of Jim's family and friends to a service at her home on the same day we had scheduled the next open house. Polly and I found out about it when Mom invited us to attend.

"I'm holding a memorial service for Jim," Mom told Polly over the phone. "I need you to be there to help."

"We had scheduled an open house that day, Wendy."

"The service for Jim is more important," Mom yelled.

"He was *my husband.*"

"On the same day as the open house? Why didn't you ask Sam or me?"

"Because I don't need your permission, Polly. I'm an adult."

"How are you going to cook for all of those people, Wendy?"

"You'll help me."

So we were forced to postpone the open house for the haphazard memorial service Mom planned for Jim, despite the increasing pressure to sell the home and end the precarious living arrangement in Hudson.

Mom was discharged on a Thursday. She was 72 lbs. when Hudson Hospital released her. She stood at a slant because of her last hip surgery. She resembled a plastic replica of the Leaning Tower of Pisa. Still, she refused to use her walker.

"She needs to start eating more," the doctor told Christie as Mom left the hospital. He also told us to keep an eye on her medication use because her liver was extremely unhealthy.

"She only drinks Diet Coke," Christie yelled back at the doctor. "*You* try to keep her from her pills!"

Meanwhile, Polly and Christie had convinced me to take the extra set of keys to Jim's Suburban and Mom's Cadillac while my mother was in the hospital to keep her from driving.

"I need my car, Sammy," she yelled at me when she learned I had the keys. "Jim used to tell me I was a good driver for a woman. Besides, the cars are *mine.*"

"With the pills you take? I'm not going to let you kill yourself, or worse, somebody else. Besides, what do you need a car for now?"

"I want to schedule my Botox surgery."

"Mom, that's silly!"

"I'm not a *child*, Sammy."

"She wants it to go buy vodka," Christie told me after

177

Mom had left the room. "She's been asking Tim and me to get her a bottle, and we won't do it."

I brought the keys with me to Minneapolis because I did not trust them with my mother.

"I need my keys immediately, Skylar... I mean, Sammy," Mom slurred as she left message after message on my answering machine. She had been confusing my name with Skylar's for years, but her mistake became more common after Jim was gone.

Polly took the Friday before the memorial off of work to drive to Mom's house and prepare food for the gathering. Katie worked on Sunday, so I braced to face my family alone.

The phone rang early on the morning of the memorial. I stepped out of the shower and answered it. It was the realtor from Hudson.

"I know we cancelled the open house," she told me, "but I have a couple that's interested in looking at the home this morning. They seem eager. Could they swing by briefly?"

"Of course," I said.

"Would you let your mother know? She doesn't like talking to me."

"Sure."

I called Mom after the realtor hung up.

"We need to the show the house this morning," I told her. "It will only take a couple of minutes."

"On the day of Jim's memorial? Absolutely not."

"The realtor told me that this couple is very interested, Mom. You'll still have two hours to prepare for the memorial."

"Excuse my language, Sam, but that realtor is a real bitch." Mom started crying. "How dare she schedule a showing on the day of the service? Who does she think she is? I'm firing her."

"We're not firing her, Mom. And we need to sell your house. You want to move, right? Just let her schedule this showing, okay? I'll be out there in a little bit, and we can talk then."

"Fine, Sammy. Whatever you think is best."

The realtor called me back as I was stepping out the door. After Mom agreed to the showing and hung up on me, she had called the realtor and fired her.

"I'm so sorry," I told the distraught woman. "My mother's not thinking straight. You're not fired. I'll be out there in an hour, and I'll calm her down."

"I told your mother not to smoke in the house this morning when she called. All of the feedback from showings has been about cigarette butts in the carpet and the smell of smoke. She lied and told me she hadn't been smoking inside. Then she started crying and screaming at me. She told me I was trying to ruin her memorial for Jim. She really needs help." The realtor's voice was shaky as she shared her story with me.

"I know." I tried to sound soothing.

I called Mom back. She started crying again. She apologized for calling the realtor and agreed to let the couple view the house.

I got to Hudson at about 11:30 in the afternoon. My sister drove Jim's Chevy into the driveway a moment after I arrived. She, Tim, Skylar, and my mother ambled out of the truck. They had two kennels with them. One was for Christie's black cat that she had brought with them from their apartment. The other was for Mom's cat, Marty. The realtor had suggested we remove the animals during each showing.

"The people never showed up!" My sister complained.

"How could they be so thoughtless?" My mother was wearing a black dress with diamond earrings. She stood at a slant. A swift breeze would knock her over.

"Marty threw up in the cage," Christie told me as though it were my fault. Marty was mewling neurotically in his carrier.

"It'll be fine, Christie." As always, I tried to diffuse the conflict.

"Do you like my new dress, Sammy?" Mom bragged.

The black dress accentuated her skeletal figure.

I looked from my gaudy, emaciated mother's outfit to Christie and Tim's jeans and sweatshirts. My sweater-vest and black tie seemed out of place.

"It looks fine, Mom."

"I bought this dress and these earrings for the ceremony."

"There are better things you could be saving your money for," I told her.

"Sam, what should I do with this fucking cat?" Christie yelled at me.

"Let's get Marty inside and clean him up. We have plenty of time to get ready for the memorial."

Skylar followed me downstairs to the laundry room. We let Marty out of his cage. He howled and darted into the corner. I cleaned up his kennel with paper towels.

Mom clung to the railing and hobbled down the stairs to join us.

"You know Jim's death was hardest on Skylar," she said to us. "You were so close to him, weren't you Skylar?"

Skylar was silent.

"Jim was like a father to you," Mom continued. "He was a better parent than your mom or Tim, that's for sure."

Mom used to say the same thing to me when I was Skylar's age. She would tell me that Jim was more of a father to me than Dad. I would humor her with silence.

"Okay, Mom," I said to change the subject. "We really need to clean Marty up."

Mom bent down to grab her Main Coon cat.

"I'll give Marty a bath," she told Skylar and me.

Skylar rolled his eyes.

"No, Mom. We'll take care of it."

"That's probably better. I don't want to ruin my outfit. Isn't it a pretty dress? I wonder if there will be any men here to see me in it?"

I stared silently at her as she shuffled upstairs. Her black dress clung to her gaunt, haggard body. She looked like a witch. I looked away and tried to clean the cat up.

This proved to be problematic. After a couple of swipes from his paws that almost took off my testicles, Skylar and I agreed that we would leave Marty in the laundry room and deal with him after the memorial. He hissed as we closed the door to lock him in the room.

Back upstairs, I helped Mom take the food Polly had prepared and place it out on the counter. I chastised her for lighting up a cigarette in the kitchen. She ignored me. After convincing Mom to go to the garage to finish smoking, Polly and Scott arrived. They helped me set up the food.

About a half-hour before the memorial was scheduled to begin, the doorbell rang. Two enormous, middle-aged lesbians and a realtor were standing at the door.

They were there to look at the house.

We told them that a memorial for Mom's recently deceased husband was about to begin.

"Can we still quickly look at the house?" The realtor asked politely.

"Of course. I'm glad you showed up!"

"About time," Christie sneered from the dining room. Tim mumbled something under his breath. It sounded like "fuckers."

I led them downstairs to the basement to start their tour.

"You can come back later in the week if you'd like to see it when nobody is here." I used the salesman's smile I had learned from my father.

The women started to explore.

They opened the door to the laundry room before I remembered that Marty was inside. An angry Main Coon covered in its own vomit pounced toward them. One of them squealed and the other slammed the door.

"So sorry about that," I muttered as they continued to the back bedroom. This was where my sister and her husband slept. Christie and Tim had pinned a blanket to the window to block out any sunlight, and the room smelled of marijuana smoke and incense. A poster of a woman with marijuana leaves covering her nipples hung from the wall.

The two women ignored the décor and commented on the intricate woodwork in the living room. Jim had built a bar and cabinets that lined the wall. I assured them that my stepfather was a master carpenter and had spent years updating and renovating the home.

I returned upstairs to where my mother was resting her slight frame on the granite counter. She was gently sobbing as she stared at a picture of Jim.

The women followed me upstairs a moment later. The realtor took them around the living room.

"What a beautiful room," one of them said. "There's so much natural light from the windows."

"Jim installed new Anderson windows throughout the house only a couple of years ago," I told them.

They came into the kitchen. The specter of my mother greeted them. Obligated to react, the realtor told my mother that she was sorry for her loss. This led Mom to explode into fits of wailing.

"Thank you," Mom moaned. "Jim was such a great man."

"God bless you," one of the women said as the other darted to the door to put her shoes on.

After they left, I told Mom that between the puke-mangled beast in the basement and the wailing specter in the kitchen, those two women must have thought they had entered a parallel dimension. We laughed.

Mom showed me some belongings of Jim's that she had found in storage before the memorial began. There were photographs of him in Alaska. That was where he was stationed during the Vietnam War. She showed me a

program of his from one of the first Super Bowls in
history. Jim had attended the game when he lived in
California. He was a huge 49ers fan. Mom also had
envelopes of photographs from his time there. Jim had
long hair in the photographs and was surrounded by many
different women. He was the quintessential hippy.

"Mom told me that Jim was into heavy drugs in
California. He got into trouble," Christie told me. "That's
one of the reasons he had to come back to Minnesota."

"And thank God he did!" Mom chimed in.

Jim had been married two times before he returned to
Minnesota and reconnected with my mother.

"He didn't have kids with any of those women, did
he?" I asked Mom as we thumbed through pictures.

"No," she snapped defiantly. "I was the only woman
he ever loved. I think I'll throw away these pictures of him
with some of these other women. I didn't know they
existed until I started looking through his things."

Finally, Mom showed me a picture that Jim had drawn
as a little boy. It was a colorful child's portrait of his
family. The meticulous drawing was very much in
character. It made me sad to see what Jim had created as a
little boy. Who could have imagined that the same little
boy would have turned into a man who was compelled to
put a pistol in his mouth?

About fifty of Jim's friends and family showed up for
the memorial. His two sisters arrived along with his nieces
and nephew. One of Mom's old coworkers from Midway
Bank even showed up. They sat in two chairs in the living
room and talked for an hour. People came and went
throughout the afternoon.

Mom pulled me aside in the middle of the memorial
and told me that the day had made her feel lighter.
Everybody was concerned with her physical condition, but
Mom seemed happier to be around people.

Jim's brother-in-law came and sat down next to me on
the sofa. I remembered him from holidays as a child. I

would accompany Mom and Jim to Jim's family gatherings at Thanksgiving or Easter. A gruff man with a thick gray mustache, Jim's brother-in-law had been in the military for most of his life. We used to sit in front of the television, watch football or baseball, and commiserate about the Vikings and Twins.

"So you're taking care of your mother now?" he asked me.

"I'm trying to help," I admitted.

"Good for you."

"My sister is staying here to take care of her," I told him.

"That's a bad idea." He frowned.

"It was our only option," I replied defensively.

"How come you didn't move out here?"

"It just didn't work with my schedule. I teach high school, and I'm working on my PhD in Minneapolis."

"That's too bad. She really needs you."

I changed the subject. "It's too bad about Jim."

"He made his decision."

"I guess. I wish he would have asked us for help if things were that bad, you know?"

"You can't think about that," he said, and stood up abruptly. "What's done is done. He's gone now."

Similar conversations happened around me all afternoon. Nobody seemed willing to discuss the reason that all of us were gathered—Jim's suicide. It made me think about my friend Nick.

Nearly ten years earlier, a group of my friends had gathered in the living room of Nick's parents' house after my friend had shot himself. We sat in silence all afternoon. We were so hesitant to talk openly about what had happened.

Jim's youngest sister broke the mold. She was a recovering addict and fearless when it came to speaking her mind. Donna had worked in a convenience store in St. Paul with my mother as a teenager. She was the one who introduced Mom to Jim. She was standing in the kitchen and talking with her older sister and my mother.

"Jim called me the night before he did it. He was complaining about his stomach—"

"He was in so much pain by the end. The VA hospital wouldn't prescribe him anymore Vicodin," my mother cut in. "I had to start giving him my pain pills. I called the VA last week and told them that I wouldn't pay any more bills because they killed him."

"Oh geez, Wendy. What good did you think that would do? Anyhow, Jim told me the pain was so bad he was going to kill himself. I told him not to talk like that, and he laughed."

"You should have called and told me," my mother said accusingly.

Jim's two sisters made eye contact. It was clear that they thought Mom had more to do with Jim's suicide than either of them.

Later, I was speaking with both of his sisters alone.

"I had no idea how much Jim was taking care of my mother by the end. I bet he was in such pain. We found a stomach cancer test in the garage that first week after he died. I wonder if he knew he had cancer and didn't want to go through the process of dying in a hospital? You know Jim. He wouldn't have wanted to end up in intensive care. I'm just so thankful he was there for Mom. She wouldn't have survived without him after she divorced my dad."

"He was no saint, Sam," Donna laughed.

"I just wish we had known. We could have helped him out before it led to this."

A couple of hours passed, and people started to trickle out. Nearly everyone had left. Mom was standing in the kitchen with a wooden box that contained the bag of Jim's ashes. She wanted the remaining family members to scatter some in the backyard.

I took the bag of ashes from her as she tried unsuccessfully to cut them open with a knife in the kitchen. The box was too heavy for her, so I carried it. We opened the bag inside. Polly, Leisa, Heidi, and my sister followed Mom and me downstairs, through the patio doors, and into the backyard.

A large patio was set underneath the deck behind the house. A small forest stood beyond the gardens Jim had planted on their plot of land.

"I want to avoid the moment from *The Big Lebowski* when John Goodman yelled at the Dude for scattering Donny's ashes so poorly," I nervously told Heidi as we stood there. "You know, after he tossed them into the wind and they blew back in his face?"

The Big Lebowski was one of Jim's favorite movies.

Heidi always laughed at my sarcasm. She had been close with our Grandma Pattye, too, so we had always shared a similar sense of humor.

Our small family watched as I led my mother through the overgrowth and into the woods behind the house. Mom clung to my arm for support and walked with a warped gait. She started crying. I supported her.

The weather was changing after a harsh winter. A warm spring breeze was picking up. Heavy clouds hung in the sky; a thunderstorm was coming. It was late afternoon now.

Near the woods, Mom reached into the box and took a scoop of Jim's ashes into her hand. She tried to scatter them by tossing them toward the trees, but she was too weak and frail. My premonition of the scene in *The Big Lebowski* came true. The wind blew the ashes back against her face. Her black dress, her wrinkled skin, and her slight body were grayed with Jim's remains.

I overcame my aversion to sifting through the ashes of my stepfather and brushed Mom off. I reached into the box to help her scatter some more into the earth.

She fell into my shoulder like a child. I hugged her as she cried.

"Open yourself to Katie, Sam," Mom said to me. "It's

time for you to have a baby."

I thought of my promise to Mom in the hospital after Jim's suicide: She would have a grandchild soon.

Then, the memory of my mother tucking me into bed as a child came to me. She once told me that I would know when I found the woman I was supposed to start my family with. Her words had stayed with me.

The woman who used to tuck me in shared so little in common with the presence clinging to me now. But something of my mother was still buried inside this ravaged, confused creature covered in her dead husband's ashes.

I missed my mom so much. I began to cry.

I held her as the storm continued to gather around us. Our family watched the sad ritual silently. Something was coming to an end.

We walked back inside Mom's house. I went from room to room and closed the windows so that rain would not get inside. Mom and Christie would not think to do so.

It started to storm as I drove home to Minneapolis. Mom was most likely passed out after taking too many OxyContin pills. Christie and Tim were almost certainly smoking pot and watching TV in their dingy bedroom. Skylar was probably left alone with his video games. Doubtless, nobody had thought to give Marty a bath.

Lightning filled the sky and the rain pelted against the roof of my car. Alone now, I started to sob. The tears made things clear to me. I grieved for my family and my inability to help them.

***

My stepmother Sarah wrote me an email the week after Jim's informal memorial service. She had some items to return to my father. Sarah asked me to pick them up since he was living in Florida, and I agreed to meet her at the elementary school where she was working as an educational aide. The school was in the Primville district, so I drove over from the high school during my lunch period. Sarah met me at the door to the school with a box full of tape recordings of Dad's radio ministry. It also contained copies of a pamphlet he wrote about finding Jesus, and t-shirts that read "Real Men Love Jesus." There were stacks of pictures from my childhood. I glanced through them quickly. Mom and Dad looked so young. My father was handsome and strong, and my mother was gorgeous. Christie was such a beautiful child. My eyes were bright and blue. We were so innocent looking.

"These are *old* pictures. I'm glad you saved them," I told Sarah.

"How are you?" Sarah asked me.

I shrugged. "You?"

"I'm free from your father, finally."

I was silent. Sarah tried to make small talk. She was never any good at pleasantries.

"What's new?" Sarah offered.

"Jim killed himself."

Her eyes grew wide as I continued talking. I explained that Christie was living with Mom, and that I was trying to set up a viable living situation for both of them.

"So your mom finally drove Jim to suicide, huh?" she laughed sarcastically.

Again, I was silent.

"I probably shouldn't have said that." She laughed again and handed me the box. "Take care of yourself, okay?"

I hugged her and carried the heavy box back to my car.

That was the last time I ever saw Sarah.

Events in Hudson unraveled quickly after the memorial. Mom was taken to Region's Hospital again because of her COPD. She was struggling to breathe. Her doctors released her to a nursing home. She needed oxygen tanks to survive. Katie and I picked her up at the hospital entrance and drove her to a facility in Ellsworth,

Wisconsin. She demanded that we buy her two twenty-four packs of Diet Coke from the gas station on the corner before we left. Mom shared a room with a woman in her late eighties.

Mom pointed at her decrepit roommate as she struggled to sit down on her bed. "I'm not an old person like her. Don't leave me here."

The staff psychologist called Polly the morning after Mom was admitted.

"Did you know Wendy is suicidal?" he accused her. "She says her family doesn't care about her. She also told me about a gun at her house. She plans on shooting herself. Aren't you worried?"

"We didn't know about a gun," Polly said.

My mother had been threatening suicide for months. This took psychologists and doctors aback. They felt empathy for her because of Jim's suicide and often agreed to prescribe the copious amount of painkillers that Mom requested. It was news to us that Mom had convinced the police department to give her the pistol that Jim had used.

My aunt struggled to explain this to the psychologist. She also struggled with her guilt about Mom's situation. Polly ended up driving to Hudson to look for the gun that night because Mom refused to tell her where it was over the phone.

Polly gave up after two hours of fruitless searching.

"As I was driving home, Sam," she later told me, "I thought about how stressful all of this was. It would be easier to drift into the other lane of oncoming traffic. What a crazy thought!"

Christie and Tim continued living at Mom's house. All of us visited my mother in Ellsworth when Easter came. Polly brought two pies—one apple and one French silk.

Mom begged Leisa for a cigarette soon after we arrived.

"They don't let me smoke here," she whispered to us. We were sitting in a small meeting room. Leisa gave in, and Mom pestered me to take her outside.

"Just let her smoke," Leisa told me.

I could not force myself to contribute to Mom's unhealthy habits.

"No. She's here because of her lungs. Mom, you can barely breathe without oxygen tanks. I won't help you kill yourself. I can't."

"Look what my family is doing to me!" Mom screamed toward the hallway. She turned to my sister. "How dare you put me here, Christie?"

"Fuck you, Mom! You put yourself here. You fucking abandoned me as a child and now I'm trying to help you. You're just a fucking bitch. You and Sam are destroying my life!" Christie snapped back.

"Fuck you, Christie! You and Tim are stealing all my money. You're an awful daughter. You always have been!"

Christie admitted that she had spent some of Mom's money. She was not sure how much.

"How about $10,000?" Mom yelled.

"We told her she could use a little money for expenses, Wendy," Polly said.

"Mom, Christie is doing the best she can," I responded.

"You both are doing this to me, Sammy. You ruined my life."

I was surprised. My mother rarely turned against me.

"We're here to help you, Mom. If you weren't so cloudy because of your pills, you'd see that. You're an addict."

"We're trying to *fucking help you*, Wendy, but you get fucked up on your pills and don't know what's happening," Tim added. "It's like you're trying to kill yourself and you don't care what you do to any of us."

"I wish all of you would just leave me alone and let me take care of myself!" Mom raged. Her eyes were mean.

Polly and Scott were irritated and overwhelmed. So were Leisa and Heidi. Skylar and Christian sat awkwardly and played with their phones. The nursing home staff watched with concern from the hallway as my family assaulted each other with words.

Katie stood off to the side. I felt ashamed for making her participate in this carnival. I was angry with my mother for causing so much trouble.

Mom kept pestering me to take her outside. Finally, I agreed to take her for a walk around the grounds.

"But I won't watch you smoke," I told her. "I refuse to watch you kill yourself."

Mom pouted but took my arm. I walked her out the front door and around the back of the building. It was a warm afternoon. A garden of flowers was planted in the yard. It was spring, and they were beginning to bloom.

"I miss my garden," Mom said as she feebly clung to my arm. Her breathing was labored. She started to name each of the flowers we were looking at. She explained their growing patterns to me with careful detail. I could not believe that the same monster who had yelled at me inside was now speaking so articulately about growing plants. It reminded me of following her through her gardens as a child.

Sadness overcame me and I started to weep. Mom was surprised.

"I'm so sorry this is happening to you, Mom," I blubbered. "I wish it weren't like this."

The anger and resentment left her face. Her eyes filled with tears as well. She held me. Blooming flowers surrounded us.

"I'm sorry too, Sammy. You can cry. It's okay."

Her permission made me cry even harder. It was tragic that our family had come to squabbling over cigarettes in a nursing home.

"I'm so sorry you had to see that," I told Katie as we drove back to Minnesota after the ordeal. I was holding her hand.

"She was so mean to all of you," Katie said. "After everything people have tried to do for her? She was so selfish."

Mom convinced the staff at the nursing home that her family was trying to steal her money after we left. They agreed to dismiss her at once despite long conversations with Polly and me about Mom's history of manipulation and addiction.

"She can't take care of herself," we told them.

"Yes, she can," they said.

Oh.

So Christie, Tim, and Skylar picked her up in Jim's Chevy. Mom demanded to drive even though she had not been behind the wheel of a car in two years. Furthermore, Jim never let her drive his truck.

"It's *my* car!" she told my sister.

Mom took the keys and swerved her way home. She stopped at a Comfort Inn hotel on the way back to her house. She kicked Christie and Tim out of the car. They screamed at each other on the side of the road.

"I'm taking Skylar with me," Mom told them. "He's better off that way."

"You fucking bitch!" Christie yelled. "You're abandoning me *again?*"

Mom drove Skylar back to her house, and Christie and Tim spent the night at the Comfort Inn. They called the secretary at the front desk of my high school the next morning at 7:15.

"Tell Sam Tanner that I'm going to come and fuck up his life like he fucked up ours," Tim told the secretary.

"Okay," she said.

The secretary was in her sixties. She was a reserved Midwesterner who was not accustomed to profanity. "I'll put you through to his classroom."

The phone rang in my room. I got up from my desk where I was grading essays about *The Crucible* from an 11th grade English class. About twenty high school students were gathered in my classroom. Theatre students used my room to socialize or do homework before and after school. These were the kids I tended to be closest with.

I answered the phone and listened to Tim. He was howling with rage.

"I'm coming to your school to fuck you up," he slurred.

Numbness spread through my chest. My whole life was spent keeping my professional life neatly separated from the chaos of my family. Tim was threatening to cross that carefully crafted boundary.

"Tim, please listen," I tried to reason with him.

"Fuck you!" He hung up. I called Christie and asked her to relax. She told me what Mom had done.

"We can talk about this later, okay?" I told her. "I promise to help you out. Do not come here. It's a high school. There's a guard at the gate. Tim won't even get inside. They'll take him to jail if he shows up here drunk and threatening violence."

"Tim doesn't care, Sam. He's been drinking all night. He says he'd rather be in jail again than keep dealing with my family. You destroyed our life, so now we're gonna fuck *yours* up."

Christie hung up the phone. My students were joking with each other as I put the receiver down.

"You okay?" one of them asked me. My face was ashen.

"Just my messed up family." I managed a resentful, sarcastic laugh.

I walked down to the office and told the secretary to let security know that my sister and her husband might come and create a problem. I described the situation in detail, and her eyes seemed to glaze over. She alerted the police. My embarrassment overwhelmed me.

Christie and Tim never came to school that day. Mom was livid when I called after school let out. She blamed the whole situation on me.

"How could you do this to me, Sammy? I'm taking back control of my life."

My plans for Mom continued to unravel. She accepted

an offer on her house for less than it was worth. Mom went to the lawyer we had found—Jenny—and transferred all the money out of the trust in Christie's name into an unprotected one in her *own*. She found a man named Shorty in the phonebook who conducted estate auctions. He organized an auction to sell all of Jim's tools. Mom received $4,000 for over $100,000 worth of tools.

Mom called me to complain about the auction.

"None of that money is protected anyway, Mom. The trust is cancelled. You'll lose all of it now if you end up in an assisted living facility. I told you to let me take care of it."

I had previously organized an agreement with a tool consignment shop in the Twin Cities. Mom's decision to hold the auction forced me to cancel it.

"I can take care of myself, Sam."

"No, you can't. You keep taking pills and making terrible decisions. You're being selfish. You're going to be out of money in less than a year."

"You sound just like your father!"

"Why, because I'm calling you out on your bullshit?"

She hung up on me for the first time in my life.

I sat at my dining room table in Northeast Minneapolis. It was a Sunday, and Katie was painting in the living room.

"I don't know what else to do," I told Katie.

"There's nothing you can do."

I called Polly and she agreed.

"There's nothing you can do, Sam."

Eventually, Christie and Tim picked up Skylar and brought him back to an apartment they found in the Twin Cities. They would not speak with me. I felt terrible for what had happened to them.

I called Dad.

"The plan was perfect," I told him. "All they had to do was live together and keep Mom alive until we sold the house. The house was so much better than where they were living, anyway. The trust would have been there to

194

take care of Mom and, after she died, Christie. I don't know what happened."

"Christie said you were lying about the money," Dad told me.

"I wasn't."

"And your mother doesn't make any sense when I talk to her."

"The pills."

"She's always been an addict, Sam."

"I know."

I told Dad about my final encounter with Sarah, and he sighed heavily into the phone.

"I'm glad I'm in Florida," Dad finally said after listening to my description of Mom and Christie's fallout. "Do you remember that book we used to read? The Stupid Family?"

I laughed.

"It's like the Stupid family," Dad told me. "Just let Mom and Christie do what they're going to do."

"What else can I do?"

"Trust God to take care of it. There's a demon inside of that woman, Sam. I always thought that. There's nothing you can do."

***

Jim's father was a veteran of World War II. By the time I met him, he was old, gray, and lecherous.

"He always pinched my ass," Mom proudly told me when we talked about him after he had passed away.

I never knew his real name, but people called him Bud. He died about seven years before his son put a bullet in his brain. I went to the wake at a small Catholic church in St. Paul. Jim wore dark sunglasses. It was chilling to look at Bud's body. I was still a teenager.

My most memorable interaction with Bud came when Jim took both him and me to a St. Paul Saints game. Jim and his dad had grown up cheering for the original minor league team at Midway Stadium. The club was formed again in the nineties. Jim must have figured that catching a game would be an apt family ritual. So we sat on a wooden bench at the refurbished stadium and watched baseball. I was twelve. Bud bought me a hotdog.

Over the years, Bud and I spent Thanksgiving and Christmas complaining about the Twins and talking about baseball.

"Call him Grandpa," Mom always told me.

"But he isn't my Grandpa," I would say.

"Yes he is. And Jim is your father."

Bud gave up drinking cold turkey in his late forties. Apparently, he had been a real lush. Bud's wife Edith told him it was either the drinking or her. Bud chose his wife.

Jim followed in his father's footsteps. He was finished with hard drugs in his thirties and booze in his forties. Jim switched to non-alcoholic beer, while Mom started hiding vodka. Unlike Bud or Jim, Mom chose drinking over her family.

As a child, I was forced to disengage with Mom after endless stints at rehabilitation clinics, any number of family interventions, and even one locked down stay at Hazelden addiction center after she flipped her car and broke her neck. Mom would not sober up, and I could not watch her drink herself to death. So I stopped telling Mom how important it was to me that she become sober. I learned it was more effective to just tune out. I would ignore our absent-minded phone conversations and check back in at the end.

"Love you, Mom," I would say.

"Love you too, Sam."

Despite what I learned as a child, I tried to reengage my mother after Jim's suicide. I did what I could to care for my family. My efforts were useless.

Anyway, Bud had two other children besides Jim— Donna and Barb. Barb and Donna were both in their sixties by the time Jim put a bullet in his brain. As I mentioned earlier, Donna was a recovering addict who had seen her fair share of addiction.

"That's why I understand your Ma and your sister, Sam," she told me after Jim killed himself. "You can't trust either of them when they're addicts."

She tried to give me advice in the wake of Jim's suicide as I tried to figure out what to do. Barb and Donna told me it was my job to take care of my mom. They had taken care of theirs after Bud had passed. I nodded and listened to them.

There had been so many questions in that moment after Jim's death. Would I move out to Hudson and supervise Mom so that she would not kill herself? Would Christie? Who would take care of her money? Who would watch her pills?

Jim kept the safe combination from Mom. He doled out pills to her two or three times a day near the end of his life.

"If I don't manage her pills, she'll kill herself," he once told me. "She'll overdose."

Jim spent nearly twenty years monitoring Mom's various addictions.

Mom spent days searching out the safe's combination after Jim's suicide. She seemed smug that she had finally figured out how to get into the safe even after the pills were gone.

Anyway, Barb and Donna kept my mother company with visits and phone calls after Jim killed himself. This continued until Barb found out something that my mother had done during the last week of Bud's life.

Bud was in rough shape at the end. Donna was taking care of him at his house in St. Paul. He was in a great deal of pain and stopped eating. Mom and Jim showed up to visit during the last days of his life. The family was taking turns holding vigil. My mom caught wind of the caliber of pain medication that Bud had been prescribed. She replaced all of the pills in his bottle with aspirin. Mom took the painkillers for herself.

Bud was in agony during the last days of his life.

Donna discovered what Mom had done and confronted her and Jim about it. Somehow, Jim convinced Donna to keep Mom's action a secret so that nobody in their family would know what she had done.

Mom called me up one evening in May after the arrangement I created in Hudson had fallen apart. It was Mother's Day.

"That bitch," she told me.

"Who?"

"Donna must have told Barb about what happened with Bud's pain medication. They aren't talking to me anymore," Mom told me after sharing what she had done with Bud's pills.

"Do you blame them?" I asked.

As we spoke, I told Mom that I could not support what she had done to Christie or the choices she was making. She did not seem to care. Instead, she complained about how much pain she was in, how suicidal she was, and how nobody cared about her.

My daily phone calls stopped after that.

The events following Jim's suicide revealed much about my mother to me. She was not harmless. Mom was manipulative. People struggled to say no to her and her destructive decisions. Doctors prescribed her pills. The staff released her from the safety of the nursing home. Psychologists refused to sign off on the paperwork that would allow Polly or me to make decisions for her.

Jim had always made sure she had cigarettes. He doled out her medication and enabled her for nearly twenty years. Jim wrote that Mom needed to be taken to a "safe house" in his suicide note. I could not make that happen despite my best efforts.

I tried to offer Mom sobriety, health, and family in the aftermath of Jim's suicide. She refused. My mother chose pain medication, isolation, and cigarettes instead of a relationship with me.

Still, I did not see a manipulative junkie when I looked at my mother. I saw the woman who gave me life and would have given hers for me. I saw her ornate stained glass windows and heard the childish stories she made up for me about Cato when I was a little boy. I saw my mother as a frightened and wounded child, bound by her limitations and scared of experiencing the pain that comes from being alive in this enormous, complicated universe.

After Mother's Day, my father's words kept returning to my mind. The energy Mom put into destroying herself was ferocious. She refused advice from those of us who cared about her in favor of her impulses. It *did* seem like a demon was in control of her. The story of her life seethed with destruction. *Something* was imprisoning her to traumatic expressions of a tormented inner world. There was nothing I could *do*.

How could my mother be such a terrible person?

Chapter 10

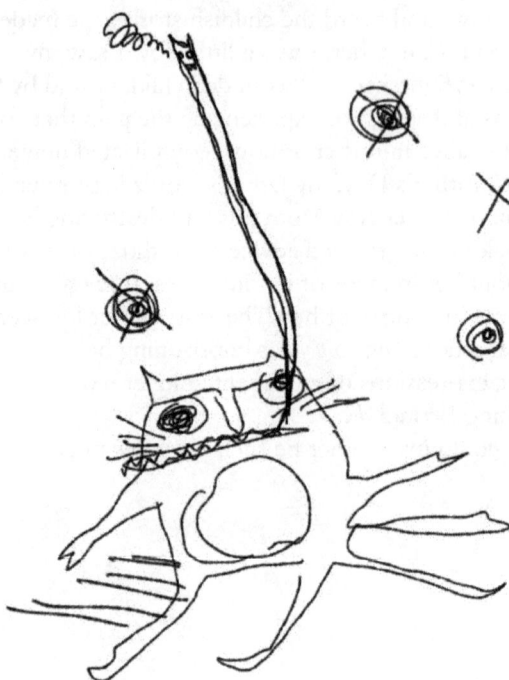

"Your mother needs to be in an assisted living facility, Sam."

A nurse called me on a Saturday morning. It was the end of summer and about two months before Katie and I were going to get married. Mom ended up in the hospital once more because she had cut her forehead on the kitchen countertop after a particularly jarring spill.

Mom was unsupervised at her house in Hudson, so she had been falling two or three times a week. Mom took her medication in the kitchen. The OxyContin and her sleeping pills were a powerful combination. Mom often passed out before she could make it to her bedroom. Sometimes, she hit her head on the granite counter. The neighbors started checking in on her after she was on the ground for an entire day because she could not get to her phone. This was why the same neighbors found her after her most recent spill. They called an ambulance for her, and she ended up at the hospital in Hudson again.

"I know she needs supervision," I told the nurse. "I tried for months to get a doctor to verify her inability to take care of herself. Can you get somebody to sign off on this so we can make it happen?"

They could not. Mom convinced yet another doctor and hospital psychiatrist that she was okay by herself. She left with another prescription and fell again the next day.

Eventually, Mom accepted an offer and was able to sell her house. She netted over $100,000 in unprotected assets. My mother was excited to have so much cash on hand, but now she needed a place to live.

Mom called me and asked if I would drive out to Hudson to help her look for an apartment shortly after selling the house. I only agreed because she told me she wanted to look at an assisted living facility. Somebody had recommended a new community in Hudson. She warned me that she had bruises on her face from her fall.

I picked Mom up on a Sunday afternoon. She had a

black eye, her forehead was purple, and she looked skinnier than when I had seen her last. My initial impression was that I was talking to a living skeleton. Mom told me that she wanted to live where people could check on her.

"That's what we wanted all along, Mom."

"Well, my family doesn't check on me. I need to find somebody else to do it." Mom sounded like a child. She was trying to make me feel guilty.

I let the tragicomedy of her statement wash over me.

"I'm glad you've decided to move to a place where people will care for you, Mom," was all I said in response. "That was what Jim wrote in his suicide note. He wanted you somewhere where you could be taken care of."

Her face got serious.

"Was it?"

"Yes."

Mom was a cheerful skeleton that morning. She spoke with a big smile underneath the black and blue bruise that was her forehead. Mom explained to me how she woke up on the kitchen floor at five in the morning

"I have no idea how I ended up there, Sam! I just keep falling."

"It's the pain medication, Mom. You need somebody to help administer it to you. You're an addict."

Mom listened quietly.

"The alcohol and the pills. You're addict," I said again.

"I know, Sam. But I need my pills. I'm in so much pain, and I have such a high tolerance to medication."

I listened to her.

Mom went on to tell me that she met the director of the assisted living facility at the hospital during one of her stays.

"Something about her eyes reminded me of my mother."

"Grandma Pattye?"

"Yes."

The director met us at the door to a beautiful, newly constructed assisted living facility. It looked more like luxury condos than a nursing home.

"This is nicer than my house in Minneapolis," I laughed as we walked into the lobby.

Mom was right. The director of the facility did resemble my grandmother. Mom told her as much.

"You look just like my mother. She was a beautiful woman in her youth."

Mom was trying to be charming. The director smiled and nodded.

"This is my son, Sammy. He's going to be a doctor."

"Are you?" The woman looked from my mother to me.

"I'm getting my PhD in education, so nothing as prestigious as that. I'm a teacher."

I chatted with the director about the facility as Mom looked around. I learned that the director had spoken with our lawyer Jenny about Mom's situation. Jenny came up with a plan so that Mom would be able to qualify for medical assistance if she moved into a one-bedroom apartment. Mom would also be able to hold onto the money she made selling the house.

"She can protect her assets *and* live here?" I was shocked.

"If she lives in a one-bedroom unit, yes."

The director showed us the one-bedroom model. It was luxurious. It had high ceilings, a washer and dryer, a balcony looking over rolling hillsides, and updated appliances and fixtures.

"Seriously, Mom. This is far nicer than where I thought you might have to live."

I was surprised that my mother was going to end up in this beautiful apartment. She would not have to pay rent. How did she keep finding opportunities like this?

"Can we see the two-bedroom unit?" Mom asked.

I looked at her intently.

"You know that you'll have to pay out of pocket if you have two bedrooms, right?"

"I have money," Mom snapped at me.

I shook my head but did not interfere. What good would it do?

Mom decided to take the two-bedroom unit. I did the math in my head. She would spend through the money she made from selling the house in less than two years just trying to pay rent for the extra bedroom, instead of protecting her savings indefinitely by choosing the one-bedroom unit.

I explained this to her again and asked what she needed a second bedroom for.

"My office, Sammy. And my birds."

Mom would not be convinced. We signed the paperwork for the unit with two bedrooms, and I drove her back to her house.

"I need the extra space, Sam. For all my stuff."

"I'm just happy that you'll finally be safe, Mom."

"I love you, Sammy." Mom bent in awkwardly to kiss me after I walked her fragile, skeletal frame to the front door.

"Love you too, Mom."

Polly, Scott, and I drove out to help Mom move the next week. Christie and Tim were not on speaking terms with my mother, so they did not join us. We took Mom's remaining furniture from her house in Hudson to the assisted living apartment.

Scott and I were dripping with sweat as my mother told us where to place the heavy, wooden china cabinet.

"This is really nice, Wendy," Polly told her after seeing her new home. "I wish you were closer to us, though."

Later, I admitted to Polly that the distance gave me comfort.

"The St. Croix river provides just enough energetic separation for me," I told her. "I don't think I want her any closer."

Polly and Scott followed me back to my house in Northeast Minneapolis after the move. They transported the expensive, leather couch that Jim and Mom purchased after the fire in Forest Lake. It would not fit in Mom's new apartment, so she told me to take it.

"It looks great in here," Polly said. "At least you got the couch out of the situation."

I laughed.

Mom had sold all the furniture in Skylar's room at the auction, despite the fact that it was nicer than what he had at my sister's house. But we convinced her to keep the new bed that Jim had bought Skylar as a gift a few years back. We brought his bed to Christie and Tim's apartment in a suburb of Minneapolis after we finished at my house. I also brought an old queen-sized bed that I had been storing in my garage to give them, because I knew theirs was in poor condition.

Christie and Tim were cordial to us as Scott and I set up Skylar's bed. They asked about Mom. I told them that the assisted living facility was far nicer than where I had imagined she would end up. Still, she could not afford to stay there for more than two years.

"If she lives that long."

"We did the best we could," Christie said defensively.

"I know, Christie. It's fine."

***

Katie and I were married in October of 2011. Dad performed the ceremony.

Katie had weathered the chaos of my family. She was still with me. What else could I ask for in a partner?

I had not been ready to start a family before Jim's suicide. What if I did to my children what my parents had done to me? After Katie suffered through the aftermath of Jim's death, I was ready to separate myself from what had been done to me. I was ready to let go of the pain and anxiety that I had learned to associate with *family*.

"Father," Dad prayed, "we ask that you bless this union."

I bowed my head. We were in the backyard of Katie's cousin's house in a suburb of Minneapolis. I had no idea what Dad would say next. He refused to do a rehearsal.

"Unlike my marriages," he joked in front of the strange ritual's participants, "we pray that this one works."

Laughter drifted through the crowd.

Mom sat in the first row. Her eyes glowed with love; they were also cloudy with pain medication. I was grateful she was there *and* I was sad to see her in such a state. Mostly, I was shocked that she had lived long enough to participate in this moment.

Katie and I had written our own vows.

"It was like you were renouncing your family," Josh, who had been my best man, told me later. "It was strange."

"I *was* renouncing my family," I laughed. "This wedding was about moving forward. I've learned what I can from the failure of my family. Now I'm ready to start my own."

Mom drank too much wine at the informal wedding reception we held at a local Thai restaurant near our home in Northeast Minneapolis. She had to leave early. Dad drove her back to Hudson.

"You can have the name Hope, Katie," Katie's Aunt Helen told us after Mom left the reception. She and her husband Bob lived in Chicago and had driven up for the ceremony. Bob was an Evangelic insurance salesman like my father. Katie shared a lot in common with her aunt. I liked both of them immediately. Helen eventually gave birth to two boys, but her first child was stillborn.

"She was a girl," she told us, "and we named her Hope. But you can have that name now."

Katie and I agreed on Solomon David Tanner if we had a boy. For me, this name would signify wisdom. It also honored where I came from. My Jewish grandfather was named David. He brought his family to America from Russia, and the name would honor the tradition of my father's line.

God chose Saul to be the king of Israel. Saul was a wild man, and his kingdom was passed to David. David was a wild, empathetic artist who followed his impulsive passions. David begat Solomon, and Solomon had his shit together. This all led to a spiritual infrastructure that begat Jesus and the redemption of the human race. This is a pretty solid narrative structure.

Katie wanted to have children with me for as long as we had known each other. The feeling was mutual, so we started banging away at it soon after we were married. There was nothing to show for our efforts a year later.

"Maybe you should go get checked out, Sam?" Katie suggested after time had passed.

So I went to a fertility doctor. An old man with white hair met me in an office.

"What's your family history?" he asked after I filled out paperwork on a clipboard.

I laughed.

"You want the short or long version?" I described my mother, my father, and my dead siblings. I told my story with great gusto, but the serious doctor offered little in the way of reaction. His white beard stared back at me. After our consultation, he told me to ejaculate in a cup.

"Here?"

"At home."

A nurse handed me a plastic bag that contained a cup and a pamphlet. The pamphlet concerned ejaculation and cups. It was riveting material and included illustrations.

I brought my supplies back home and waited until inspiration struck. A week later, I had some time on my hands. So I filled a plastic cup with semen, drove from Minneapolis to St. Paul through heavy traffic, and handed it to an old woman with blue gloves.

"Enjoy," I told her.

She was not amused.

They called me with the results a couple days later. Not good.

"We'd like you to come back in," was the nurse's cryptic conclusion.

I was not the only problem. Katie's period was irregular as well.

"When are you going to have babies, Sam?" My mom left weekly messages on my answering machine. Somehow, she kept living. Years of smoking left her voice rough and scratchy. The COPD had worsened. She sounded like a demon when she reminded me of her impending mortality. "Who knows how long I'll be around?"

All of Katie's family and friends continued to post pictures of babies on their Facebook pages. Katie scrolled through them while I sat next to her on the couch in our little Northeast Minneapolis home.

"Whatever is going to be," I told her sadly, "will be."

"I know."

We held each other.

Nothing was ever simple for me, but I was learning that it was *okay*. I was releasing my emotions. Unlike my mother, I was becoming an adult.

***

I visited Mom in her apartment early the next summer. This was near the time that Katie and I were learning that we might be unable to conceive a child. It was a warm weekend morning. The sun was bright as I left St. Paul and drove through the countryside toward Hudson.

Mom had settled into her two-bedroom apartment in the assisted living facility. She convinced Polly to go with her to buy an African grey parrot at a farm in Wisconsin. Mom spent $4,000 on a bird that would probably outlive her by fifty years.

"You bought what?" My shock was evident even over the phone.

"Jim always wanted one," she shot back.

"Can you afford that, Mom? Will they even let you have a parrot at your facility?" I made it clear to her that I did not think it was a good idea for her to buy an African grey parrot.

"I have money. And they let me have my other birds here," she said. "I just won't tell the director."

African grey parrots live between 50-70 years, mimic human speech, and have the cognitive ability of four to six-year-olds. They can understand up to 100 words. Mom already had her other lovebirds, but was thrilled to have this parrot.

"He's my little boy. Besides, you can have the bird when I die."

"I don't want it," I laughed. "Give it to Christie."

"Christie doesn't want it either."

"She'd probably pawn it."

I disapproved of Mom's new pet but did not get involved. Mom named the bird Gabby. Mom came up with this name before learning that Gabby was actually male.

"Gabby is like my child." She left messages about the bird's daily routine on my answering machine. It ate grapes, told her he loved her, and rested on her head when she took him out of the cage.

Mom started getting into fights with the staff at her assisted living facility about her use of medication, her pets, and her smoking. But at least people were looking after her and her assortment of animals. She stopped falling because her medication was being controlled. Mom was in rough physical and mental shape. Still, she was alive. This was more than most people—doctors included—had predicted. Say what you might about her—my mother was surviving.

The tenacity to which I attributed her survival was evident when I arrived to visit her on that summer morning. Her fierce work to evade the facility's no smoking policy impressed me.

Mom proudly showed me the camouflage she created to hide her smoking. She arranged pots and hanging plants to create a beautiful garden on her third story balcony. Stunning daisies hung above towering tomato plants. The design was aesthetically pleasing as well as cunningly utilitarian. Mom lit a cigarette behind the canopy as I looked out on the rolling hillsides across the parking lot from the assisted living facility. A warm breeze blew over the land.

"It's beautiful out here," I told her.

"This wasn't in bloom last night." Mom pointed at a flower that was opening up. "It bloomed for you, because it knew you were coming."

I leaned in to smell the flowers, like I had done as a little boy when Mom took me outside to work with her in the garden.

"They kicked a woman out of here last year for smoking on her porch." Mom coughed and flicked an ash into a vase.

Mom went on to tell me a story. She had been smoking on her porch earlier in the spring. She was standing at a slant because of her osteoporosis. So she accidentally lit one of her plants on fire.

One of Mom's nurses had told her to buy an electric wheelchair in the winter, because the staff worried that she should not be walking. She kept falling and hitting her head. Mom used her savings to purchase the most expensive model. It was controlled by a joystick and took up most of her living room.

My mother used this bulbous contraption to race to the kitchen when her balcony started on fire. She filled a jug of water and raced back to the deck. The plant was still burning, so she returned to the kitchen. Mom filled both the jug and the watering can.

"I knew one jug wouldn't be enough."

Mom doused the plants, but the fire had spread. So she raced back to the kitchen in her wheelchair. The kitchen was now flooding. Mom had used the sink's hose and positioned it so that it was spraying water all over the floor. The wheelchair would not work in the kitchen due to the water. My mother got out of the wheelchair and started crawling back and forth from her flooded kitchen to her burning deck.

"The deck was on fire and my apartment was flooding. I was so worried somebody would find out I had been smoking," she told me.

I started laughing. So did she.

Eventually, Mom was able to put the fire on the deck out. Now there was standing water in her kitchen.

"I cleaned all night so the nurses wouldn't find out I had been smoking," Mom told me.

"What about the neighbors below you?" I asked. There was a balcony directly below hers on the second floor.

"I think they were really pissed at me. I got water all over their deck."

I shrugged my shoulders and started laughing. So did she.

Mom introduced me to her African grey parrot after telling me her story. Gabby had a large cage in the second bedroom. His cage was next to another cage that contained my mother's two lovebirds.

"Don't all these birds make too much noise?" I asked.

"They're fine. Say hello, Gabby."

Gabby squawked. It was a guttural, demonic utterance.

"What the hell was that?" I asked.

"Gabby said he loves you," Mom answered.

"Oh."

I could not believe that Mom had not been kicked out of the assisted living facility yet.

Mom was surprisingly lucid that morning, so we

continued to talk. She brought me a red popsicle from her freezer. It was the same kind she used to give me as a little boy.

Our conversation drifted into the past, and we talked about the seven years we had lived together. It was interesting to hear my sober mother talk about my childhood since the nurses had been monitoring her pain medication. Our talk led us to a discussion about my best friend from childhood, Jordan.

"You started playing with him as soon as you could go outside, Sam."

"I was probably looking for any excuse I could find to get out of our crazy house," I laughed. Mom laughed too.

Jordan lived two doors down from us on Mt. Curve in St. Paul. Recently, I had checked the value of that old house online. It was now worth nearly a million dollars. It was too bad that Dad did not hold onto that property.

I became close friends with Jordan when I was little. We played with each other whenever we could. He and I watched He-Man on television or built towers out of Legos in the morning. We chased each other around our yards with plastic swords during the afternoon.

Mom packed us lunches one day when we told her that we were going on a journey to Boogie-Land.

"What's Boogie-Land?" Mom had asked us.

We told her that it was a magical, distant place full of boogers in the sky. She laughed, and we went out in the backyard. I remember looking up at the sun with Jordan. Both of us were trying to figure out how to climb the electric meter behind my house in order to get to the clouds.

Jordan left when I was six.

"You were so upset after Jordan told you his family was moving to New Jersey," Mom told me. "You were so angry that you refused to see or talk to him."

I did not remember that.

"How old was I?" I asked.

"You were six. His mother kept calling our house. Jordan was crying because he missed you so badly. It hit you hard when he left, Sammy. It's because you're sensitive. Like me."

"I still remember watching him drive away with his parents," I admitted.

"I do, too."

"That's the last time I ever saw him."

"I wonder where he is now? He's all grown up, like you."

Mom and I talked for nearly three hours that morning. I even watched her swipe a pill from the nurse who came to deliver her medication. She convinced the nurse to check on something in her bathroom and took an extra sleeping pill from the tray. I rolled my eyes. Again, I refused to get involved. But it was nice to see that she was safer than she had been.

Mom followed me down to the parking lot in her state-of-the-art wheelchair. She exchanged a contentious glare with the director as we passed her in the lobby. I politely said hello.

In the parking lot, Mom showed me her new car. She had bought the vehicle with the money she made from selling the house. Mom spent nearly $30,000 on this brand new Chevy Malibu. It was dangerous for her to drive. Furthermore, she had nowhere she was required to go. It was foolish of my mother to spend so much money. She needed her savings money for rent. Again, I could not involve myself in her decisions, so I feigned polite interest as she told me proudly about her new car.

I waved at Mom as I drove away. She sat in her wheelchair and waved back. My mother was alone. But she pointed up to the deck that overlooked the parking lot and smiled. It was covered with beautiful flowers and plants.

Mom reminded me of a child.

Once again, I was overcome with emotion as I drove West toward Minnesota through peaceful Wisconsin farmland. Her little garden was more evidence of Mom's tenacious, creative gifts. She had spent her life running from pain and self-medicating instead of learning to use her creativity productively. Now, she was stranded in an assisted living facility in the aftermath of Jim's suicide. But she was stubbornly clinging onto things. Whether it was having access to her pills, buying parrots, or smoking cigarettes—Mom was a determined weed who refused to be tended by others.

That was where I came from. Mom refused to let her doctors tell her that she could not have a healthy baby.

Regret washed over me as I drove. Mom's story about Jordan came to mind. My friend Nick and my stepfather Jim appeared in my imagination as well.

"You're sensitive," Mom had told me.

Mom was right. Experiencing pain was hard. But I would experience it. I would not try to numb it or avoid it. That was the difference between her and me.

A little prayer for my mother escaped my lips and drifted up into an enormous, complex universe.

What else could I do with the complexity of what I was feeling?

Let it go.

***

Mom was kicked out of the assisted living facility soon after my visit. She had passed out with a lit cigarette in her hand *and* left the burner to her stove on. The director called both Polly and me to let us know that this most recent offense was *too* egregious. Mom was a hazard to others, so she was being transferred to a nursing home in the area.

"That bitch is out to get me, Sammy," Mom explained when I called her to find out what happened. "I filed a complaint about her with the state."

Mom was being moved to a new nursing home near

the assisted living facility. She sold most of her furniture, put the rest in storage, and gave her cat Marty to one of the nurses. Mom sold her lovebirds, but refused to give up her African grey parrot. My mother convinced her most recent doctor to take care of Gabby. This man listened to my mother weep about Jim's suicide and her uncaring family. He felt so badly for her that he bought a cage and put Gabby in his office. Eventually, he returned Gabby to Mom, who snuck the bird into the nursing home. Mom convinced the staff to let her keep the bird in her room when she told them that Gabby was the only family she had.

Mom returned to Region's Hospital in St. Paul soon after she was admitted to the nursing home. Her nurses found her passed out in her bathroom. She had pneumonia and was having trouble breathing. They put her in an induced coma for nearly a week. Katie and I were the only ones who went to visit her after she woke up. It was a Saturday afternoon, and the hospital was empty. If Jim were alive, he would have been sitting with Mom in her room with a copy of the St. Paul Pioneer Press, looking at Twins box scores. But now Mom was alone.

Mom looked as though she was dead. Her eyes sunk into her skull, her hair was stringy, and she struggled to breathe. I looked around for a doctor or a nurse. I wanted to ask somebody what was happening. We were all alone in her hospital room.

"Where's your doctor, Mom?" I kissed her forehead.

She looked up at me. Recognition flashed in her cloudy eyes, but she struggled to speak.

"Katie and I came to visit you," I told her. I just wanted to fill the silence with words.

Mom started to writhe in her bed. She was tangled in wires, and I was worried that something would be unplugged. Her voice was hoarse as she started to squawk. Mom kept repeating the same thing.

"I need you to," she moaned. "I need you to, I need

you to…"

Mom could not find the words she was looking for. This continued for five minutes. Her motions became more emphatic, and she started sneering and repeating her mantra. Mom was frustrated about something, and she kept pointing toward Katie's stomach.

I tried to decipher what Mom was attempting to communicate to me.

First, I thought she might be asking for a cigarette. Next, I thought she might be asking me to pull the plug on her life support system. Finally, I thought she might be asking me to get Katie pregnant.

My mother kept trying to climb out of bed. Again, I looked around for a doctor or a nurse. This was frightening to me. Katie watched in silence.

"Mom, you need to lay back down."

"I need you to, to, to…" she was twitching and trying to come toward me.

Katie and I left the room.

"What do you think is wrong with her?" I asked Katie.

"I don't know."

"Maybe her mind is finally gone?"

We eventually found a doctor. He explained that Mom was doing okay, but he was worried that her most recent coma might have led to brain trauma.

I returned to the room. Mom's lunch arrived. I fed her from a container of applesauce with a plastic spoon. She was like a baby.

"How long will you keep her here?" I asked the nurse.

"We don't know."

Katie and I left. Mom was returned to her nursing home a few days later after returning to her senses. She demanded to be released from the hospital. Her doctor gave her a clean bill of health.

Time moved quickly. The summer turned to fall, and then it was winter again. I remained busy teaching high school, working on my PhD, and trying to give time and energy to my wife. Our fertility problems continued, and I was growing more and more convinced that Katie and I would be unable to have children.

We were at another one of Katie's aunts' houses the following Christmas Eve. Katie had a huge family. As a little boy, I spent Christmas Eve with Mom and Jim at their house in Forest Lake. That was over now. Jim was dead, and Mom was alone in a nursing home with her parrot.

I was blowing my nose into a Kleenex at Katie's family gathering. Her aunt sat down next to me.

Katie's aunt was sloshing wine in her cup. It was a different sort of slosh than my mother used to make. Katie's aunt's slosh was festive, celebratory, and cheerful. My Mom's slosh was far darker than that.

"How's your mom doing, Sam?" Katie's aunt knew my mother had been moved from the assisted living facility to the nursing home. She had recently put *her* mother into a nursing home, so she was trying to empathize. I appreciated that.

"Oh, you know."

I could not figure out how to answer her question. Mom was alive. But nothing about her was *okay*.

"It must be tough for her. Is she settling in yet?"

Again, it was hard to answer. I started to stutter about her drinking, about her pain medication, and about her selfishness. I sounded like a confused child rather than a sensible adult.

"I met her at your wedding," Katie's aunt continued politely. "She was a wonderful woman."

"Yes, she can put that face on," I said.

"Well, it must be hard for her."

"That's one way to put it."

How could I explain my mother?

Katie and I woke up early that Christmas morning. We had agreed to bring my mother to the annual family gathering at Polly's house. Polly did not want Mom driving

217

her new Malibu in the snow. Mom had already had two minor accidents with the car. She sped into a light post and backed into a parked car. Mom did not have car insurance, so she paid for the repairs out of pocket. Katie and I drove out to Wisconsin to pick her up.

"I didn't know how to answer that question when your aunt asked me last night," I told Katie on the drive. "How can I possibly explain the complexity of my mother and her situation to somebody who's never been around it? I mean, you get it, right?"

"Your mother always feels so *heavy* to me," Katie said.

"That's the right way to describe it. And your aunt thinks that we're just talking about an alcoholic or a woman being put in a nursing home, but that isn't quite it, right?"

"Right."

I asked Katie to do the Christmas shopping for my mother because my schedule was so busy. Katie purchased two bird figurines and a silver swan that doubled as a ring holder.

We arrived at Mom's new nursing home early in the morning. It was located a mile from the assisted living facility in Hudson. Again, I was shocked at how nice Mom's new home was—it was brand new. The lobby was adorned with decorations, and her room had a view of the forest behind the building.

I knocked on Mom's door and she answered. She was wearing a red sweater, and Gabby was standing on her head.

"Hello, Sammy."

"This nursing home is beautiful, Mom." I made small talk and ignored the fact that a bird was nesting in my mother's hair.

"The food is terrible," she told me.

"Do you need a jacket?"

"I can't find it. I'll be fine. But I need a Diet Coke and my cigarettes."

Mom complained about the nursing home during the drive into St. Paul. She was in the backseat. Katie held my hand as we sped through the countryside.

My small family sat around a Christmas tree in Polly's living room. We were opening presents after a surprisingly pleasant morning of eating and talking. My sister and Tim were sitting near the tree with Skylar. Leisa and Heidi were on the couch. Mom was sitting in a rocking chair, the same chair that her grandmother—my Gammy—used to sit in when we opened presents as children.

Mom opened the gifts that Katie had bought her. Her face beamed.

"Thank you so much," she told us.

Katie mentioned that the silver swan was a ring holder. Mom's eyes shifted, and she turned accusingly to Polly.

"I want my ring," she snarled at her sister.

Polly was holding onto Mom's valuables after helping her move into the nursing home. Mom's room in the nursing home did not have a lock, so all her jewelry was at Polly's house.

"I'm holding your ring, Wendy," Polly told her calmly. "Jenny doesn't want you to have it at the nursing home. They aren't safe there."

Polly had continued to communicate with Jenny, even though Mom had fired her after a fight. Mom was resentful that Jenny had tried to help manage her finances more carefully. Still, Polly kept in touch with her. Jenny helped to arrange Mom's transfer to the nursing home.

Anyway, Mom spent nearly $1,000 after Jim's suicide to have all of the rings she had accumulated during her life—including the wedding rings my father and Jim had given her—melted down and combined into one gaudy ring. It was a hideous, bejeweled monstrosity on her skeletal finger. Mom had it appraised after it was finished. It was worth nearly $20,000.

"Polly, that's my ring and I want it."

"Wendy, it won't be safe in a nursing home."

"Shouldn't I be able to wear my own wedding ring? Especially after my husband killed himself?" Mom pouted.

Mom continued to use the tragedy of Jim's suicide to try and get what she wanted. She used the story to convince doctors to fill her medication, psychiatrists to babysit her African grey parrot, and was trying to use the same technique on her family. The irony in this instance was that she had destroyed Jim's ring in order to have this new monstrosity forged.

"You don't have a lock on the door, Mom," I chimed in. I was trying not to get involved, but she was being impulsive and reckless again. This was too much.

"I don't care," she howled, "I want them."

"They won't be safe, Mom," I reasoned calmly with her. "They're safe here with Polly."

"I'm not leaving here without that ring."

Polly gave up. She went into the back, brought out a box, and gave Mom the ring. Mom put it on. The monstrous ring was so out of place on her bony, emaciated finger.

"Mom, what could you possibly need that ring for at your place? That's the last asset to your name, and you're going to bring it to a nursing home? You're just going to throw it away?"

"I'm not going to the throw it away, Sam." Mom sneered like a child.

I knew the ring would either be lost or stolen because of Mom's carelessness, the pain medication abuse, or her forgetfulness. It was as though I was watching her toss her last $20,000 into the breeze. I was working tirelessly to pay my student loans, make my mortgage, and be financially prudent. Her carelessness with money astounded me.

Mom continued to bicker with Polly. I listened silently. I began to grow angry.

How in the world did a woman who had never worked a day in her life have a ring that was worth $20,000? For that matter, how did she have all those assets after Jim's suicide? How was she managing to spend and lose all of those assets in under a year? How did she keep ending up in these nice long-term care facilities? How had it never occurred to her to help out her son with his education or her daughter with her disabilities? Why did she refuse to take care of herself? My mother continued to squander her good fortune in the most frustrating ways.

I was so angry with her.

"Oh Polly, I can stop somewhere in Hudson and buy a safe for the ring," I heard my mother say.

"We're not stopping anywhere." I spoke loudly and my voice was firm. Its ferocity surprised me. Everybody stopped talking and looked at me. I was not going to be a part of this madness anymore.

The sneer on Mom's face vanished. The tone of my voice affected her. She looked like a hurt, dejected child. Why was my mother behaving so foolishly?

I was seething with anger during the ride back to Hudson to drop Mom off at her nursing home. She was silent in the backseat.

"I don't understand why I got so upset," I told Katie after we dropped Mom off. "I've learned that it's impossible to help her. But this is so frustrating to me."

"You bottle up your emotions, Sam."

Katie was right.

Mom had walked into the nursing home in Hudson without a jacket on her back. She had stumbled behind her walker, sipping a flat Diet Coke. My mother had a $20,000 gold ring on her finger. She had looked like a corpse returning to its crypt.

I kept talking to Katie.

"Is it selfishness? Do I want that money to be given to me? Maybe I'm just frustrated that she'd rather have a gaudy, golden ring than any relationship with her family."

"That's what she's become, Sam. You can't do anything about it."

"I know. So I shouldn't still get angry about it."

"Yes, but she's still your mother."

I thought for a moment.

"You know the story she tells about my birth?"

Katie nodded.

"The amniotic sac was unbroken. I was surrounded by water when I came out."

"Yup, I've heard it." Katie had heard this story from my mother countless times. Mom repeated herself ad nauseam.

"Maybe that's what kept me safe?"

"You weren't contaminated by her?" asked Katie.

"No, I was the only kid that came out of her body healthy. Three babies died, Christie was born premature and has suffered ever since, and I came out fine."

Katie listened to my wild rant.

"Mom's destroyed almost everything she's ever touched. Think of all that destruction: Her children, her homes, her marriages, her body, and her relationships. Jesus."

"And the water kept you safe?"

"Jesus, I don't know."

"Safe from what?"

"From whatever that heaviness inside of her is?"

Katie let me continue.

"Safe from whatever demonic force is inside of her?" I laughed.

I held Katie's hand as we raced back into St. Paul, leaving Hudson, a $20,000 ring, and my mother's heaviness behind.

***

Katie and I met my friends Todd and Tina for dinner in Minneapolis that winter. Todd and Tina had both attended our wedding. We met at a trendy diner in Uptown. Todd commented on the specter of my mother at our ceremony.

"She looked like a skeleton," he told me.

"Don't I know it?" I told both of them about our experience with Mom at Christmas. I described the ring in detail.

"Your mother is like Lord Sauron," Tina said. She was an avid *Lord of the Rings* nerd.

"One ring to rule them all," I laughed.

"And you were like Gandolf when you refused to help her get a safe. This shall not pass!" Todd added.

"I feel more like Frodo," I said. "But I have no idea how to take the ring to Mount Doom."

"Frodo didn't either, Sam," Todd laughed.

We had drinks after dinner. I described a particularly chilling message that my mother had left on my answering machine. My mother continued to leave weekly messages for me. I did not answer often. I reinstated careful boundaries to protect myself from her.

"I've found a doctor to deliver Katie's baby," she had growled on the most recent message.

"It was like a demon was talking to me," I told Todd. He laughed as I took a swig of a Krautini—we were at a German restaurant in Minneapolis after dinner, and I had ordered the strangest drink on their menu. It involved gin and sauerkraut.

"It's like the movie *Rosemary's Baby*," Todd said after I did my best impersonation of the Anti-Christ.

"That's the same thing my father said," I laughed.

It was. I wrote my father an email earlier in the week to tell him I was worried that there was some sort of evil in my mother. I did not want it to be passed into my child if we had a baby. My father responded by writing about watching *Rosemary's Baby* with my mother when they were younger.

"She was so excited to see that movie when it came out, Sam. It was sick."

I told Todd and Tina about Dad's email.

"What do you think about all this, Katie?" Todd asked.
She laughed.

"What can I think?"

Todd told me that listening to my stories about my mother was like watching a movie.

"This is another book," he said. I had been telling them both about trying to write about my friend Nick's suicide.

I nodded. I thought for a moment and responded.

"It feels like a sequel to the book that I wrote about my friend Nick. They're connected."

"And the third book," Todd said, "can be called Return of the King. It'll be about what you learned from carrying the ring."

"A trilogy," I laughed.

"The third book should be about your teaching. You should show what you've learned from Nick, your mom, your dad, and your childhood, and how that's all shaped your teaching. Return of the king."

"That isn't a bad idea," I told Todd.

Like it or not, I did owe whatever I was becoming in adulthood to Mom and Dad.

***

Scott planned a surprise birthday party for Polly in March. She was turning 60. He asked if Katie and I could pick my mother up from Hudson. The party was in St. Paul. I begrudgingly agreed.

It was the first day of spring break. I had been looking forward to a little respite from my intense schedule. Instead, I would be tangled up with my mother again.

I called Mom the morning of the party.

"We'll come pick you up at your nursing home at 4:00 this evening, okay?"

"I can drive myself," she told me.

I pictured her swerving all over the road, running down small children, their pets, and their grandparents.

"Really, it's okay Mom. Isn't your car in the shop anyway?"

"The whole front end is damaged, but I have it back now."

Mom had driven over a stop sign a couple weeks back. It took the front end of her car off.

When she got into accidents, Mom would tell the police that her husband Jim knew her she was a good driver. Then she would cry and tell them her husband had killed himself if they would threaten to take her license. The police would feel sorry for her and let her off the hook.

One time, Mom drove all the way from her nursing home in Wisconsin to Polly's house in St. Paul. A concerned driver was worried about her erratic driving on I-94. This woman followed my mother all the way to St. Paul and confronted her when she parked.

"You shouldn't be driving," the driver told Mom in front of Polly's house. "You're dangerous."

Mom started yelling at this woman until the police arrived and broke them up. Mom convinced the police that she would be careful, and no action was taken to revoke her license.

Katie and I drove to Wisconsin on a rainy Saturday night to pick up my mother. A grey mix of ice and rain coated the cars as I swerved in and out of traffic.

"Slow down, Sam," Katie told me. She held my hand.

"I'm a good driver," I told her and squeezed her palm. Then I laughed. "Jesus, I sound like my mother."

I slowed down, and we exited in Hudson. I asked Katie if she was ready to see my mother.

"I just said a little prayer," she admitted.

We walked into the nursing home lobby after arriving. Three old women were sitting in the front room. They were bouncing a large beach ball back and forth. The large fireplace was roaring, and the room was warm.

"That's my fantasy," I told Katie. "To be in a nursing

home and have nothing better to do than to watch the fire and play catch with a bouncy ball!"

Katie rolled her eyes at me.

We walked up to my Mom's room and knocked.

She opened the door. Gabby was standing on her head. Mom was standing at an angle because of her osteoporosis and had caked makeup all over her face to cover her wrinkles.

"I have to put Gabby in his cage. We were playing lovies on the bed." She laughed at herself. "That doesn't sound good."

Katie and I exchanged glances.

The bird squawked, and Mom guided him into his cage.

I helped my mother to the front door. She left her walker in the foyer and took my arm. I lifted her into the backseat of my car and we drove to St. Paul.

Mom asked whether or not Katie and I were trying to have children. I told her about the fertility testing, and she listened quietly as I worried aloud that we might be unable to have babies.

We arrived at the restaurant where the party was being held in St. Paul. We were the first guests to arrive. I helped Mom into her seat. The waitress came around and took our orders. I asked Mom if she wanted a Diet Coke. She said sure. Then the waitress came to me. Mom's alcoholism be damned—I was feeling tangled, and the place made its own vodka.

"I'll have a Bloody Mary," I said.

Mom's ears perked up immediately.

"Give me one of those too," she told the waitress. "Cancel the Coke."

I was too tired of trying to police Mom to fight. I sighed heavily and whispered to Katie.

"I shouldn't have ordered a drink," I said.

"Oh well," she said.

Heidi and Leisa showed up with my nephew Christian. Polly's friends arrived, and a large group gathered around the table. Two ridiculous balloons that read six and zero sat at the head of the table.

Heidi could not help herself at the party store.

"I wanted to buy everything that said 60 on it," she laughed. "The gaudier the better!"

Polly arrived. She was surprised to see all of us waiting for her. Her husband Scott rarely planned surprises for her, so she was shocked. I was happy to see that the party pleased her.

Polly ordered a Bloody Mary as well. She did not comment on my mother's drink, despite Mom's documented history as a recovering alcoholic.

We had a cordial evening, and it was nice to see both my mother and her sister in a celebratory situation after so much chaos and trauma.

"This is the first time I've been out at a restaurant on a Saturday night in years," Mom told me.

I asked Mom about her history with surprise parties. The Bloody Mary was making me chatty.

She reminded me of Jim's 50th birthday. She had rented out an event center in Forest Lake and invited all of his friends and family. I was eleven. I remembered the venue had an indoor driving range, a batting cage, and a putting green.

This memory got us talking about birthday parties that her and Polly had when they were children. We started remembering Grandma Pattye.

Heidi and I exchanged creepy stories about spending the night at Grandma's house.

"Remember the Alfred Hitchcock records?" I asked her.

"I do. Who does that to children?" Heidi laughed.

"My mom was a neat woman," Polly told Katie. "She was creative."

"I always felt uncomfortable at her house," Heidi said. "It felt heavy there."

"Mom's house was haunted," my mother told us.

"It was," Polly agreed earnestly.

Polly told us a story I had not heard before. Polly was sleeping in the basement as a teenager. She had moved her bedroom downstairs. A pressure pushed on her chest in the middle of the night. She was unable to move for fifteen minutes. When it was released, she ran upstairs to where Mom was sleeping. Polly woke my mother up to tell her what had happened.

"Why do you think I don't sleep down there, Polly?" Mom had asked her.

My mother chimed in after Polly told her ghost story.

"That happened to me too. It got so bad that I refused to sleep down there anymore. That's why Polly moved her bedroom to the basement."

All of us listened to Mom intently. She continued talking.

"One night, I ran up the stairs at three in the morning. Mom was sitting at the table smoking. She looked at me and asked what was wrong. I told her what happened, and she just nodded. She knew there was a ghost in that house."

Somebody changed the subject and eventually, Katie and I were driving Mom back to Hudson. It was still raining, and the sky was gray. Thick clouds obscured the moon.

Mom did something strange as we pulled up to a stop sign near her nursing home. The road was empty, and we were alone as the rain beat down on the windshield.

Mom reached up behind Katie and touched her on her head. She breathed in her ear.

"I love you," she whispered into Katie's ear. Katie looked at me with wide eyes.

We dropped Mom off at the nursing home. Mom thanked me as I walked her through the door.

"This was a special night, Sam."

"Love you, Mom."

"Love you too, Sam."

"What the hell was that?" I asked Katie when I got back in the car.

"I don't know!"

"Did she breathe in your ear?"

"Yes. She leaned in and whispered that she loved me."

"Jesus. And after that story she told us about my grandmother's house? I'm glad you said a prayer before coming out here."

"That was really weird."

I sighed and took Katie's hand. We drove home through the darkness and the rain.

***

Katie came downstairs the next morning. We sat on the couch.

"I had the weirdest dream last night," she said.

"What?"

"I had a baby even though I wasn't pregnant. You were upset."

"Why?"

"I named her without asking you. You didn't like the name."

"What was the name?"

"Hope Elizabeth Joyce Tanner."

"I like that name."

"The baby came out like it was already born. It had teeth," Katie laughed darkly. "I thought it had fetal alcohol syndrome because it had a big forehead."

"Well, that's terrifying."

Mom left a message on my answering machine later in the day.

"You should really bring Katie to visit." Mom's voice was raspy. "I have some things to give her. Some family things."

Her voice was ominous, and she did not sound like herself. I shivered. I did not call Mom back.

Spring break ended, and I returned to teaching. I came home from school and Katie was waiting for me at the front door.

"Can I show you something?"

"What is it?"

She led me into the kitchen. Katie had taken the last pregnancy test that was stashed in our kitchen drawer. She held up the results for me to look at.

"What is this?" I asked her again.

"I'm pregnant."

Chapter 11

Katie was enormously happy about the pregnancy. I was not ready to celebrate anything. There was a long road ahead. I was so afraid.

What if there was a miscarriage? What if something went wrong? My family history was downright traumatic when it came to reproduction.

What if the baby had nine heads and sixty-five toes? My sperm count *was* irregular. We had struggled to conceive.

What if this was my son, Solomon?

What if this was my daughter, Hope?

What if I could not put into practice the things I had learned from watching the failures of my own parents? What if I caused harm to my child?

I was learning to accept my cosmic inability to control my circumstances, but a baby was serious business.

Katie and I sat together on our couch after she showed me the pregnancy test. We held hands. Fluffalufagus jumped up and settled onto my lap. Yara eyed us nervously from her perch on the armrest of the recliner in the living room.

"I suppose you better cancel your appointment at the fertility clinic," I told Katie.

"Yes."

"Maybe you should call your regular doctor instead?"

"Yes."

"I'm scared."

"Me too."

I called my Dad soon after Katie's first appointment confirmed that, indeed, she was pregnant.

"What a blessing!" my father exclaimed. "Praise God!"

Dad came up to Minnesota from Florida to visit shortly after my call. We met to have a drink at the Aster Café in Northeast Minneapolis. It was a Tuesday night, and we were sitting on a patio near the Mississippi River. It was unseasonably cold for June, so we were alone. A wedding was happening in the adjacent pavilion. A live band accompanied the ceremony.

"Is that a mariachi band?" Dad asked as he sat down.

I had arrived early to get some work done. I spent most of Katie's pregnancy catching up on reading, writing, or planning my teaching. I put away my academic burden when my father arrived.

"Something like that," I shrugged.

"How's Katie?"

"Still pregnant," I laughed.

"What a blessing. Mazel tov!"

"Mazel tov."

We celebrated the baby growing inside of Katie. Each of us ordered a Bloody Mary to make a Jewish toast. We sipped our drinks and enjoyed the breeze off the Mississippi.

The waiter returned to check on us. "You guys going to order any food?"

"I think we're probably just going to get drunk," Dad laughed sarcastically. I always stopped after a couple drinks. Dad did not drink much in his old age either. He was trying to sound cool.

Dad was wearing a leather jacket with a Corvette insignia. He bought another used Corvette before driving up from Florida. The jacket came with it.

"Just drinking? That's my style." The waiter laughed with my father.

"Say, can I smoke this out here?" Dad referred to his cigar.

"I don't think so," the waiter said. Then he looked around and reconsidered. "You know, you guys are the only ones out here, so why not?"

Dad lit a cigar and started puffing away. In moments, a woman in a gown came rushing over.

"Can you put that out? We're having a wedding over there, and I can smell the cigar."

"Doesn't it smell good?" Dad asked with a smile. His Jewish sarcasm was a kneejerk response. Next to his pack of Backwoods cigars on our metal table were his journal and a book he had just bought about Jewish wit.

The woman laughed. "It smells great. But can you put it out?"

"Sure," Dad said.

People loved my dad. This was true even when he was blowing cigar smoke into their wedding ceremonies. He was magnetic.

"You would have been angrier about that when you were younger," I told him after the woman walked back to the wedding.

"Would I?"

"Yes. You've mellowed in your old age."

"I guess that's what happens." His hair was grayer than I remembered. I had not seen Dad in months.

Dad kept checking his cell phone as we talked. He was playing two girls against each other on this trip to Minnesota. One owned a company in Seattle. The other was one of his born again Christian friends. Dad had been drifting between women like he drifted between Florida and Minnesota over the last four years. He was staying with old acquaintances like his friend Dave on this trip. He was also staying with new ones, like the director of ministry for a local Messianic Jewish organization called Good News for Israel. Again, people loved my Dad. They let him sleep on their couches for free.

Dad did not ask to stay with me.

Years ago, my father used my address for a brief period of time after I bought my house in Minneapolis. This was so he could have health insurance in Minnesota, even though he lived in Florida. Bill collectors began sending threatening notices to my address, and the phone rang off the hook because people were looking for Dad. My father was upset with me when I finally demanded, over the phone, that he stop pretending he was living in my house. I could tell that, even though he was angry with me, he did not want to be a burden to me. It made me sad. But all of that was years before my marriage to Katie, Jim's suicide, and our evening together in Minneapolis.

I updated my dad as we sat on the patio. I told him about Mom blowing in Katie's ear.

"That's creepy," Dad said.

"I know, right?"

I worried aloud about whether or not the baby inside of Katie's stomach was going to be okay.

"You and Mom lost three babies and had all of that trouble with Christie, you know?"

"Relax, Sam," Dad said. "You're not us. You need to have faith."

Dad lit another cigar after the wedding ceremony next door was finished and the party had moved inside.

"I can't imagine how hard it was for you and Mom to lose those babies."

"You have no idea. But your mother was so determined. I knew that God wanted us to have children."

"Still, it must have been painful."

"Christa was the hardest." His eyes got watery. "She was so peaceful when I held her after she was born. She was going to be special. It was hard to watch her die."

"It would have been nice to have another sister."

"Christa is in heaven now. Christie was hard because she was in the hospital for such a long time. The doctors thought I was crazy because I just sat with her and prayed. You would never have been born if she hadn't lived. I know it's hard sometimes, but you should be grateful to Christie and your mother. You wouldn't be here right now if it weren't for them."

Dad seemed more open than usual, so I found myself telling him about what I was learning from writing a book about my friend Nick.

"We have to release emotional charges and pain," I ranted. "Otherwise it eats us up. It kills us."

"Nick was so loud." Dad smiled as he remembered my friend.

"You were always in your room smoking pot while we played video games. Nick would ask what you were doing. I would say 'smoking pot,' and he would laugh."

Dad laughed loudly.

"Writing that manuscript was a way for me to release that pain," I told him. "The book isn't very good, but it was important for me to write. It brought me closer to Nick's mom and dad."

"How are they?"

"Doing as well as they can. The next book is probably about you and Mom."

"Were we that bad?"

"No. You were exactly the parents that I needed in order to become who I am. But it still hurt."

Dad told me he remembered asking God if he had made a mistake by giving him the wrong parents when he was a boy.

"I just couldn't believe that I came from those Russian immigrants. They were so strange. They embarrassed me. Nobody could understand that," he said.

"Oh, I think I could." I smiled at Dad knowingly.

He laughed.

"I don't have any animosity toward you," I echoed from our earlier conversations. "I've turned out exactly as I should have, but you guys were something else. I think I always sensed that there was great instability in that household."

"We were only a family for six or seven years."

"Yeah, the first six or seven years of my life. That time formed me."

Dad nodded.

"You escaped by smoking pot or going on business trips. I had to learn to survive in that house with Mom and Christie."

"I suppose you're right."

"I had to live with whatever that heaviness is inside of Mom."

236

Dad's eyes grew serious.

"A demon?" he asked.

Dad's Christianity grew more complicated as he aged. It was a mixture of the zealous Christian right, the inebriated hippie left, ancient Jerusalem, Orthodox Judaism, and his own intuitive sense of spiritual survival as a first generation, Russian immigrant in America. Talk about confusing.

"I don't know, Dad," I laughed. "After what I've learned these last couple of years? Mom was probably sacrificing goats or something in the basement."

Dad laughed again.

"You aren't all that far off base," he said. He told me about the time that he caught Mom throwing up before bed.

"She was bulimic as long as I had known her. I finally confronted her. She lashed out at me, and I saw a side of her that I'll never forget."

"What did you see?"

"It's hard to explain. There was something else there. It was *evil*."

"I think I saw that in her after Jim's suicide."

Dad thought for a moment and started talking.

"She was so manipulative, Sam. She would convince me to buy her cigarettes or to do whatever she wanted, and I just went along with her. Jim was the same way. The angriest I have ever been is when your mother got in that car accident with you during that thunderstorm back when you were seven. What was she thinking, taking you out into that? How could she do that? If you hadn't had the sense to put your seatbelt on, you would have been dead. She went through the windshield. She destroyed that car. Do you know that she promised me she would give up smoking if I bought her that car? She didn't. And she ruined it. When I got to the hospital that night, I was ready to kill her. You were the one who protected her from me. You stood up in the hospital room and stepped between us. You stood up for her, even though she almost killed you that night."

"Somebody had to make peace," I said.

"It was you. I remember that you had power that night. When you told me to calm down, I did. You were only seven."

"On some level, as stupid as her decision to get into a car and drive that night was, I understood why she did it. Mom was worried you were cheating on her. She made that choice because she wanted you to be home with her instead of buying pot or finding another woman. I don't know. Emotionally, it made sense to me."

"I went to Poser's that night," he remembered.

Dad was talking about my Uncle Dan. Dan smoked too much pot, treated Polly poorly, and got along famously with my father. They loved getting high together.

"Mom didn't want you to leave, Dad. She wanted you around. So even though it was a stupid decision, I understood her emotional motive. She was hurt. She just didn't know what to do with that pain. I don't think she ever did. That might be her fatal flaw."

"I wanted to kill her, Sam. She'd taken the most important thing in the world to me, my son, and risked his life."

"Haven't you learned that you need to give your possessions up? You need to give them to God? Isn't that what you always tell me? Have faith?"

"Isaac." Dad was referring to the Bible story where Abraham was asked to sacrifice his son that he had waited so long to conceive.

I thought for a moment.

"If Mom ever put my child in danger…well, I don't know, I just don't…" I trailed off, thinking about Mom blowing in Katie's ear, leaving messages on my phone, and infecting my new family with her heaviness. I so badly wanted the child growing inside of Katie to be healthy, to be safe.

"See?" Dad recognized something in my face. "It's hard."

We were silent for a moment.

"You can't get in the way of God, Sam. You need to trust that if you are walking with Him, all of this is happening as it needs to be." He gestured with his hands. I took his movements to be a reference to the enormous, complicated universe around us.

Dad took a puff off his cigar and kept talking.

"Your mother has no power. Still, she is your mother. She gave everything that she had to have you. And she was a great Mom to you when you were little. You don't know how hard it was for her during those pregnancies. If it weren't for her, you wouldn't be here. Don't forget that, regardless of what you decide to write about us."

I listened quietly and took another sip of my Bloody Mary. A peaceful breeze drifted over the Mississippi River.

"I often think about the prayer you made when you were a little boy," Dad told me.

"On the park bench?"

"About your mother. You asked God to take care of her. I don't know how else to explain how she's still alive."

"Divine intervention?" I laughed.

"How else would you explain it?"

"God knows the doctors can't explain it to me. They've been telling me that she's dying for years."

"See?"

It was getting darker out now. The moon was rising over Minneapolis, reflecting on the river.

***

Mom left a message for me on my answering machine after I met with my father.

"I just wanted to remind you that you haven't called me in a long time. I know how you forget, Sammy. I'm so lonely."

Gammy used to call me and make me feel guilty about not talking to her enough as well. Mom would laugh and tell me that it was just a guilt trip. It still made me feel bad.

I called Mom the next day.

"I'm really busy, Mom," I told her.

I always was. My dissertation project had started. I was directing and conducting research on a student written play about whiteness. My days were being gobbled up.

"You always are, Sammy. You need to make time for your mother."

She went on to tell me about how she had joined a psychiatric group.

"We meet every day from 9-3," Mom said. "They even give us a free lunch."

"I'm glad you're getting out of the house."

Gabby squawked in the background.

"I still want to kill myself, Sam. I even have a plan." Mom told me she was suicidal any number of times after Jim died. I always reacted calmly.

"Who would watch Gabby if you died, Mom?"

"I don't know." Mom turned from the phone and spoke to Gabby. "Mommy loves you."

"You have to be there for Gabby." I wanted to tell Mom that Katie was pregnant. But I could not make myself do it. Something was holding me back. I was worried about Mom knowing that a little being was growing inside of Katie. Could she harm it somehow?

"I just miss Jim so much." Mom started crying.

"I know, Mom."

"Is Katie pregnant yet? You know that's the only reason I'm staying alive." It was like she was reading my mind.

Did she want a grandchild only to infect it with the same curse that had ruined her life and the lives of everybody she loved?

"Not yet," I lied to her. "We're trying."

"Keep practicing." Mom laughed.

"Love you, Mom," I said.

"Love you too."

I hung up the phone.

I took the morning off of work when it came time for Katie's twelve-week checkup.

The doctor attached a device to Katie's stomach, and we listened to the baby's heartbeat. It sounded so anxious, so nervous. I said as much to the doctor as a joke.

"Maybe you're the one who's nervous, Sam?"

"Maybe."

I was sweating and holding Katie's hand as I listened to the rhythmic thumping of a new life inside of her.

Katie and I decided not to find out whether our unborn child would be a boy or girl.

"Do you want to know?" Katie was excited.

"I don't want any preconceived notions about it," I said.

That was not quite true. I had a couple of notions: Solomon for wisdom and Hope for something better.

I began to tell people about Katie's pregnancy after that appointment. This included coworkers, friends, my dentist, etc. Even my realtor knew before my mother.

Katie and I contacted my realtor because the housing market was coming back in Minneapolis. We decided to wait another year after weighing the pros and cons of selling our house. With the upheaval of finishing graduate school and having a baby, we decided against moving.

I called Polly and let her know. I asked her not to share the news with Mom.

Polly was ecstatic and agreed to keep our secret.

"I understand," she told me. "Tell Katie how excited I am for you guys!"

"I'm not ready for your mother to know," Katie told me.

"I get it," I said. "Me neither."

Dad assured me that Mom had no power to harm to my child. I believed him. Still, I felt uncomfortable telling my mother.

I continued to worry that *something* inside my mother would infect the good news of Katie's pregnancy. I was so used to things not working out the way I wanted them to. I felt powerless to protect Katie or our baby.

I took a trick out of my father's playbook on an early morning run before school. My mind was electric as I raced through the silent streets of Northeast Minneapolis at 4:30 in the morning. Visions of my dissertation, my writing projects, my teaching, and my family suffocated my imagination.

"I give this child to You," I prayed out of desperation to the God of Abraham, Isaac, and Jacob. "In Jesus' name, amen."

The sky was silent overhead, and a large moon hung motionless in all that blackness.

Who can say how this enormous, complicated universe works?

***

Mom's doctors agreed that she was healthy enough to live without supervision after she berated them for months to do so. Against the advice of the staff at the nursing home in Hudson, Mom rented an apartment near Polly in St. Paul. This meant she gave up her health insurance through the state of Wisconsin. Jenny advised her against leaving both the state and its benefits as well as the nursing home. Mom told Jenny to fuck off.

I did not help Mom move. I told her that I agreed with Jenny when she shared the idea over the phone.

"What do you and Jenny have against me?" Mom asked indignantly.

I laughed and told her I cared about her. It was unwise for her to be living without nursing help. I could not support such a silly, destructive choice. Mom told me she needed to have privacy and that she could care for herself.

I shrugged, and she paid a moving company to transport the furniture that had been in storage during her extended stay in a nursing home. Polly did not help her move either.

It was June before I visited my mother in her new apartment. Skylar's birthday was coming up. Mom and Christie had been trying to make amends. Mom invited Christie, Tim, and Skylar over to celebrate his birthday and see her new place. She invited me as well. I decided this would be an opportunity to share the news about Katie's pregnancy with my family. I put $40 in an envelope as a present for Skylar and drove to St. Paul alone.

I pulled up to a depressing, tired looking building near Gammy's old house on Como Lake. Polly's house was only two miles away. The complex had accommodations for low-income housing but, again, Mom chose to take a unit with two bedrooms and did not qualify for any rent reduction.

I found my way up to the fourth floor and knocked on Mom's door. She answered. As always, my mother was frail and too skinny. Mom hugged me and led me into her apartment.

There were stacks of mail scattered throughout the apartment. Boxes had been left unpacked, and there was not nearly enough room for her furniture. The television was on as I pushed aside a pile of papers to sit down in the living room. Gabby's cage dominated the space. He squawked menacingly at me after I sat down.

This was a heavy room.

Mom told me that she had made a cake for Skylar's birthday. Memories of childhood birthday parties in our house on Mt. Curve washed over me. Mom would spend the mornings baking an ornate cake. She would stencil my name on it. All of my friends and family would be invited over. This was before the divorce.

Now, a meager angel food cake, dripping with chocolate frosting, sat on a paper plate in her dirty kitchen.

"How do you like this place?" I asked her.

243

"The apartment manager is a bitch. But at least I have privacy now."

"Oh."

"I quit smoking, Sammy," Mom bragged. "They don't let you smoke in here."

"Good for you," I told her. This was the same thing I always told her when she said she quit smoking or drinking.

I was prepared to tell Mom about Katie's pregnancy, but she started rambling about how the manager of this new apartment was already causing her trouble. My mother was so angry. I could not bring myself to share my news.

Christie, Tim, and Skylar arrived soon after me.

I hugged Christie and shook Tim and Skylar's hands.

"How are you guys doing?"

"You know," Christie shrugged. "After everything that happened."

"I know." I shrugged too.

We spent a moment sitting in the front room.

"This is my new E-Cigarette." Christie puffed on a stick. "Tim and I gave up smoking."

Tim qualified for a new disability program through the state. A huge check arrived with two years' worth of back payments. They had just come from the store.

"I want to put some of the money away," Tim told me. "What do you know about savings accounts?"

"The first of the month is coming, and we don't have anything in pawn," Christie continued. She went on to tell me about her schooling. She was taking online nursing classes with National American University. We started comparing the cost of credits.

"The University charges something like $1,500 a credit," I told her.

"Geez, mine are only $257 a credit." She told me that, over the course of a year and a half, she and Tim had taken out over $25,000 in student loans. She took out the maximum amount of loans and used the money on living expenses, cell phones, or whatever.

I had managed to do most of my PhD by only taking out $20,000. I felt guilty about that. Christie and Tim saw their loans as free money.

"Show us the place, Mom," Christie said.

"Sure." Mom ambled to her feet.

"I love you," Gabby said after we left the living room. Skylar and I exchanged looks. Gabby's voice had a gravely quality. It sounded like scream metal mixed with a garbage disposal.

Katie's uncle has two African grey parrots. They live down in Arizona near Lake Mead.

"When they talk," Katie had told me, "they sound just like Paul. We thought Paul was in the other room when we visited, but it was only the birds."

Gabby sounded like a creature from the seventh layer of hell. I wondered what Gabby had overhead in Mom's presence?

I commented on Gabby's voice.

"That bird sounds like a demon," I told Skylar.

He laughed. So did Tim.

"He does not, Sammy." Mom laughed too.

Mom lit a cigarette near the window after she brought us into her bedroom.

"I thought you quit, Mom?"

"Oh, this is just a butt."

Christie was standing next to Mom as she smoked. Christie leaned in and took a drag from Mom's cigarette.

Tim and Skylar were standing near Mom's TV. They were trying to figure out how to make the cable work. Mom complained that she could not get reception. Tim looked up and saw that Christie was smoking.

"Christie," Tim said. "I just bought you that new E-Cigarette. What the hell are you doing? I thought we were trying to quit smoking?"

"Geez, sorry, if it bothers you, don't look."

"I love you," Gabby said again in the other room.

"One of you will inherit Gabby when I die," Mom told Christie and me.

Christie and I looked at each other and laughed.

"We'll see," I told Mom.

Mom spent most of our time together sobbing and telling us she was suicidal. She served us cake on paper plates. I did not eat mine.

Jim's ashes were on top of the television cabinet in the living room. They were still in the wooden box he had made.

"We might go to the pawn shop. They have a guitar that was signed by Dimebag Darrell nineteen days before he was shot!" Tim told me. "Skylar and I could get on Pawnstars with that shit!"

Tim had always been a Pantera fan. I remembered listening to the tapes he would let Christie borrow when they were teenagers.

"I need to go pick something up from a friend's house, Wendy," Tim eventually said. "But it was good to see you."

I shook Tim's hand and gave Christie and Skylar a hug as they walked out the door. I did not give Skylar the envelope in my pocket with forty dollars in it. It did not seem right to me to do so.

I turned to Mom after Christie left with her family.

"I need to leave too, Mom."

But I did not leave. I sat down at her dining room table with her. I wanted to tell my mom that my wife was pregnant. I was looking for a moment.

"How have you been, Mom?"

"I've been so lonely, Sam."

Mom started to cry again.

"Why are you more lonely now than before?" I asked her.

"At least I would go down and eat with people for meals back in the nursing home in Hudson. That was before Jenny screwed me over."

"Why do you think she was screwing you over?" I asked Mom.

"She started lying about me." Mom was earnest. "She told people I was abusing my medication, that I was drinking."

Mom went into the other room to grab a document she told me would prove that Jenny had taken money from her. She smelled like alcohol when she came back.

It was then that I decided that I was not ready to tell Mom that Katie was pregnant. Not in this sad apartment, not during this delusional conversation, not like this.

"I need to go, Mom."

"I love you, Sammy." She hugged me.

"I love you, too." I hugged her back.

"I remember when you were hiding from me in the corn," she told me as I stood in the doorway. "When you were just a little boy."

"I know, Mom."

I walked out into the hallway. It smelled of rot and mold. Back in my car, driving home, I felt an indescribable emptiness inside of me.

There was such sadness here.

***

I started sharing stories about my experience with Mom with my friend Angus Poulin after Jim's suicide.

Angus was an English teacher. He specialized in mythology and took different spiritual traditions and beliefs very seriously. Angus was tall. He had frenetic eyes that glowed beneath a mop of black hair. Imagine Shaggy from Scooby Doo, Merlin the wizard, and a restless shaman of the universe disguised as a white, Midwestern American in the 21st century.

Angus was a trip.

He was also safe to speak openly with. We were both in our thirties, in touch with our emotions, and a little frenetic. Angus and I taught together in the same English department for nearly eight years.

Angus had a classroom on the second floor. Mine was on the first. I would walk up to talk with him before or after school or during our lunch periods.

The lights were dim in his room, and masks created by students adorned the walls. It felt to me that his room was populated with a diverse collection of unseen beings. That is the effect being around Angus had on me.

Anyway, we were discussing our difficult interactions with a female colleague in the school. As always, Angus' self-reflection proved insightful.

"Oftentimes, my frustration with Avery is more about me than her."

I laughed, and he continued.

"I can be so naïve. I think I look for female approval because of my relationship with my mother. So maybe your relationship with your mother has something to do with your interactions with Avery?"

I thought for a moment. I was tired. It had been a long year. Teaching was hard work. I began.

"Have I told you about how my mother came to see my play?" I asked him.

"You have not."

I told Angus about Mom coming to see a play I had recently directed at the high school.

It was the product of my dissertation research. My students had created an original play about whiteness, and I was analyzing the theatrical process and the students' conclusions. Local and national media picked up the project, so the performances felt extremely high-stakes to me. Also, my doctorate depended on it. My professional and personal worlds had always been kept closely separated. Still, Mom had heard about the play because Polly had attended. Mom was jealous that Polly went, so she called and left a message on my answering machine on a Sunday morning.

"I'll be coming to your play, Sammy. I need to see you."

I tried to call her back and tell her not to come.

I imagined Mom arriving in the parking lot. She would struggle with her walker and amble into the theatre. Mom would not be able to keep up with the play. She would fall asleep. That was the best scenario. The worst scenario would involve her bursting into hysterics to my professional colleagues and mentors from graduate school about Jim's suicide, or about how her son did not call her enough. Students and parents at the school would be taken aback. I had enough to manage without my mother's presence.

I could not get a hold of Mom on the phone. She pulled into the parking lot an hour before the performance started. I was watching for her out the window. I raced outside and met her.

She was struggling to light a cigarette as she tried to set her Diet Coke onto her walker. She could barely stand up, let alone walk the distance to the school, climb the steps, and sit through the play.

"Mom?" I called out.

"Sammy?" She smiled.

"I was trying to call you."

"I was shopping," she told me. Mom had $200 worth of groceries in her trunk.

I told Mom that she would not be able to make it up the stairway, that the play was really long, and that I would not have much time to talk with her because I was so busy managing the production.

She resisted leaving at first. Finally, she agreed that the ice cream she bought would melt if she sat and watched the two-hour performance.

"You reminded me of when you were a little boy, when you came running out to greet me, Sam," Mom told me. She looked sad.

"I love you, Mom."

"I love you too."

We hugged, and she climbed back into her car.

I walked back inside the school feeling relieved, embarrassed, and solemn.

Of course I wanted my mom to attend the play. I wished that I had a mother who could share my life. I wanted her to be involved with me. I knew this could not happen.

Angus listed quietly as I related this story.

We kept talking, and I told him about Mom blowing into Katie's ear after the surprise party for Polly. I talked about the baby growing inside of Katie, about listening to its heartbeat, about being afraid that Mom would infect it.

"That's heavy energy, Sam," Angus finally said.

"It always is when I'm talking about my mother."

Angus was a powerful listener, so I spoke an irrational, confused fear aloud. I was admitting it to both of us.

"I suppose my fear," I told Angus, "is that whatever spiritual force has infected my mom will infect my baby. I suppose her curse is broken. My life has been taking what is good about my mother and separating it from what is wrong. I survived. But that survival might come from Mom. She's like a determined weed. Maybe that's what will be given to my child from her. That's a family gift. But it comes with baggage. Maybe the child is a way to forever break that curse. I said as much at my wedding, when I said the ceremony was a spiritual break from the family that had come before and a step toward the family that would come next."

I paused.

"I guess I'm afraid that my mother will die when my baby is born, and that the darkness in her will transfer to him. Maybe she's staying alive just for that? How else can she continue to exist despite such poor health?"

"Holy shit wrinkles." Angus laughed. "You think your mother wants to reincarnate in your baby?"

"Maybe," I laughed.

I paused and thought about how my mother had influenced the rest of my life. I responded to Angus' original question after my long, rambling story.

"Maybe that's the root of my frustration with Avery. Like you, maybe I'm looking for nurturing and warmth from an older female, and maybe I need to know that I'll never get if from her."

Angus laughed. A student came in the room.

"I'll be with you in a second," he told her.

"Take it easy, man," I said. "You've got work to do."

"You too."

I left the sanctuary of Angus' classroom and stepped back into my day as a teacher, a husband, a son, and a potential father.

***

My mother called me with news. It was spring and, though Katie was thin, her belly was starting to show signs of pregnancy.

"I'm moving again, Sam."

"Already?" I asked. "Have you gotten out of the lease you signed for your current apartment?"

"No, I'm just going to walk out on it. The apartment manager here is a bitch."

"Okay Mom," I told her, "but I'm busy all week. I won't be able to help you move."

"Christie and Tim are going to help me. But I need you to come over. I want to give you Gammy's good china dinnerware."

This collection of plates, serving dishes, and cups were given to Mom after her mother died.

"I'm busy, Mom."

"This is important."

Finally, I agreed to come over and pick up the items she wanted to give me. Polly called me later that afternoon. She told me she would come over and help Mom pack.

I arrived before Polly. Mom's apartment was in a state of disarray. Boxes were piled in the corner, and items were haphazardly scattered around the room.

We sat down at Mom's dining room table and started packing. She was careful to wrap each delicate item in newspaper.

"It's really expensive, Sam," Mom reminded me.

Mom was sober and cognizant as we worked together to box up Gammy's china. I decided that I was ready.

"Mom, I have something to tell you."

"Yes?"

"Katie's pregnant."

Mom began to cry.

"I knew it," she said.

I hugged her.

"I'm so proud of you, Sammy."

Polly arrived shortly after.

"Did you know that Katie is pregnant, Polly?"

Polly hugged me.

We finished packing the dishes. Polly helped me bring them to my car. We spent a moment together after bringing a load down.

"Mom looks pretty terrible, doesn't she?"

"Yes, she's skinnier than last time."

"I just don't know how she can keep drinking and abusing her medication."

"I don't think the bulimia helps."

"You think she's doing that, too?"

"She always has. Your mother used to hide pans around the house when she was a teenager. We would find vomit in them. She would eat so much food that she'd throw it all up. She's never really quit doing that."

"My dad used to say the same thing about her."

"That was part of the problem with her pregnancies. Her cervix wouldn't hold the babies in because of her bulimia. The doctors actually stitched up her cervix when she was carrying you to keep you in. They scheduled a C-section."

Polly's words stayed with me, and I considered the enormity of my mother's dysfunction, her evil.

Polly and I stayed an extra couple of hours to help Mom pack up the rest of her belongings.

"You're moving this Saturday, Wendy?" Polly asked with doubt. Mom's apartment was filled with stuff. Most of that stuff was not yet packed.

"Yes, Christie and Tim are going to help me."

Christie, Tim, Skylar, and their friend showed up on Saturday to help her move. I agreed to help and showed up alone.

"Katie's pregnant?" Christie asked when I got there.

"Yes," I admitted.

"Wow, my little brother's going to be a dad!"

I smiled.

"Congratulations." Tim smiled at me.

The friend Christie and Tim brought with to help was wearing a shirt that read

"DON'T FUCK WITH SATAN." I politely introduced myself and shook his hand.

They worked tirelessly that day to help Mom move. It took ten hours, but they were able to cart Mom's furniture from her apartment to a moldy building in the suburbs of St. Paul. I helped by driving boxes over in my car.

"Is it a senior place?" I asked Mom after we arrived at her new apartment complex.

"I'm too young for that, Sammy," my mother said as she stared at me vacantly from a wheelchair.

"Okay."

Anyway, I took the china home after Mom was moved in. I weeded through four boxes of dishes. The artifacts brought back memories of holidays at Gammy's house when I was a child.

I tried to make room for the dinnerware. I kept items from the boxes that seemed valuable. The rest of the items ended up in front of my house near the street.

A little girl from down the block came up to me as I was setting the items out.

"Are you giving those away?" She had an African accent.

"Absolutely, do you want them?"

"I'll come back."

She came back and took three boxes of dishes, cups, and serving platters. Later that evening, she knocked on my door.

"Do you have any more stuff?"

"Sorry, that was it."

The girl left.

"If Gammy knew that the family from down the street had all her good china, she'd roll in her grave," I told Katie later that day.

Both of us laughed.

I hung out on the couch and turned on my Xbox after putting the china away. Katie played with her laptop. We went upstairs and fell asleep together.

I woke up at three in the morning. My heart was beating fast, and I was drenched in a cold sweat. My mind was filled with abstract, irrational fear. I had dreamed that an intruder was in my house.

I went over the dream as I lay in bed. Mom's china came to mind.

A cold realization set in. I did not want any items in my house that had belonged to my mother or her family.

It was this irrational train of logic that got me out of bed at three in the morning. I found myself downstairs, taking the china out of the hutch in my living room, boxing it up, and carting it out to the street. It took me twenty minutes to pack and transfer Gammy's expensive china to the sidewalk in front of my house. Fluffalufagus eyed me with suspicion as I worked. The street was silent and the moon glowed overhead as I carted boxes out to the curb.

I went back upstairs and climbed into bed. I was

careful not to wake Katie. The boxes were gone by the time I woke up in the morning.

I thought about the baby growing in Katie's stomach. There was *something* that I wanted to protect that child from.

It was the same thing that had been with me since I was born.

Chapter 12

I awoke in a cold sweat.

Katie was fast asleep next to me. It was three in the morning.

I had been dreaming again. I was finishing my doctorate, exhausted from teaching high school, and Katie was due in one month. I was overwhelmed and anxious. My dreams were vivid and my mind was *traveling*.

In the dream, Mom had been standing by the shores of the Mississippi River. She had thick stacks of money in her hands. Mom was using the money to feed birds that were gathering around her. The creatures were devouring hundreds of dollars.

I grabbed onto a railing and started to scream like a newborn.

"Why wouldn't you give that money to your children, Mom? What kind of a mother are you?"

She ignored me and continued feeding the birds. In the dream, Mom was both a child and an old woman. She was human and spirit.

"You and Dad could have raised our family out of poverty, Mom. We could have had a better life if both of you hadn't been so selfish and foolish. Instead, you're broke. I'm broke, and my child will be born that way as well."

My whining embarrassed me even in my dream. I sounded like a spoiled child. I was frustrated with myself.

Mom turned toward me after I was finished yelling at her.

"Are you finished? You want this money, Sam?" Mom's face twisted into a cruel smile.

I was terrified. I turned and ran.

Mom chased me. My feet stumbled through overgrowth. Suddenly, I was in the neighborhood where I grew up. I climbed up a hill. I rushed through the forest and made my way to our old house in St. Paul. I ran through the front door, up the stairs, and into the hallway. Mom rounded the corner as I made my way to my old bedroom. She was on all fours. Her eyes were ferocious and red. I slammed and locked the door. It barely held as she banged against the wooden frame.

"Let me in, Sammy!" Mom howled. Her voice was throaty and demonic.

I held the door and reached for a phone. I dialed 911. The phone rang and rang. Nobody answered. Finally, Mom's voice came through the receiver.

"Nobody can help you, Sammy," my mother growled at me.

I braced my body against the door as she tried to make her way in.

"Help!" I cried out.

The room vanished and I was floating. Mom was gone. *Something* else was near me. It took the form of a child.

I reached for a hand. It grabbed onto my finger.

We were connected in that *space between spaces* for a moment. I pulled the child near and held it as tightly as I could. It was upset.

"It'll be okay," I said.

This being and I were deeply connected in that blank space, gathered together as great storms of energy, alive forever as gusts of great wind.

Then the dream ended, and I was in my bedroom.

My mind seethed. I made sure the door to the room was closed. Next, I spoke to the baby inside of Katie's belly.

"It'll be okay," I told it. "I'm here."

I thought about what Katie had said the day before.

"I've been dreaming about your Mom the last couple of nights," Katie had told me.

We had been in a parenting class on a Saturday morning. Our doctor suggested we take a course for new parents. The teacher mentioned something about being very careful about who you let stay in the room during your delivery. I looked over at Katie and laughed. She had too. We were both thinking about my mother. I whispered in her ear.

"Mom will try and send her spirit if we keep her out."

"I know." Katie giggled.

Anyway, I woke up from my dream. Anxiety and confusion overwhelmed me. I was unable to fall back asleep. I went downstairs and made a cup of coffee. I sat in my office and worked on an essay about ethnographic research. I graded papers for a section of 11th grade English. I thought about my mother.

It was Sunday morning.

***

I was one of the last people I knew to avoid getting a cell phone. I rolled my eyes when Katie ordered the iPhone 5.

"Enjoy being connected to the Matrix," I told her with a sarcastic laugh.

She rolled her eyes at me.

My refusal to get a phone was always a nuisance to people.

"How am I supposed to contact you?" people would ask me.

"Smoke signals?" I joked.

My friend Mike complained whenever we planned something together.

"How are you going to get a hold of me? Stop at a coffee shop? Connect to Wi-Fi and check your email?"

"My laptop is pretty portable," I offered sheepishly.

Mike scoffed at my stubbornness.

I had no desire to be *connected*. Mostly, I did not want my mother to have unabated access to me. I could not handle her calls four or five times a day.

Anyway, my lack of a cell phone became more problematic as Katie's belly grew larger.

"How am I supposed to contact you when I go into

labor?" Katie asked me.

Katie and I went to dinner at my friend Nick's parents' house a month before Katie's due date. Mr. and Mrs. Wiseman also invited my friend Josh. He came with his wife and two little girls. I shared that I was still without a cell phone while we ate.

Mrs. Wiseman was concerned.

"How is Katie going to let you know when she goes into labor? I'm going to let you use my cell phone," she told me. "You need it more than me."

"Thank you Mrs. Wiseman," I laughed. "I promise I'll get one soon."

"Make sure you do."

I gave in begrudgingly. I ordered what was colloquially referred to as a "burner" about three weeks before Katie's due date. This is the sort of prepaid phone that meth dealers use so that the police in *The Wire* cannot trace their calls.

"What is that thing?" Katie asked when I showed it to her after it arrived.

"My new cell phone," I laughed.

I registered my new phone online. It was working after a great deal of futzing. I am pretty sure that I gave my personal information to a Columbian drug lord in order to activate it.

Anyway, I gave Katie's iPhone 5 a call so that she would have my new number. Now she could call me when our baby decided to climb out of her womb.

"What's my number?" I asked her after calling.

She told me. The first three digits were 666.

"The sign of the beast?" I asked.

"I guess."

"Great." I rolled my eyes.

I had a conversation with Mom's newest caseworker before activating the phone. She had been assigned to my mother by the state. This caseworker had good intentions, but was utterly clueless.

We talked on my landline. The caseworker told me a story.

Mom had been in an alcohol detox center the previous night. She was being evicted from her newest apartment because, once again, she had started a fire after passing out in her kitchen. Mom's neighbors alerted the apartment manager. Smoke was coming out of the crack between the floor and the door. The police were called. Mom was taken to detox because the responders found empty bottles of vodka in her apartment. She kept telling the police that she wanted to kill herself.

The caseworker was incredulous at my calm reaction. I was unable to work myself up over this newest incident. It was the same story I had heard time and time again since Jim's suicide.

"Sounds about right," I said with a shrug after she finished trying to shock me with the story.

"She looks terrible." The woman seemed to blame me.

"I know she does. I really don't understand how she's survived since her husband's suicide," I told her. "It's confounding. I don't understand why doctors keep letting her out of care facilities."

"She'll be homeless if she's evicted, Sam. She's out of money and doesn't have any options. Maybe you could let her stay with you?"

"Honestly, I love her, but I just don't think there's anything I can do for her. I've tried. I don't want to sound heartless, but it's her fault that she's out of money. We tried to set up a plan to protect her assets and take care of her. She ruined it because she wanted to be alone. My mother abandoned me when I was seven. I tried to step in and take care of her after Jim's suicide. She wouldn't let me. She chose pills and isolation. She's spent through hundreds of thousands of dollars in assets in foolish and careless ways. I worried this would happen. But it just wouldn't do anybody any good if I tried to help. And my wife and I are expecting a baby in a month."

The caseworker paused. She continued after a moment of silence.

"I understand. But she's looking forward to your baby. That seems like the one thing she's excited about."

"Great," I thought to myself as I hung up my landline.

I went for a run early the next morning before heading to school. It had recently snowed, and my neighborhood was freezing.

The wind howled as I ran through Northeast Minneapolis.

There was goodness in my mother, and I wanted those traits to be passed along to my child. But I wanted the *badness* gone. I mumbled something of a prayer to that effect toward the silent sky. The name of Jesus escaped my lips.

My feet crushed fresh snow as I ran. It was so peaceful.

I breathed deeply, ran with all my might, came home, showered, dressed in a sweater vest and tie, and went about my day as a high school teacher, doctoral student, and theatre director.

I was bracing myself for whatever was coming next.

Mom called the next evening. I was exhausted, so I let her speak into the answering machine. I did not give her the number to my burner. Mom was crying as she spoke.

"You need to call me, Sam. This could be it. I can't do it anymore. I know that I have a grandchild on the way, but I don't think I can make it. They're taking my apartment away. It's too much."

She rambled on for about a minute or two. Mom talked about Jim. She said she was going to kill herself.

Katie and I were sitting on the couch. We were watching *The Walking Dead* on Netflix. Fitting, right?

I sighed loudly, but I did not answer the phone.

Mom hung up, and I glanced over at Katie's stomach. It was huge. She was due in a week or two. An irrational thought occurred to me.

"I don't want her to die the same day that our baby is

born," I said to Katie.

She shrugged.

"That would be pretty creepy," I continued.

"Yes, it would."

I got up from the couch and emailed my father. He had moved back to Minnesota a month earlier. Like Mom, he walked out on a rental lease. Dad packed up his belongings and found a place to live in the suburbs of Minneapolis.

"I'm sick of Florida," he told me. "I'm coming home."

Anyway, this is what I wrote to him in the email:

How are you doing out here? Enjoying the cold? Baby is due any day now. Mom is leaving creepy messages on my machine. Same old, same old.

Keep praying.

Love,
Sam

Dad responded the next morning. This is what he wrote to me:

Of course I keep praying. Your mom's behavior has nothing to do with you or the baby. I believe she is literally struggling with demons and needs spiritual intervention. I can't wait to see Solomon. Bet he smokes cigars when he is older.

Love,
Dad

I thanked Dad for his quick note. I also reminded him that the baby might be a girl named Hope.

But I was still worried after Mom's message.

Would Mom kill herself at the same moment that Katie gave birth? Would her death coincide with the birth of our baby? Would Mom reincarnate in my new child?

These insane and cosmic thoughts plagued my glowing mind as I ran through the streets of Northeast Minneapolis the next morning. Fresh snow coated the sidewalks.

I got to school and sat down at the computer in my classroom. I was prepared for another frenetic day of teaching high school. Students were already milling about my classroom.

Avery, the same colleague that Angus and I had discussed earlier, came down to see me.

"I've got something for you, Sam. Well, it's for the baby." She handed me a package.

"You didn't have to get me anything."

"It isn't much," she said.

"I'm always awkward when I get presents," I admitted.

"I knit a swaddling blanket."

I took the blanket and held it up.

"Thank you, Avery," I told her.

"Sure."

This kind gesture was one of the few moments that I felt valued by my colleagues at Primville. I wandered upstairs. My feet took me through a crowded high school hallway and into Angus' classroom. I told him about the gift.

"That was one of the nicest things an adult has done for me at this high school," I told him. Students showered me with gifts and adoration all the time. My colleagues, besides Angus and Tina, were far colder toward me.

"It was thoughtful," he smiled. "I'm surprised."

Angus and I started talking. I told him about the message my mother had left on my machine.

"I just hope Mom doesn't kill herself the same day that the baby is born," I laughed. "I don't want any demon spirit trying to possess my child!"

Angus laughed too.

I collapsed on my couch when I got home from school that night. I was exhausted from teaching. I saw there was another message on my machine. I listened to it. It was the caseworker that had called me earlier about Mom.

"Sam, you need to go buy a tackle box for your mom. She has agreed to let us monitor her medicine. It would be best to buy one with a combination lock. So just go pick that up. Thanks."

Was I really supposed to monitor Mom's pain pills? Jim had tried. He kept them in a safe and ended up putting a bullet in his head.

I had not actually seen my mother in a couple of weeks. I had never met this caseworker. My schedule offered very little in the way of wiggle room, particularly with a baby on the way.

So I erased the message and went into the kitchen. Katie was cooking spaghetti on the stove. Her stomach was huge.

"A tackle box?" Katie asked me after I told her about the message.

"Yup," I said.

"Great."

"Yup."

Later that night, we were cuddling on the couch and watching South Park. I spoke.

"It would be way too dramatic if she killed herself at the moment our baby was born, wouldn't it?"

"Yes."

"I hope she doesn't do that."

"Me too."

"Do you think she will?"

"Who knows?"

It is impossible to completely cut ourselves off from where we come from, but I was spiritually severed from my mother. My baby was, too. The wedding ceremony with Katie marked a separation from Mom. So did the moment in the parking lot outside of the psychiatric ward, three days after Jim's suicide, when Mom lit a cigarette and Katie started crying. The moment I erased the message from Mom's latest social worker was just another along a similar trajectory.

Mom was dead to me nearly ten years ago when she woke up from a coma. I told her goodbye then. Everything since then had been her terrifying death wail. But the terror was subsiding now. My relationship with my mother was being liberated. The demon was letting go of me. *Something* was being released into the universe. It was necessary to give up where I had been in order to move where I was going.

God knows what would happen next, but I was learning that everything was going to be okay.

***

"I think we should go."

Katie woke me up. She was sitting up in bed. It was two in the morning. Katie had been groaning since early in the evening. It was a week before winter break started at my school. We still had two days until Katie's due date. This was not good timing. I was hoping Katie's labor would coincide with my time off from school. No such luck.

"Are you going into labor?"

"I think so."

"Okay."

My heart started thumping as I gathered our things.

My Honda CRV raced through the frozen, empty streets of Minneapolis. I ran red lights. We arrived at North Memorial hospital fifteen minutes later.

We were admitted into a room. I stood by Katie's side as contractions wracked her body. I was powerless to help.

Katie's mother and father arrived around five in the morning. I used Katie's iPhone 5 to contact the substitute teacher that agreed to help in case Katie went into labor early. He responded and told me he was ready. I wrote four days of lesson plans—enough to get the classes to winter break—as Katie's labor pains subsided. I emailed them to Angus to give to my substitute.

My father did not respond when I texted him. I did not contact my mother.

Katie and I had discussed pain medication. She figured that she wanted to try to have the baby without it. The pain grew worse and worse. The doctor convinced her to have an epidural later in the morning. She was fully dilated before the pain medication kicked in. I had never seen a human being sustain that much physical pain.

The pain subsided after the epidural started working. Katie started to push. Katie's mother held one of her legs, and I held another.

I could not bring myself to look at what was happening.

"Are you going to be okay?" the nurse asked me.

"I'll be fine," I grunted.

The nurse timed Katie's pushes. She cheered my wife on.

Finally, I heard crying and saw a shock of light hair.

"It's a boy," our doctor told us as the nurse lifted a newborn into her arms.

Solomon David Tanner was born at 11:54 AM on December 17th, 2013.

I started weeping. So did Katie.

The doctor handed Solomon to Katie. He started crying into her chest. Then he calmed down. His eyes were open and wide.

"Is he a ginger?" I asked the doctor.

"Really?" Katie laughed. "That's the first thing you're going to say?"

"Look at that hair," I laughed through my tears.

"He's blonde," Katie's mother said.

I placed my hand on his head and gazed at him.

His hair was blonde. It was the same color that mine was when I was a child. Later, my hair turned to dark brown.

The nurses examined Solomon after he rested on Katie

for a couple of minutes.

He was healthy, but one of his testicles looked abnormal to a nurse. They sent me down to radiology with Solomon to have an ultrasound.

Solomon clutched onto my finger with his tiny hand as the nurse wheeled him through hospital hallways.

I looked at him and told him that it would be okay.

The radiologist looked over the X-rays when she was finished. She told me that it was not life threatening, but that we should also have it checked out by a specialist.

"Life for a Tanner isn't easy," I told Solomon on our way back up to Katie's room.

He did not cry. He just held onto my finger.

Katie and I spent that first evening drifting in and out of sleep. Katie fed Solomon, we changed diapers, and our new son cried. I played the album *Seven Swans* by Sufjan Stevens on my laptop when our boy fell asleep. I felt like the three of us were in a safe bubble, protected from the quiet, freezing Minnesota winter outside.

"Is this what it's going to be like?" I asked Katie with tired eyes.

"I think so," she said.

Katie took a shower early the next morning. I stood over Solomon and touched his head with one hand and his feet with my other. He was greedily sucking at a pacifier.

Solomon looked up at me with big eyes. Something in his face reminded me of my father. I kissed his forehead.

I went home later that morning to take a shower and get some things Katie wanted. We were going to spend another evening in the hospital. I heard Mom leaving a message on my machine as I walked through the door. I picked up the phone.

"Mom?"

"Sammy!"

Katie had texted Polly after Solomon was born. Polly told Mom.

"How's Solomon?" Mom asked.

"He's fine," I told her.

"I'm so happy!" She paused. "I don't know if I can drive all the way to the hospital."

I sighed with relief.

"Don't worry about it, Mom. He's doing great. I just came home to take a shower. You'll meet him soon."

"I love you, Sammy."

"Love you too, Mom."

I returned to the hospital with our car seat, nursing pads, and some essays to grade. Katie was in the room with her mom and dad when I returned.

"Did you see your dad?" Katie's mother asked me.

"You just missed him," Katie told me.

"He sat here with Solomon for an hour," Katie's mom said.

I took Katie's phone and called Dad. I chased him down in the atrium of the hospital. He and I sat in the lobby and talked.

"He's beautiful," Dad told me. "I'm proud of you."

"Solomon David," I shrugged.

"I think he's going to be a prophet," Dad laughed.

I laughed too.

Dad paused and thought.

"There was a peacefulness about him as I held him. I *felt* it. It reminded me of when I held Christa after she was born."

"He does seem peaceful," I told Dad.

"Is your mother coming by?"

"I told her not to."

"That's probably best."

Dad and I talked about what rough shape Mom was in.

"Your mother was always determined to get her way," Dad said. "That's why you're here. It's why Solomon's here, too. She wanted so badly to have a healthy child. The doctors told her it was impossible. It was like she wanted a baby to spite them. I was ready to give up. But she was on a mission."

"And here we are now. I'd like to think that I have some of that same determination. But without all that nastiness."

"I always thought there was *something* wrong with her," Dad told me.

I paused and thought.

"I survived my mother. But I survived *because* of her as well. And now there's Solomon." I smiled.

"Yes." Dad was thoughtful for a moment. His lips twisted into a sarcastic smile. "You know she's gonna want to hold him. Just be ready for that."

Dad and I laughed together.

"King Solomon," Dad said. "Wisdom."

Nurses and doctors were passing by and giving us strange looks.

"You'll circumcise him here?" Dad asked.

"Yes."

"You don't need a rabbi, but make sure you're in the room with him."

"Is that what you did with me?"

"I put on Tefillin and stood next to the doctor saying Hebrew blessings. Everybody in the room thought I was crazy," Dad laughed.

"I'll be in the room," I said.

"Make sure you pray when they do it, okay?"

"Sure."

"I'm proud of you," Dad said as he stood up and hugged me. "The line will continue on."

"I love you." I hugged him back.

"Love you too."

Two friends had come to visit by the time I got back to Katie's room. They were standing near Katie's bed. Solomon was gone.

I looked around the room. "Where's Solomon?"

"He's getting circumcised."

"What?"

Was I really going to miss the circumcision?

"Where is he?" I asked frantically.

"The nursery," Katie's mom said. "Do you want to be in there with him?"

"Yes!"

I bolted out of the room and went to the nursery. I asked a nurse if I could go in and watch. She looked at me like I was a lunatic. She let me enter the room after a conference with some other nurses. The doctor had already begun the procedure. He looked up at me with an irritated expression.

"My father was raised an Orthodox Jew," I tried to explain to him. "He would kill me if I weren't here for this."

The doctor laughed. I sat down and watched as Solomon slept underneath a lamp and had his foreskin cut off.

"He's so peaceful," the nurse said as she sat with me.

"He isn't even bleeding," the doctor said.

I made small talk with the nurse and doctor. I prayed under my breath as the doctor worked. Any of the prayers I had learned from my father came to my mind. I uttered the Lord's Prayer. Once more, I spoke in the name of Jesus.

I chanted in Hebrew when he finished.

"Baruch Ha Ta Adonai," I said aloud. Then I laughed and turned to the doctor and nurse.

"I'm no rabbi, but I had to give him a little something."

They both laughed awkwardly.

They checked my ID bracelet as I was leaving.

"It would be weird if I was some random guy just watching circumcisions, right?"

"Well, if you were, the psychiatric ward is just down the hall," the nurse told me.

I thanked them for letting me be there.

I wheeled Solomon's cart back to the room, and we spent the night being visited by friends and family.

"He's so peaceful," everybody told us.

We brought Solomon home after two nights in the hospital. He started sneezing early in the evening. I drove to Walgreens and bought a humidifier.

He spent that first night eating, pooping, and crying.

The glory of his birth was being replaced with the routine of staying up all night, wiping his butt, and wrapping him in blankets. Fatherhood was unexpected and strange.

Mom had left another message on my answering machine while we were still at the hospital.

"Sammy, I know you're there. I need to see Solomon. I should've been there when he was born."

I called her back the next morning.

"It's okay. He's here waiting to see you."

"I'm so proud of you, Sammy. I can't wait to meet him."

"I know, Mom."

Mom finally came over to see Solomon on a Sunday morning three days later.

Katie and I were sleep deprived.

Polly agreed to drive Mom over to our house. She had visited Solomon in the hospital but wanted to see him again.

I decided to invite Christie over, too. She also wanted to meet Solomon and had not come to the hospital. She reminded me that she was his aunt over email, and that she had a right to meet him.

Christie arrived ten minutes before Mom and Polly. Skylar was with her. Skylar had stubble on his face. He sat on the couch as Christie played with Solomon.

"Are you breastfeeding?" Christie asked Katie.

"Yes," Katie said.

"That's what I should have done with Skylar," Christie told Katie. "We would have a closer bond. That's why we don't get along."

"You think that's the reason?" Skylar snarled at her.

"See how they get when they're teenagers?" Christie asked sarcastically.

"He'll be moving out soon," I told her.

"I hope so. Who knows? Look at him. How can he get along in the real world? He might stay with us."

"I'd rather live in the streets," Skylar said.

Skylar looked through my XBOX 360 games as Christie held Solomon in our living room.

"Can I take this one?" He held up a copy of *Bioshock Infinite.*

"Sure," I told him. "I don't have time to play video games these days anyway."

He left with six games.

"You better make sure you get those back to Sam," Christie told Skylar.

"Don't worry about it," I said.

Christie left before Mom arrived. I watched her and Skylar amble down the steps, get into her car, and drive away. The video games seemed to be the only thing I had to offer that either of them could receive.

Mom arrived with Polly about five minutes after Christie was gone. I watched out the window as she hobbled out of the passenger side door of her car. Polly had driven.

Mom was hunched over and fragile. She reminded me of broken glass. I went outside and held her arm as Polly parked the car. Mom had a black eye and looked distracted. I realized that she was heavily medicated.

"I love you, Sammy." Mom kissed my cheek. I hugged her gingerly.

"What happened to your eye, Mom?"

"I fell again."

Polly came around the car, stepped over a snow bank, and hugged me.

"I'm so excited to see Solomon again!"

Polly and I helped Mom get to the sidewalk.

"These steps?" Mom pointed at my neighbor's house.

"No, Wendy, their house is the blue one," Polly said. "You remember. You've
been here before."

We walked to my house and up the steps to the front door. It was snowing. It took Mom nearly five minutes to climb the five steps up to my house. Inside, she opened a Diet Coke and stared at Solomon.

Solomon was wrapped up in a blanket. He was sitting in a rocker that Polly had given Katie at her baby shower. It was vibrating and making bird noises—Solomon was fast asleep. Katie was sitting next to him.

Mom did not try to hold or touch him. She just looked at him.

"He's beautiful," my mother said.

Mom sat down on the couch and started nodding off as Polly and I made small talk. Polly made coffee cake like Gammy used to. She set it in the kitchen. Polly handed us presents for Solomon. She bought him an outfit, two pairs of socks, and two hats. Polly thought that a sweater vest, a flannel shirt, and a pair of corduroys would fit my fashion sense.

"You can dress him in it when you bring him to school," Polly told me.

"Thanks, Polly."

Polly tried to wake my mother up by involving her in the conversation. "Wendy was sick when she heard that I had visited Solomon at the hospital."

Mom looked up from her stupor. "You should have brought me."

"It's fine, Mom. Polly just stayed for a moment."

Polly told my mother that it was time to go. Mom was nearly passed out on the couch. We woke her up and walked her to the door. I helped her into the car and said goodbye.

"Thank you so much, Polly," I told her.

"I love you guys," she said.

"Love you too."

"Love you, Sammy," Mom told me.

"Love you too."

I walked back in the house, and Katie was sitting with Solomon.

"That wasn't so bad, right?"

"Nope."

Katie and I were trying to catch some sleep later that night.

I dreamed about Mom again. She was haggard and worn. In my dream, she walked into a dimly lit liquor store to buy a bottle of Vodka. The people behind the counter eyed her with contempt. So did the other customers. I was embarrassed for my mother. There was nothing I could do. I started to cry in my dream.

I awoke to find that Katie was up. She was feeding Solomon.

Our white noise machine was running, and the heat in our bedroom was turned up.

I imagined my mother. I pictured the strong, determined woman who had survived four traumatic pregnancies, ignored the advice of her doctors, and given birth to me. I thought about the woman who had stayed sober during the first years of my life. Like Katie was doing for Solomon, Mom fed and took care of me. She read to me and kept me safe and warm. My mother really had loved me.

I was not worried anymore that the heaviness inside of her would hurt my baby. I knew that the work of my life had carried me beyond whatever force was weighing her down. I was bruised and battered, but I had survived. *Something* had been released. *Something* was coming to an end. I could not place my finger on what either of those things might be.

So I realized that—even if Mom killed herself now that she had seen Solomon—that force could not do any more damage to me.

Yes, Mom had become a haggard addict. She was a

275

self-destructive and narcissistic old woman. But there was more to her. It was complicated. She was *also* an empathetic, sensitive being with an enormous soul.

I reminded myself to remember Mom as the woman who had nursed me, defied all logic to give birth to me, and loved me with all of her heart.

Though he would never see that woman, I wanted Solomon to know that *this* was his grandmother, too.

A week later, I parked my car outside of a grocery store in Northeast Minneapolis. It was winter break at my high school now and Katie, Solomon, and I were starting to settle into a routine. We were nesting.

I heard knocking when I got out of my car. I turned and saw Angus Poulin. He was sitting in the passenger seat of the car that I had pulled up next to. He rolled down his window.

"Hey!" Angus called out. "What up brother? Father?"

I laughed.

"How's it going, man?"

My social skills were lacking after spending so much time holed up with Katie and Solomon. It was my first time out of the house alone. Still, I smiled to see my friend.

"Fine, it's great to see you!"

Angus' stepson was driving the car. He was a student of mine at the high school.

"How's Solomon? How's fatherhood?" Angus asked. He was holding a stalk of celery. His black hair was tangled beneath a winter hat.

"Well, he screams, poops, and eats. That's about it," I said.

They laughed.

Angus kept talking.

"I'm telling people at school that Solomon David is going to be the savior." Angus howled with laughter. "Like Jesus! A prophet! The redeemer!"

"That's the idea," I laughed with him.

We said farewell, and I headed to the store.

I smiled. I was so tired, but I was also proud and relieved to have Solomon at home. It was the day before Christmas Eve, and snow fell onto the traffic in the parking lot as I walked inside to buy groceries.

Katie and Solomon were asleep in the nursery rocking chair when I returned. Solomon was nestled to her breast. The house was warm and quiet.

Katie would make a good mother.

I hoped I would be a good father.

Regardless, I would *try*.

Blooming

Mom was almost evicted from her apartment after
Solomon was born. Instead, she talked the apartment
manager into letting her stay at the last moment. Once
again, Mom got her way.

Mom's interactions with my family became sporadic
and harmless after this near eviction. I would bring
Solomon and Katie over to her sad apartment, and Mom
would spend twenty minutes gazing vacantly at her
grandson before we came up with an excuse to leave.
Solomon eyed her with interest.

Bottles of pills were scattered around her living room.
Mom's body was thin, frail, and desiccate. Her survival
continued to baffle me.

Dad joined us for one of these short visits. I picked up
lunch and met him at Mom's apartment. Dad sat with
Mom on her couch as Solomon crawled around her carpet.
Katie and I watched from across the room.

"I wish I would have known this day was coming when
we were in the hospital, all those years ago," Dad told my
mother. His was earnest and sincere.

I thought about my brother Jayson and my sister
Christa. I turned away as I began to cry.

I finished my doctorate a couple of months later.
Katie's parents attended my graduation ceremony. So did
Polly. Mom and Dad did not. Katie took a picture of me in
my graduation gown with Solomon in my arms. I posted it
on Twitter with the caption: "Dr. Tanner and son. We will
check your pulse. For free. With a scalpel."

I accepted a position in the Pennsylvania State
University system that fall. My new job would begin the
following August.

Mom called me and asked if I would take her grocery
shopping. This was soon after I knew we would be moving
to Pennsylvania. I drove her to the store. I told my mother
the news about my new job after we finished shopping.
Mom started weeping ferociously.

"You're leaving me, Sammy?"

"It isn't that far."

"Pennsylvania? Yes, it is. Don't go."

"I have to."

Mom wept on the ride back to her apartment. I dropped her off at the door.

"I love you, Mom."

"I love you too, Sammy."

Polly came over to visit soon after I told Mom we were moving to Pennsylvania. As always, she brought gifts for Solomon. Polly got down on the floor and played with him as we spoke.

Our discussion, as it often did in the aftermath of Jim's suicide, turned to our experiences with my mother. Polly told a new story as she played with my son.

Back when Jim was alive, Mom had revealed to Polly that a letter had arrived in the mail. It was from a woman and addressed to Jim. Jealous, my mother intercepted the long letter and read it. This woman believed that Jim was her father and wanted to arrange a meeting. Her mother was one of Jim's ex-wives.

Mom tore up the letter and placed it in the garbage. She never told Jim about it.

"I didn't want her to mess up what Jim and I have," Mom later told Polly.

Polly was speechless. I was too as I listened to this story.

The more I learned about my mother, the more complicated my feelings toward her became.

Polly left, and we thanked her for bringing Solomon gifts.

Katie found out she was pregnant again that winter. It would be another boy.

"You're moving across the country, starting a new career, and having another baby?" Angus asked in disbelief. We were talking about my next journey in his classroom before school.

"After everything else? This is nothing," I laughed.

Angus laughed too.

My new family moved to Pennsylvania in June.

Katie's parents drove her and Solomon in one car. I drove our two cats in my CRV. Yara was still alive. Fluffalufagus had died the summer before. We replaced Kitty with another black kitten. I named this new cat Meow-A-Saurus. The stupid name was meant to pay homage to Fluffalufagus. The blackness of her fur was meant to pay homage to Cato.

My childhood stayed with me in the form of a black cat.

I left Minnesota early in the morning. The sun reflected brightly in my rearview mirror. I stopped at a Caribou Coffee shop to get some caffeine for the drive. A former student was working as a barista.

"Hello, Mr. Tanner."

"Hello."

We chatted for a moment. I told her I was moving to Pennsylvania. She wished me luck.

I listened to the soundtrack to *The Last Temptation of Christ* by Peter Gabriel as my car sped East. It was in a collection of CD's that I had forgotten in my classroom. This was the soundtrack I had played for my high school students during journaling or quiet reading time ten years earlier. YouTube and iTunes were not yet available.

Listening to heavy, Aramaic music made me emotional as I crossed the St. Croix River and left Minnesota. Visions of my childhood raced through my mind. I felt like I was leaving something of my past behind. Images of Mom's smiling face appeared in my imagination. Distant impressions of being held safely in her arms as I fell to sleep were buried somewhere inside of me. Ancient memories of my parents came to me. I pictured Dad, Mom, and Christie sitting with me at the kitchen table in St. Paul. We were so *young*. The desolation of our dissolving family was now within me. These histories would always be a part of me. I made my lonely way forward. As I did so, I felt something inside of me begin to transform.

Something was with me in that car.

All that had been, all that was, and all that would be were converging inside me as the car coasted through farmland. Inarticulate visions and energies were taking shape. They were speaking to me, through me. Something was being conjured. I was making real peace with the universe now. I was growing.

Yes, my family was somehow *there*. Friends, former students, blood relatives, and peripheral connections were *with me*. Jim and Nick were alive. Christie, Mom, and Dad appeared. Jayson and Christa were *there*. But not as the imperfect beings that had existed here. Their released spirits were not bound by the inordinate limitations of a shrouded universe. *Something* was being loosed into the cosmos through my continued existence. Energy was running wild. The creation was alive as the freeway melted into horizon. I was eternal, and so were my stories, because once something is conjured, it never goes away. I was an essential part of an infinite design. *We were alive. We were at peace.*

So I sped along, a determined weed, struggling to find my way in an enormous, complicated universe.

***

Mom died on November 13th, 2015 at 11:30 in the morning. I was in Pennsylvania when she passed away. It was only four months after I left Minnesota.

On my birthday, Mom would call me at the exact time I was born. She would sing happy birthday. I loved her singing as a child. I stomached it as an adolescent. I ignored it as an adult. After singing, she would tell me the entire story of my birth. She would glow with pride as she described how I was removed from her stomach in a sac of water.

"You were perfect," she told me. "I was so proud of you already. I knew you were special. You were the reason I was born."

Eventually, these phone calls dissolved and I drifted into adulthood. Mom suffered from the confusion that resulted from a lifetime of destructive addiction.

The mother that I loved from my childhood had been gone for a while by the time Polly called to tell me that my mother was dead.

Still, I wept.

A mother's love is an energy that transcends time and space. That energy exists regardless of addiction or harmful and selfish decisions. This love conquers demons. It repels compulsive destruction.

So I forgive my mother. I reciprocate her love without pause, safe in the knowledge that we have been made as we are to contribute to the design of an infinite universe, running wild with powerful life.

I was no longer afraid of what would come next. I knew that it would be *okay*.

www.ingramcontent.com/pod-product-compliance
Lightning Source LLC
LaVergne TN
LVHW041211080426
835508LV00011B/908